Dungeon

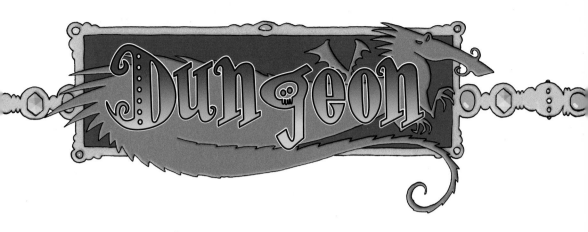

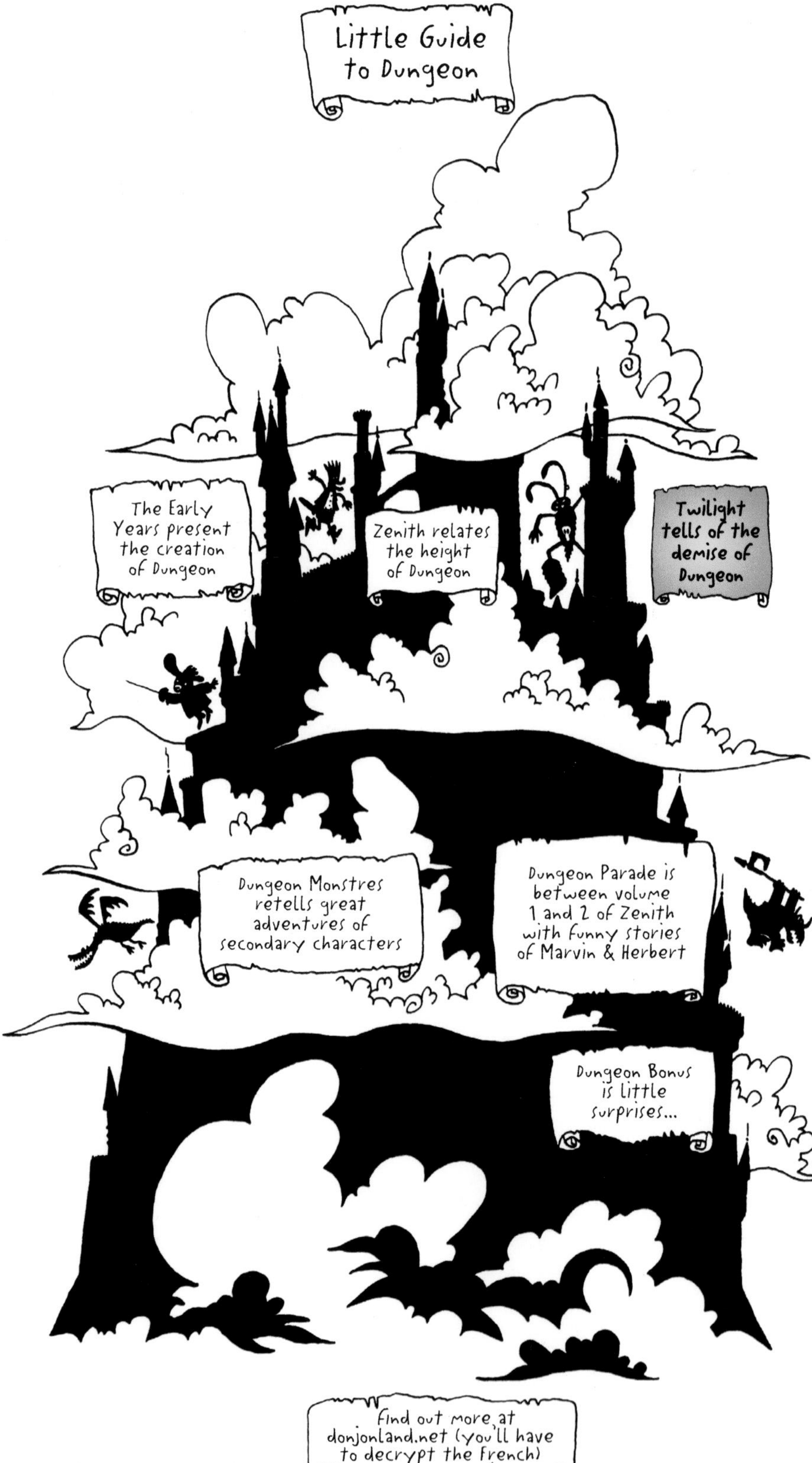
Little Guide to Dungeon
The Early Years present the creation of Dungeon
Zenith relates the height of Dungeon
Twilight tells of the demise of Dungeon
Dungeon Monstres retells great adventures of secondary characters
Dungeon Parade is between volume 1 and 2 of Zenith with funny stories of Marvin & Herbert
Dungeon Bonus is little surprises...
Find out more at donjonland.net (you'll have to decrypt the French)

GN
SFA

Twilight
Volume 2:
Armageddon

Joann SfAR • Lewis TRONDHEIM • KERASCOET

NANTIER • BEALL • MINOUSTCHINE
Publishing inc.
new york

Also available
Dungeon, Zenith, vols. 1, 2: $14.95 each, 3: $14.99
Dungeon Early Years, vols. 1: $14.99, 2: $12.95
Dungeon, Twilight, vols. 1, $12.95, 2: $14.99, 3: $12.99, 4: $14.99
Dungeon, Parade, vol. 2: $9.95
Dungeon, Monstres, vols. 2: $12.95, 3: $12.99, 4: $14.99
Also by Trondheim:
Little Nothings, vols. 2, 3: $14.95 each
Mr. I, $13.95
with Thierry Robin:
Happy Halloween, $14.95

See previews, get exclusives and order from:
NBMPUB.COM

we have over 200 titles available
Catalog upon request
NBM
160 Broadway, Suite 700, East Wing
New York, NY 10038
If ordering by mail add $4 P&H 1st item,
$1 each addt'l

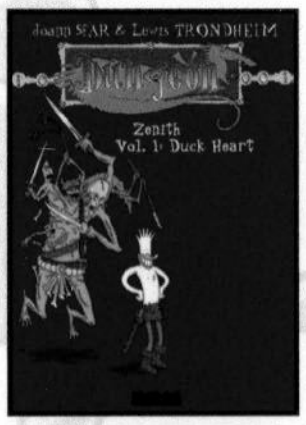
Zenith
Vol. 1: Duck Heart
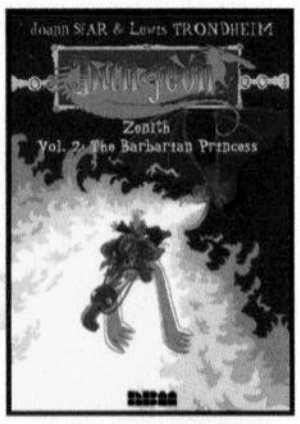
Zenith
Vol. 2: The Barbarian Princess
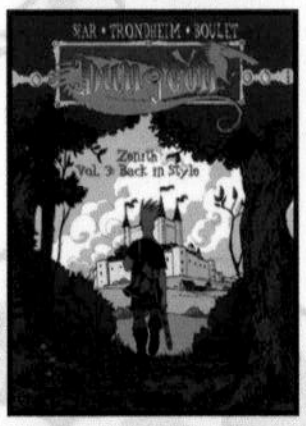
Zenith
Vol. 3: Back in Style
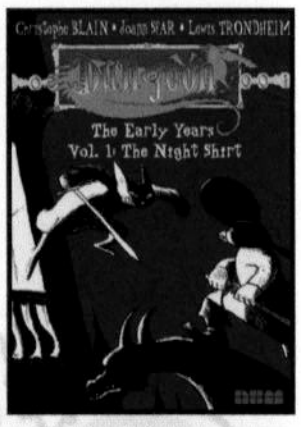
The Early Years
Vol. 1: The Night Shirt
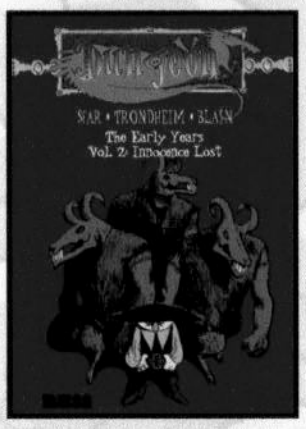
The Early Years
Vol. 2: Innocence Lost
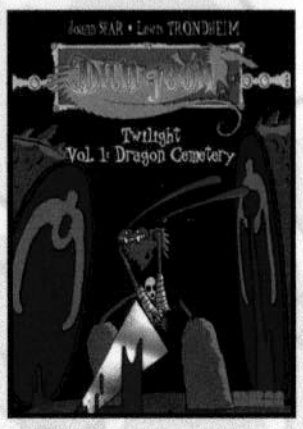
Twilight
Vol. 1: Dragon Cemetery
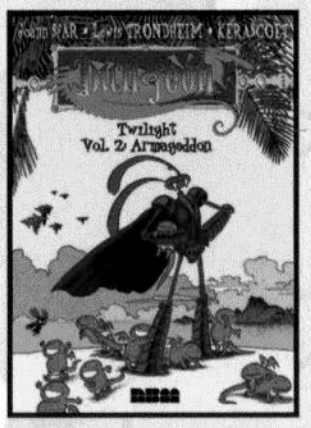
Twilight
Vol. 2: Armageddon
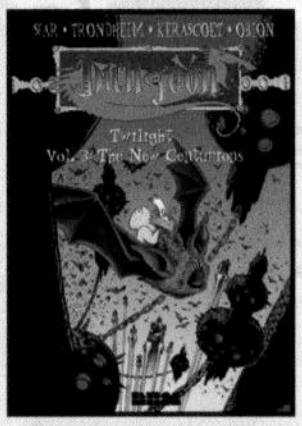
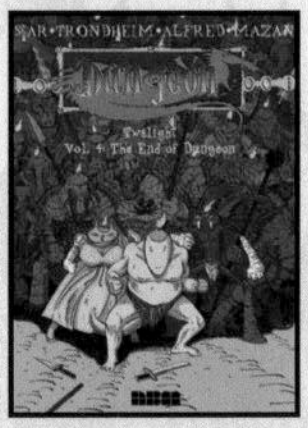
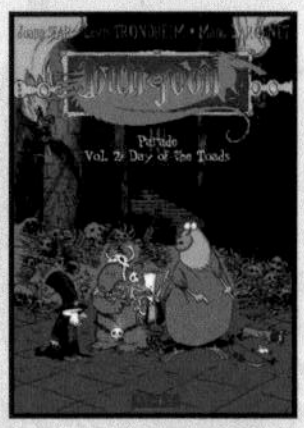
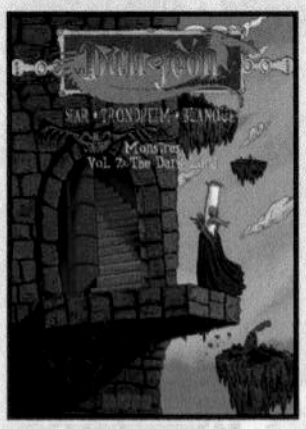
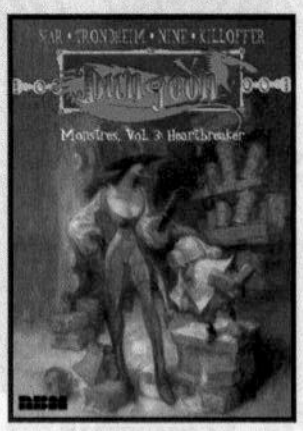
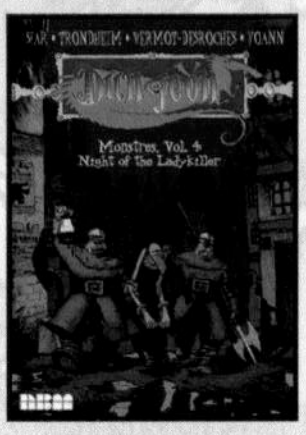

Originally published in French in 2 books:
Donjon Crepuscule:
Armaggedon and *Le Dojo du Lagon*
ISBN: 978-1-56163-477-4

Translation by Joe Johnson
Lettering by Ortho

2nd printing December 2014

T 108497

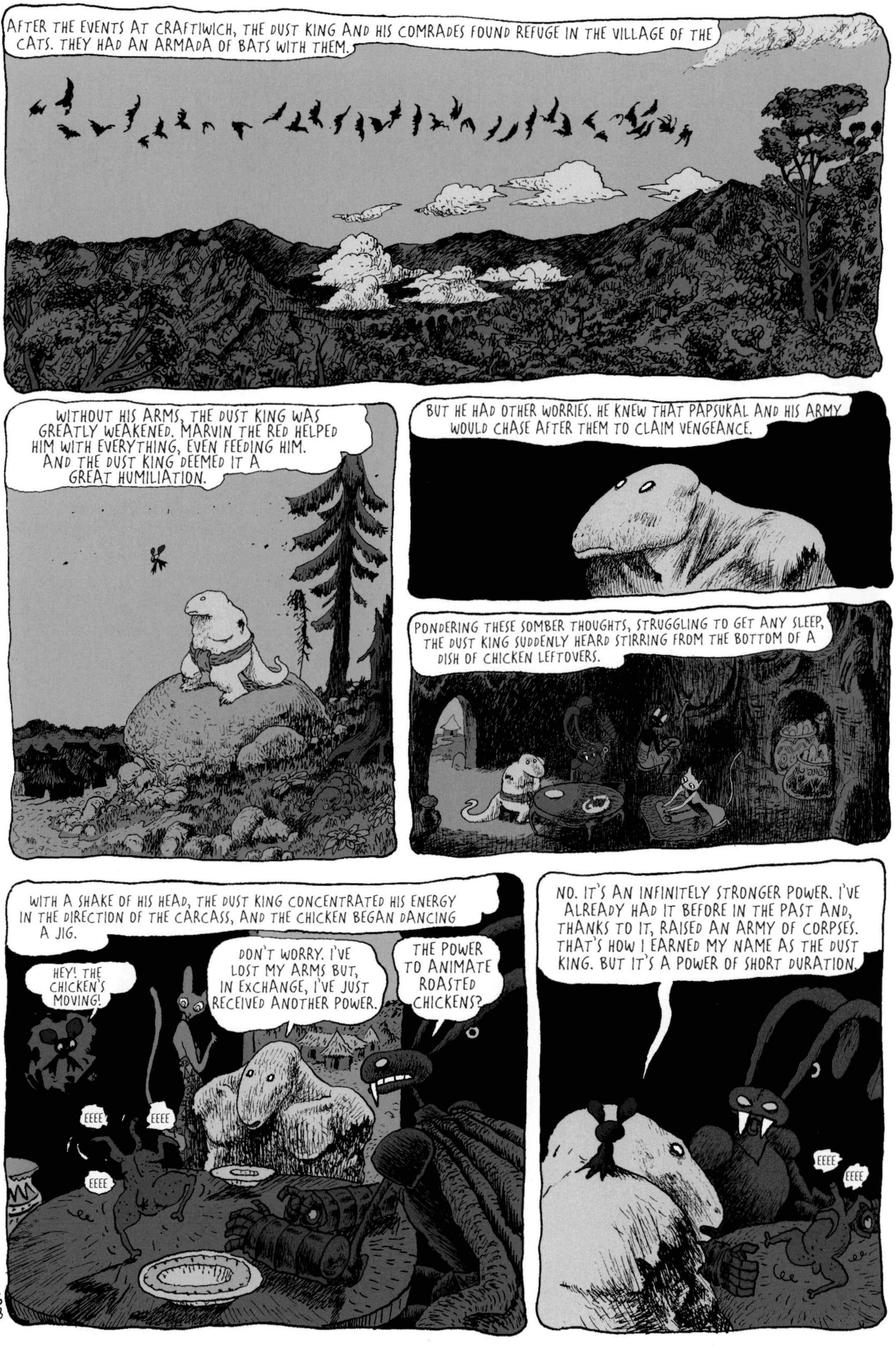

AFTER THE EVENTS AT CRAFTIWICH, THE DUST KING AND HIS COMRADES FOUND REFUGE IN THE VILLAGE OF THE CATS. THEY HAD AN ARMADA OF BATS WITH THEM.
WITHOUT HIS ARMS, THE DUST KING WAS GREATLY WEAKENED. MARVIN THE RED HELPED HIM WITH EVERYTHING, EVEN FEEDING HIM. AND THE DUST KING DEEMED IT A GREAT HUMILIATION.
BUT HE HAD OTHER WORRIES. HE KNEW THAT PAPSUKAL AND HIS ARMY WOULD CHASE AFTER THEM TO CLAIM VENGEANCE.
PONDERING THESE SOMBER THOUGHTS, STRUGGLING TO GET ANY SLEEP, THE DUST KING SUDDENLY HEARD STIRRING FROM THE BOTTOM OF A DISH OF CHICKEN LEFTOVERS.
WITH A SHAKE OF HIS HEAD, THE DUST KING CONCENTRATED HIS ENERGY IN THE DIRECTION OF THE CARCASS, AND THE CHICKEN BEGAN DANCING A JIG.
HEY! THE CHICKEN'S MOVING!
DON'T WORRY. I'VE LOST MY ARMS BUT, IN EXCHANGE, I'VE JUST RECEIVED ANOTHER POWER.
THE POWER TO ANIMATE ROASTED CHICKENS?
EEEE
EEEE
EEEE
NO. IT'S AN INFINITELY STRONGER POWER. I'VE ALREADY HAD IT BEFORE IN THE PAST AND, THANKS TO IT, RAISED AN ARMY OF CORPSES. THAT'S HOW I EARNED MY NAME AS THE DUST KING. BUT IT'S A POWER OF SHORT DURATION.
EEEE
EEEE

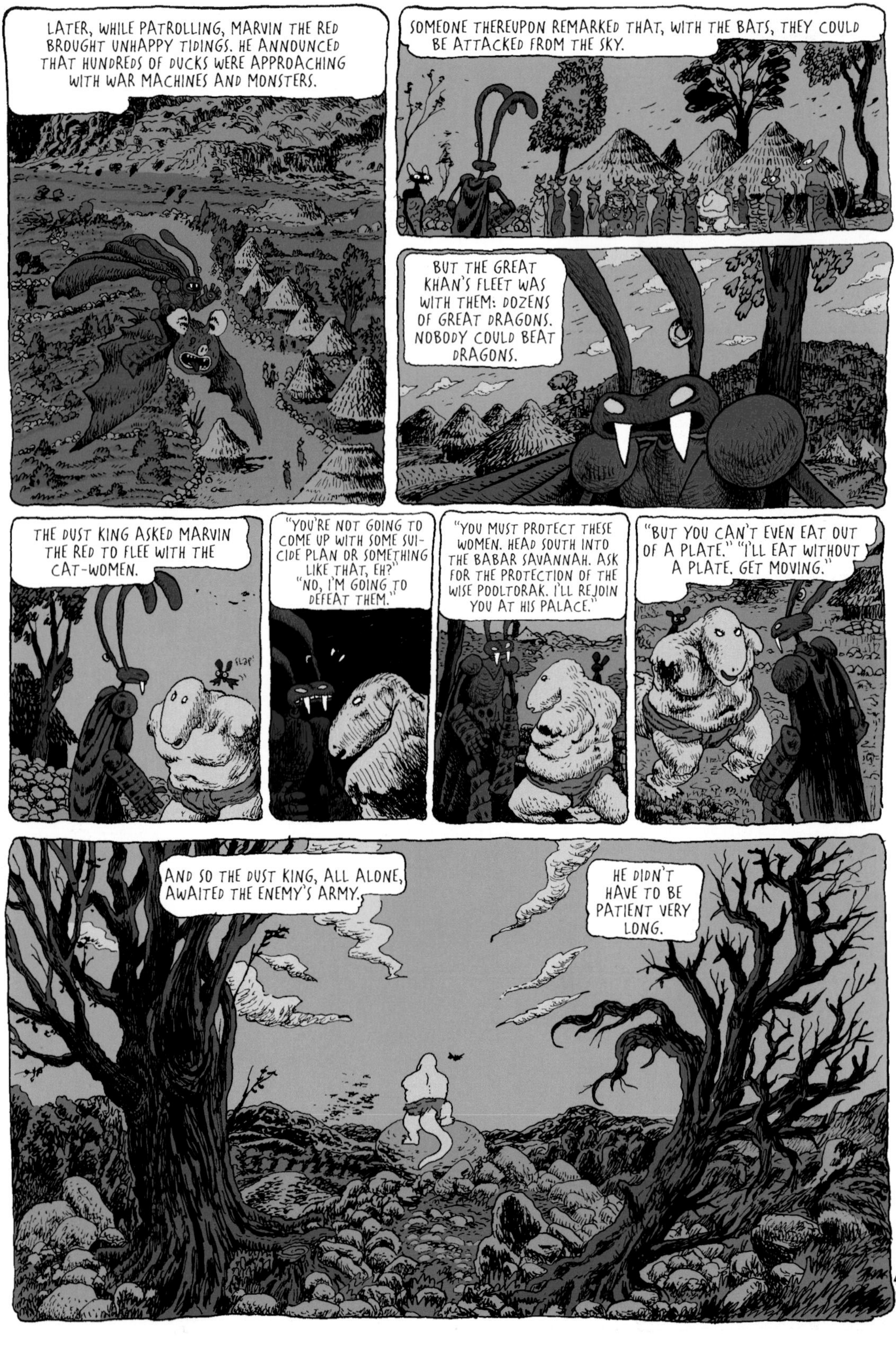
LATER, WHILE PATROLLING, MARVIN THE RED BROUGHT UNHAPPY TIDINGS. HE ANNOUNCED THAT HUNDREDS OF DUCKS WERE APPROACHING WITH WAR MACHINES AND MONSTERS.
SOMEONE THEREUPON REMARKED THAT, WITH THE BATS, THEY COULD BE ATTACKED FROM THE SKY.
BUT THE GREAT KHAN'S FLEET WAS WITH THEM: DOZENS OF GREAT DRAGONS. NOBODY COULD BEAT DRAGONS.
THE DUST KING ASKED MARVIN THE RED TO FLEE WITH THE CAT-WOMEN.
"YOU'RE NOT GOING TO COME UP WITH SOME SUICIDE PLAN OR SOMETHING LIKE THAT, EH?"
"NO, I'M GOING TO DEFEAT THEM."
"YOU MUST PROTECT THESE WOMEN. HEAD SOUTH INTO THE BABAR SAVANNAH. ASK FOR THE PROTECTION OF THE WISE POOLTORAK. I'LL REJOIN YOU AT HIS PALACE."
"BUT YOU CAN'T EVEN EAT OUT OF A PLATE."
"I'LL EAT WITHOUT A PLATE. GET MOVING."
AND SO THE DUST KING, ALL ALONE, AWAITED THE ENEMY'S ARMY.
HE DIDN'T HAVE TO BE PATIENT VERY LONG.

THE ENTIRE ARMY WAS COMING, BURNING EVERYTHING IN ITS WAKE.

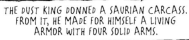

POW

POW

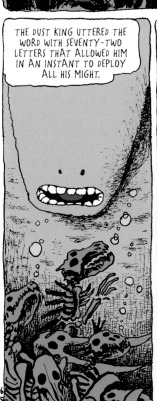

THE DUST KING UTTERED THE WORD WITH SEVENTY-TWO LETTERS THAT ALLOWED HIM IN AN INSTANT TO DEPLOY ALL HIS MIGHT.

THE SKELETONS OF DRAGONS OF THE PAST THEN SURGED FORTH FROM THEIR LACUSTRINE CEMETERY. THE MUMMIFIED WINGS WHIPPED THE AIR SAVAGELY. EACH REGAINED ITS POWERS OF YESTERYEAR, INFINITELY MORE FORMIDABLE THAN THOSE OF THE FEEBLE DRAGONS OF THE BLACK FORTRESS.

THE DUST KING DONNED A SAURIAN CARCASS. FROM IT, HE MADE FOR HIMSELF A LIVING ARMOR WITH FOUR SOLID ARMS.

46
95

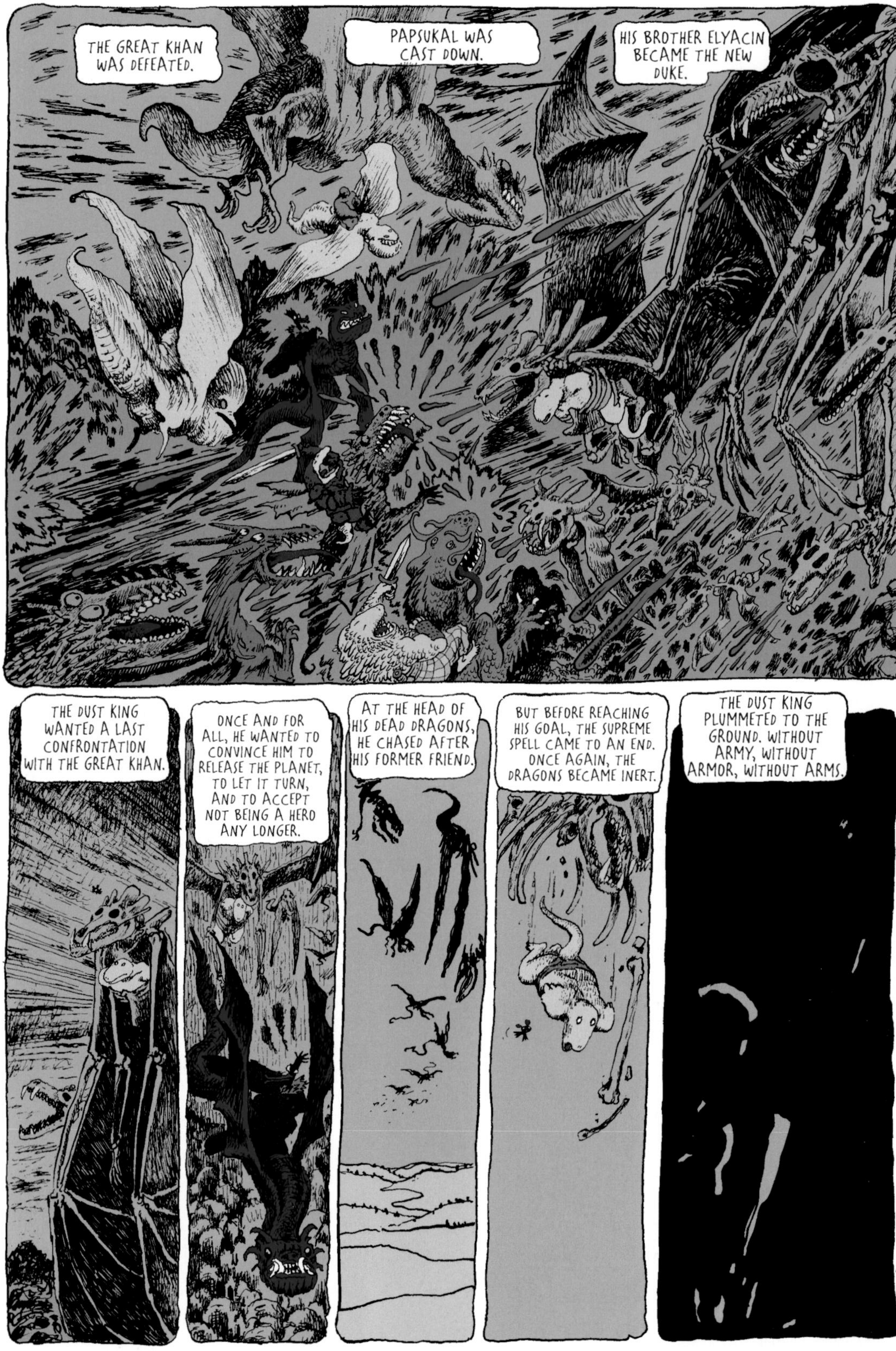
THE GREAT KHAN WAS DEFEATED.
PAPSUKAL WAS CAST DOWN.
HIS BROTHER ELYACIN BECAME THE NEW DUKE.
THE DUST KING WANTED A LAST CONFRONTATION WITH THE GREAT KHAN.
ONCE AND FOR ALL, HE WANTED TO CONVINCE HIM TO RELEASE THE PLANET, TO LET IT TURN, AND TO ACCEPT NOT BEING A HERO ANY LONGER.
AT THE HEAD OF HIS DEAD DRAGONS, HE CHASED AFTER HIS FORMER FRIEND.
BUT BEFORE REACHING HIS GOAL, THE SUPREME SPELL CAME TO AN END. ONCE AGAIN, THE DRAGONS BECAME INERT.
THE DUST KING PLUMMETED TO THE GROUND. WITHOUT ARMY, WITHOUT ARMOR, WITHOUT ARMS.

HE LOST CONSCIOUSNESS.

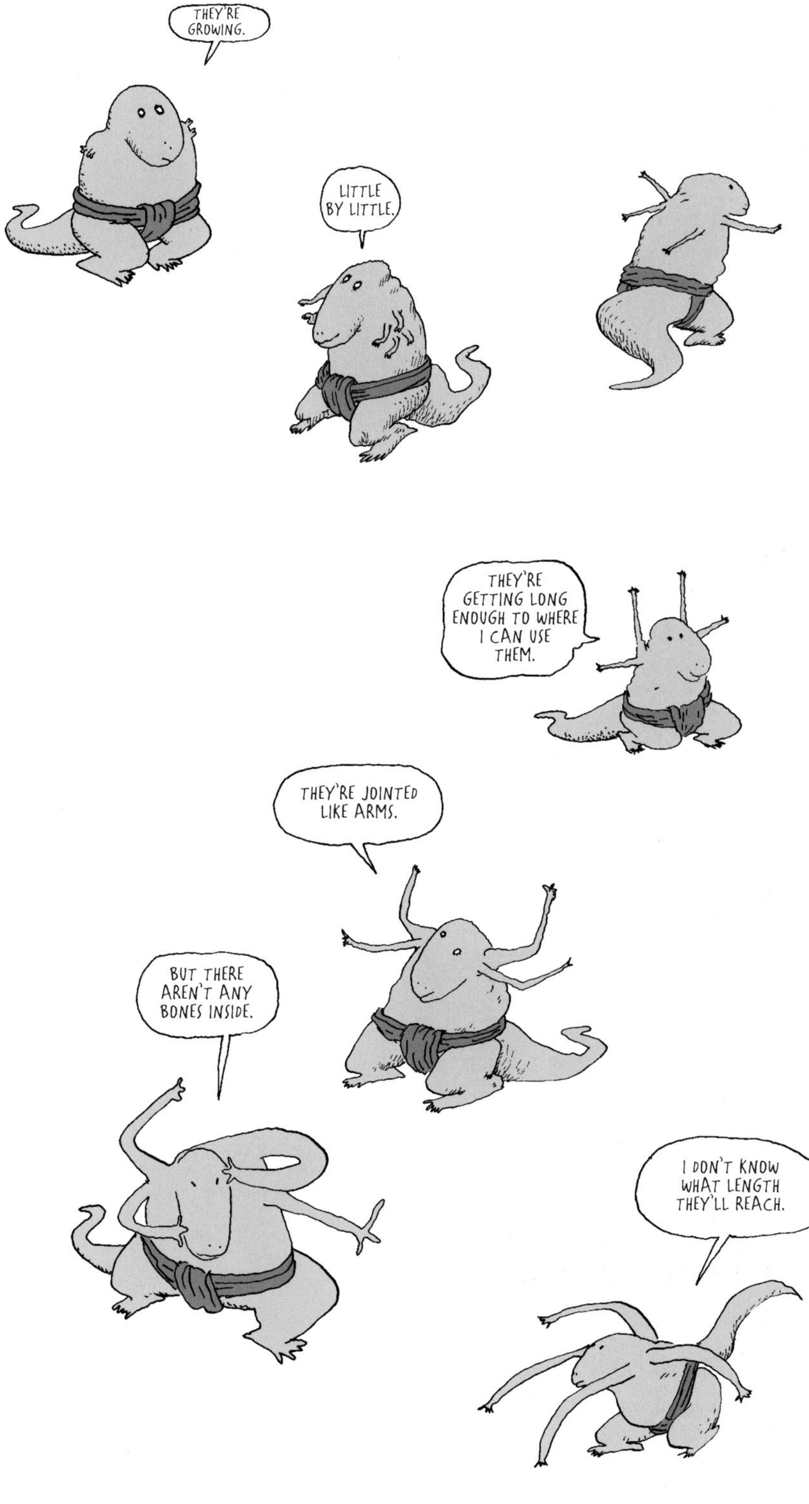
THEY'RE GROWING.
LITTLE BY LITTLE.
THEY'RE GETTING LONG ENOUGH TO WHERE I CAN USE THEM.
THEY'RE JOINTED LIKE ARMS.
BUT THERE AREN'T ANY BONES INSIDE.
I DON'T KNOW WHAT LENGTH THEY'LL REACH.

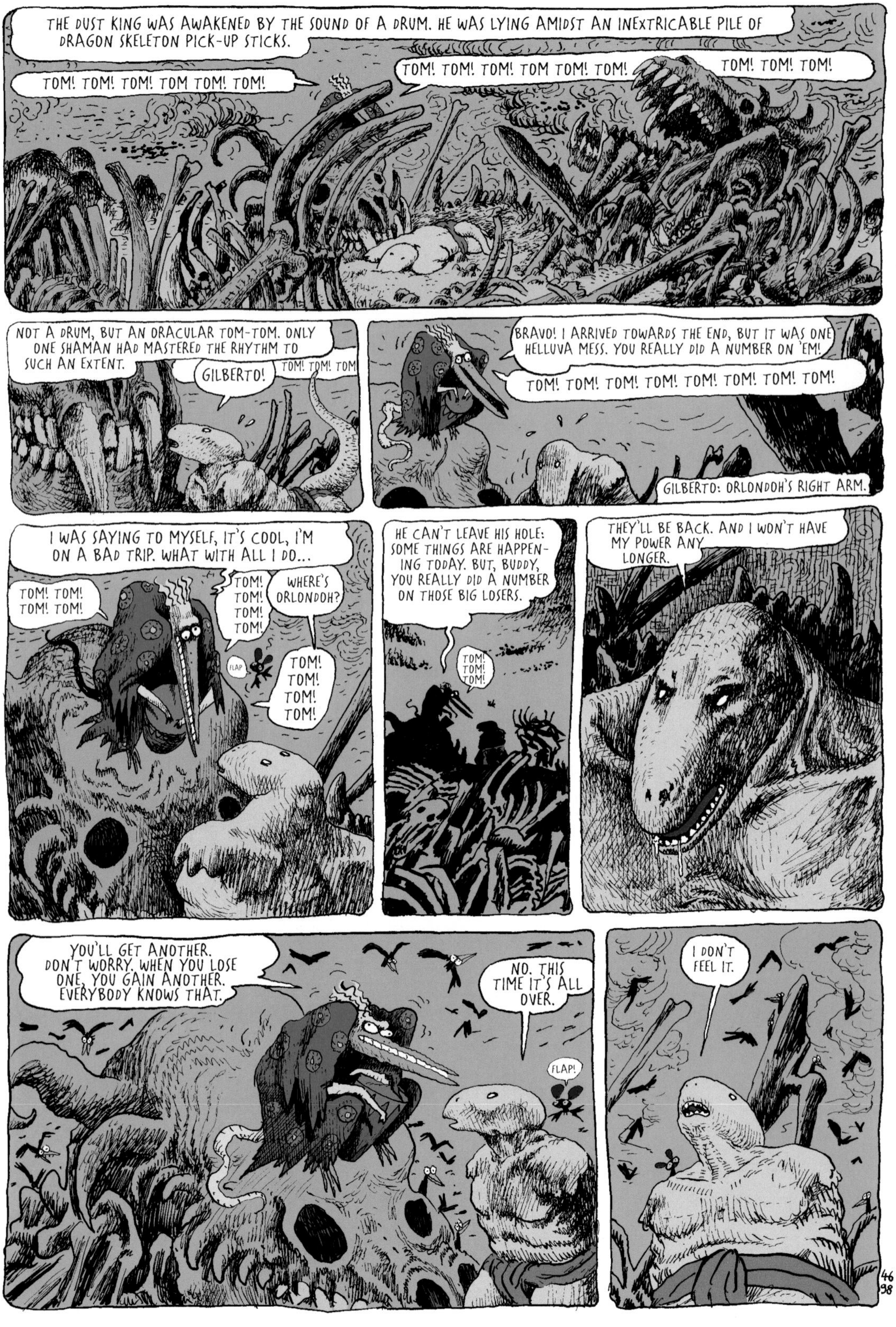
THE DUST KING WAS AWAKENED BY THE SOUND OF A DRUM. HE WAS LYING AMIDST AN INEXTRICABLE PILE OF DRAGON SKELETON PICK-UP STICKS.
TOM! TOM! TOM! TOM TOM! TOM!
TOM! TOM! TOM! TOM TOM! TOM!
TOM! TOM! TOM!
NOT A DRUM, BUT AN ORACULAR TOM-TOM. ONLY ONE SHAMAN HAD MASTERED THE RHYTHM TO SUCH AN EXTENT.
GILBERTO!
TOM! TOM! TOM
BRAVO! I ARRIVED TOWARDS THE END, BUT IT WAS ONE HELLUVA MESS. YOU REALLY DID A NUMBER ON 'EM!
TOM! TOM! TOM! TOM! TOM! TOM! TOM! TOM!
GILBERTO: ORLONDOH'S RIGHT ARM.
I WAS SAYING TO MYSELF, IT'S COOL, I'M ON A BAD TRIP. WHAT WITH ALL I DO...
TOM! TOM! TOM! TOM!
TOM! TOM! TOM! TOM!
WHERE'S ORLONDOH?
FLAP
TOM! TOM! TOM! TOM!
HE CAN'T LEAVE HIS HOLE: SOME THINGS ARE HAPPENING TODAY. BUT, BUDDY, YOU REALLY DID A NUMBER ON THOSE BIG LOSERS.
TOM! TOM! TOM!
THEY'LL BE BACK. AND I WON'T HAVE MY POWER ANY LONGER.
YOU'LL GET ANOTHER. DON'T WORRY. WHEN YOU LOSE ONE, YOU GAIN ANOTHER. EVERYBODY KNOWS THAT.
NO. THIS TIME IT'S ALL OVER.
FLAP!
I DON'T FEEL IT.

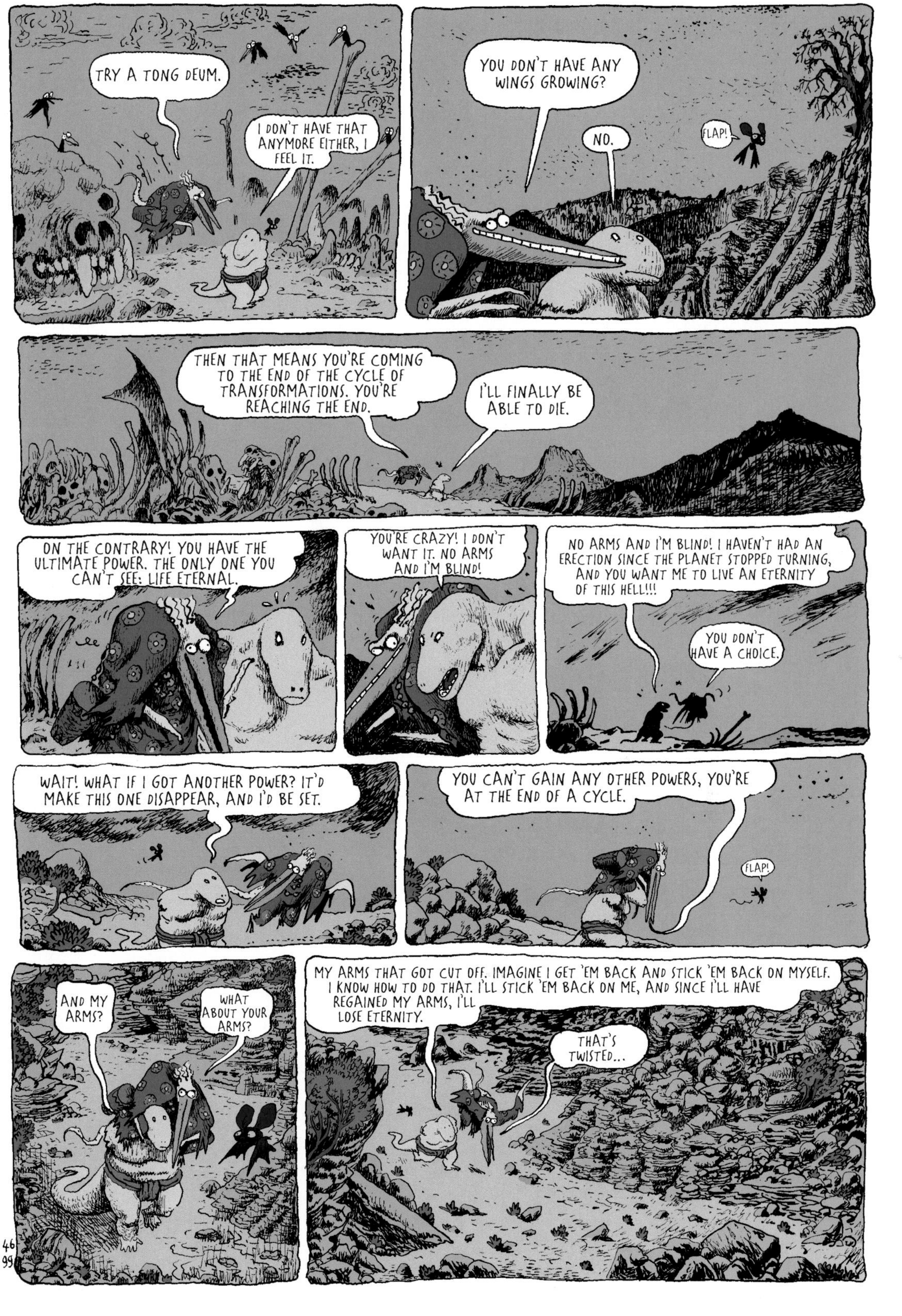
TRY A TONG DEUM.
I DON'T HAVE THAT ANYMORE EITHER, I FEEL IT.
YOU DON'T HAVE ANY WINGS GROWING?
NO.
FLAP!
THEN THAT MEANS YOU'RE COMING TO THE END OF THE CYCLE OF TRANSFORMATIONS. YOU'RE REACHING THE END.
I'LL FINALLY BE ABLE TO DIE.
ON THE CONTRARY! YOU HAVE THE ULTIMATE POWER. THE ONLY ONE YOU CAN'T SEE: LIFE ETERNAL.
YOU'RE CRAZY! I DON'T WANT IT. NO ARMS AND I'M BLIND!
NO ARMS AND I'M BLIND! I HAVEN'T HAD AN ERECTION SINCE THE PLANET STOPPED TURNING, AND YOU WANT ME TO LIVE AN ETERNITY OF THIS HELL!!!
YOU DON'T HAVE A CHOICE.
WAIT! WHAT IF I GOT ANOTHER POWER? IT'D MAKE THIS ONE DISAPPEAR, AND I'D BE SET.
YOU CAN'T GAIN ANY OTHER POWERS, YOU'RE AT THE END OF A CYCLE.
FLAP!
AND MY ARMS?
WHAT ABOUT YOUR ARMS?
MY ARMS THAT GOT CUT OFF. IMAGINE I GET 'EM BACK AND STICK 'EM BACK ON MYSELF. I KNOW HOW TO DO THAT. I'LL STICK 'EM BACK ON ME, AND SINCE I'LL HAVE REGAINED MY ARMS, I'LL LOSE ETERNITY.
THAT'S TWISTED...

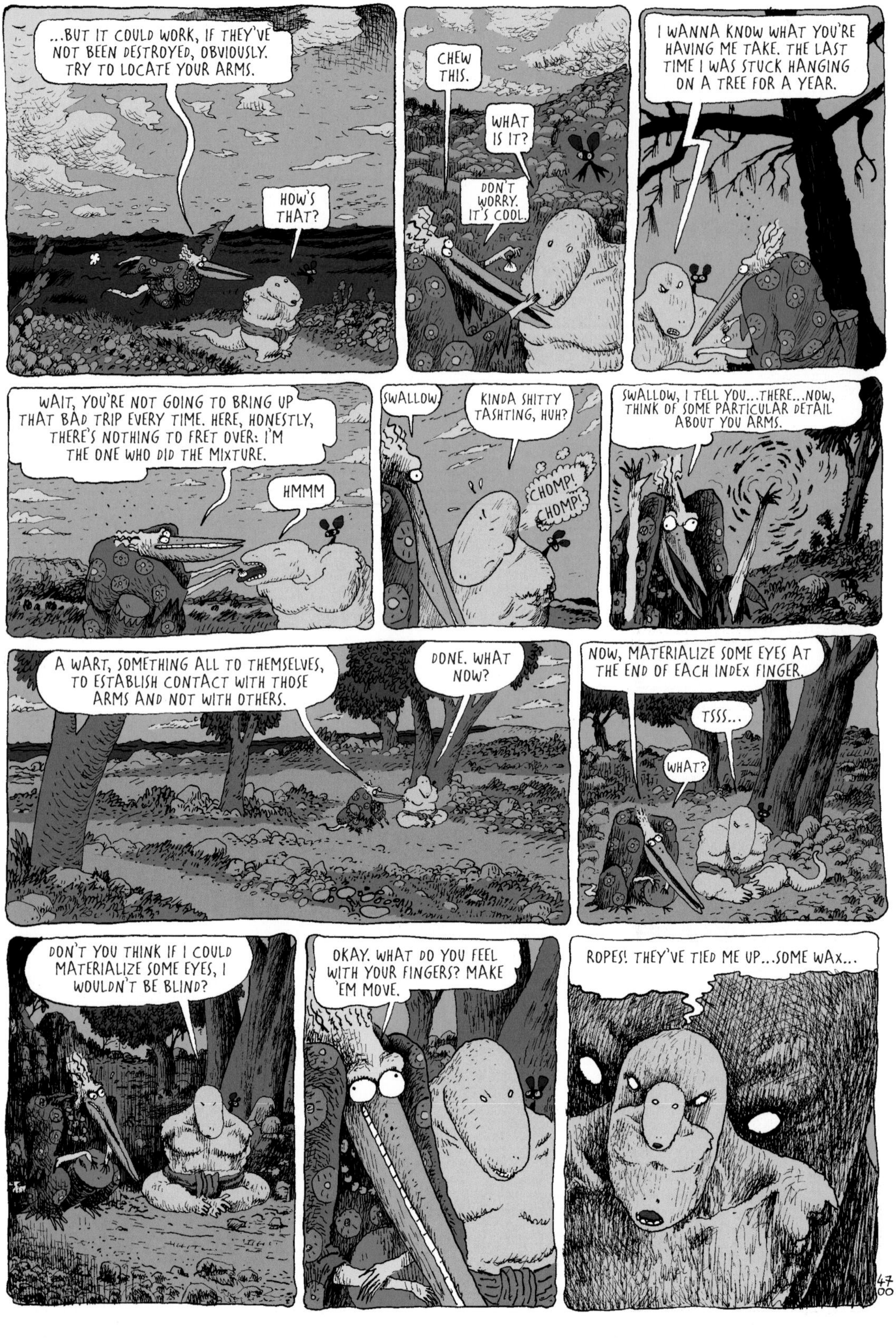
...BUT IT COULD WORK, IF THEY'VE NOT BEEN DESTROYED, OBVIOUSLY. TRY TO LOCATE YOUR ARMS.
HOW'S THAT?
CHEW THIS.
WHAT IS IT?
DON'T WORRY. IT'S COOL.
I WANNA KNOW WHAT YOU'RE HAVING ME TAKE. THE LAST TIME I WAS STUCK HANGING ON A TREE FOR A YEAR.
WAIT, YOU'RE NOT GOING TO BRING UP THAT BAD TRIP EVERY TIME. HERE, HONESTLY, THERE'S NOTHING TO FRET OVER: I'M THE ONE WHO DID THE MIXTURE.
HMMM
SWALLOW.
KINDA SHITTY TASHTING, HUH?
CHOMP! CHOMP!
SWALLOW, I TELL YOU...THERE...NOW, THINK OF SOME PARTICULAR DETAIL ABOUT YOU ARMS.
A WART, SOMETHING ALL TO THEMSELVES, TO ESTABLISH CONTACT WITH THOSE ARMS AND NOT WITH OTHERS.
DONE. WHAT NOW?
NOW, MATERIALIZE SOME EYES AT THE END OF EACH INDEX FINGER.
TSSS...
WHAT?
DON'T YOU THINK IF I COULD MATERIALIZE SOME EYES, I WOULDN'T BE BLIND?
OKAY. WHAT DO YOU FEEL WITH YOUR FINGERS? MAKE 'EM MOVE.
ROPES! THEY'VE TIED ME UP...SOME WAX...

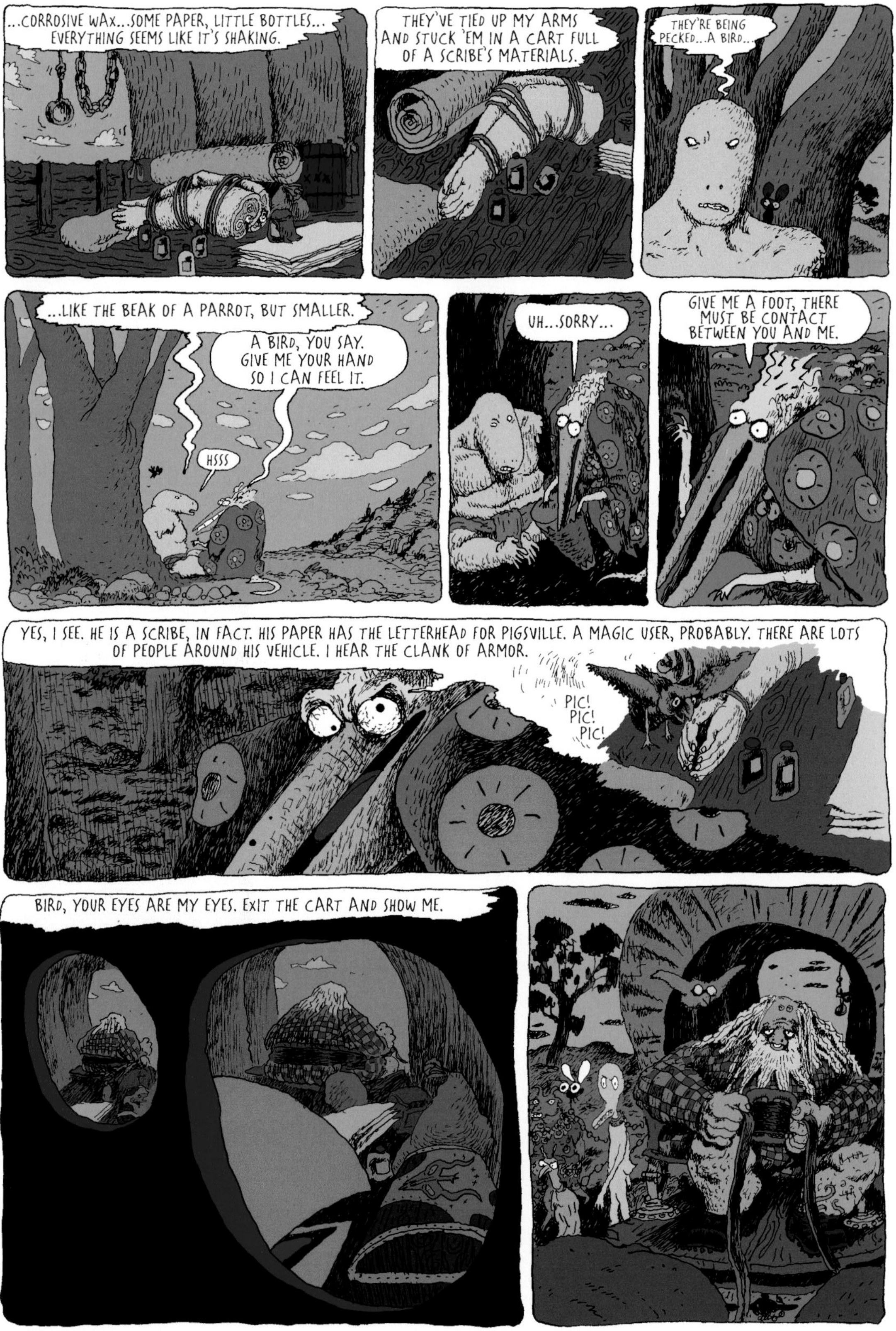
...CORROSIVE WAX...SOME PAPER, LITTLE BOTTLES... EVERYTHING SEEMS LIKE IT'S SHAKING.
THEY'VE TIED UP MY ARMS AND STUCK 'EM IN A CART FULL OF A SCRIBE'S MATERIALS.
THEY'RE BEING PECKED...A BIRD...
...LIKE THE BEAK OF A PARROT, BUT SMALLER.
A BIRD, YOU SAY. GIVE ME YOUR HAND SO I CAN FEEL IT.
HSSS
UH...SORRY...
GIVE ME A FOOT, THERE MUST BE CONTACT BETWEEN YOU AND ME.
YES, I SEE. HE IS A SCRIBE, IN FACT. HIS PAPER HAS THE LETTERHEAD FOR PIGSVILLE. A MAGIC USER, PROBABLY. THERE ARE LOTS OF PEOPLE AROUND HIS VEHICLE. I HEAR THE CLANK OF ARMOR.
PIC! PIC! PIC!
BIRD, YOUR EYES ARE MY EYES. EXIT THE CART AND SHOW ME.

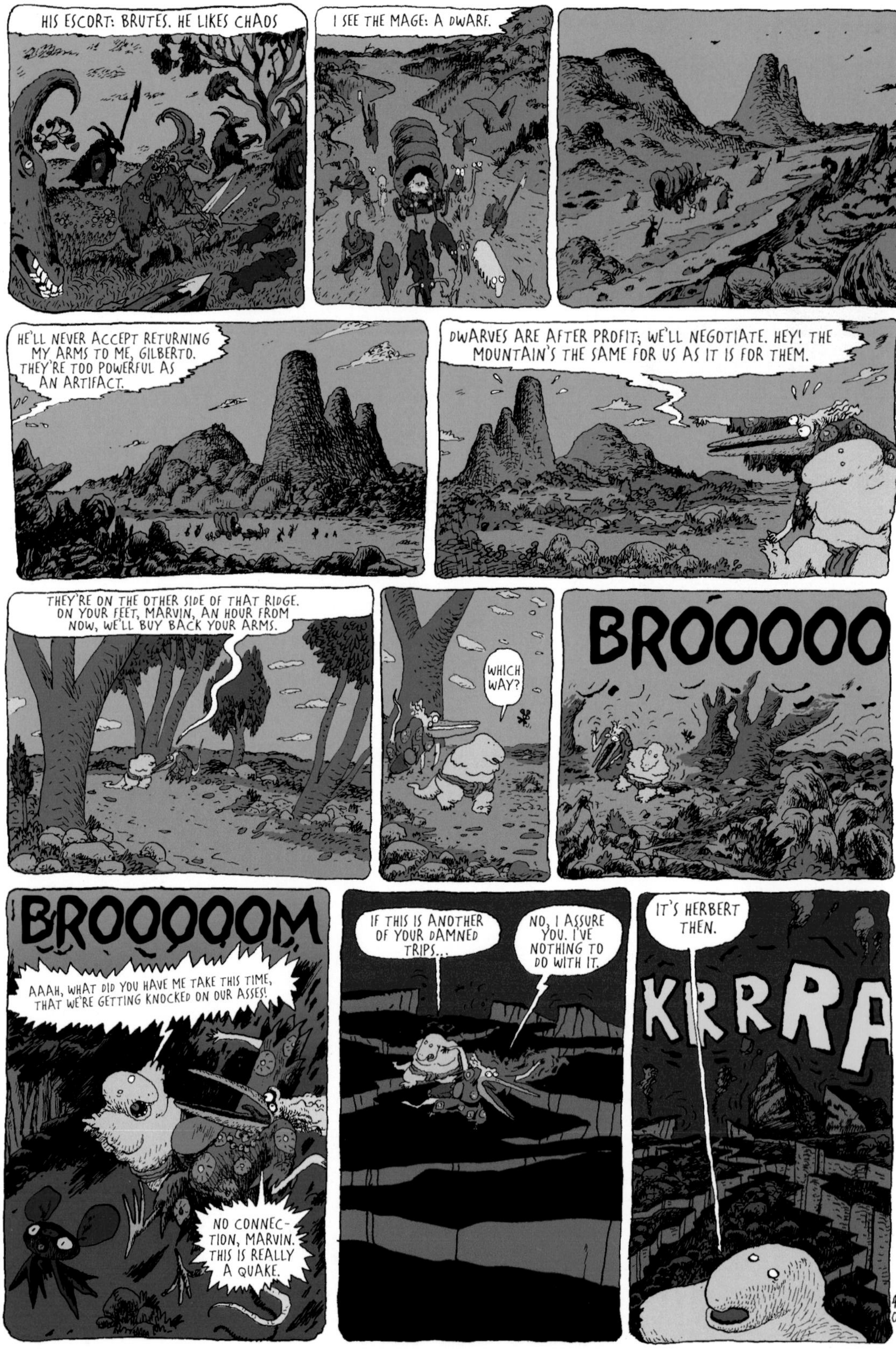

HIS ESCORT: BRUTES. HE LIKES CHAOS
I SEE THE MAGE: A DWARF.
HE'LL NEVER ACCEPT RETURNING MY ARMS TO ME, GILBERTO. THEY'RE TOO POWERFUL AS AN ARTIFACT.
DWARVES ARE AFTER PROFIT; WE'LL NEGOTIATE. HEY! THE MOUNTAIN'S THE SAME FOR US AS IT IS FOR THEM.
THEY'RE ON THE OTHER SIDE OF THAT RIDGE. ON YOUR FEET, MARVIN, AN HOUR FROM NOW, WE'LL BUY BACK YOUR ARMS.
WHICH WAY?
BROOOOO
BROOOOOM
AAAH, WHAT DID YOU HAVE ME TAKE THIS TIME, THAT WE'RE GETTING KNOCKED ON OUR ASSES!
NO CONNECTION, MARVIN. THIS IS REALLY A QUAKE.
IF THIS IS ANOTHER OF YOUR DAMNED TRIPS...
NO, I ASSURE YOU. I'VE NOTHING TO DO WITH IT.
IT'S HERBERT THEN.
KRRRA

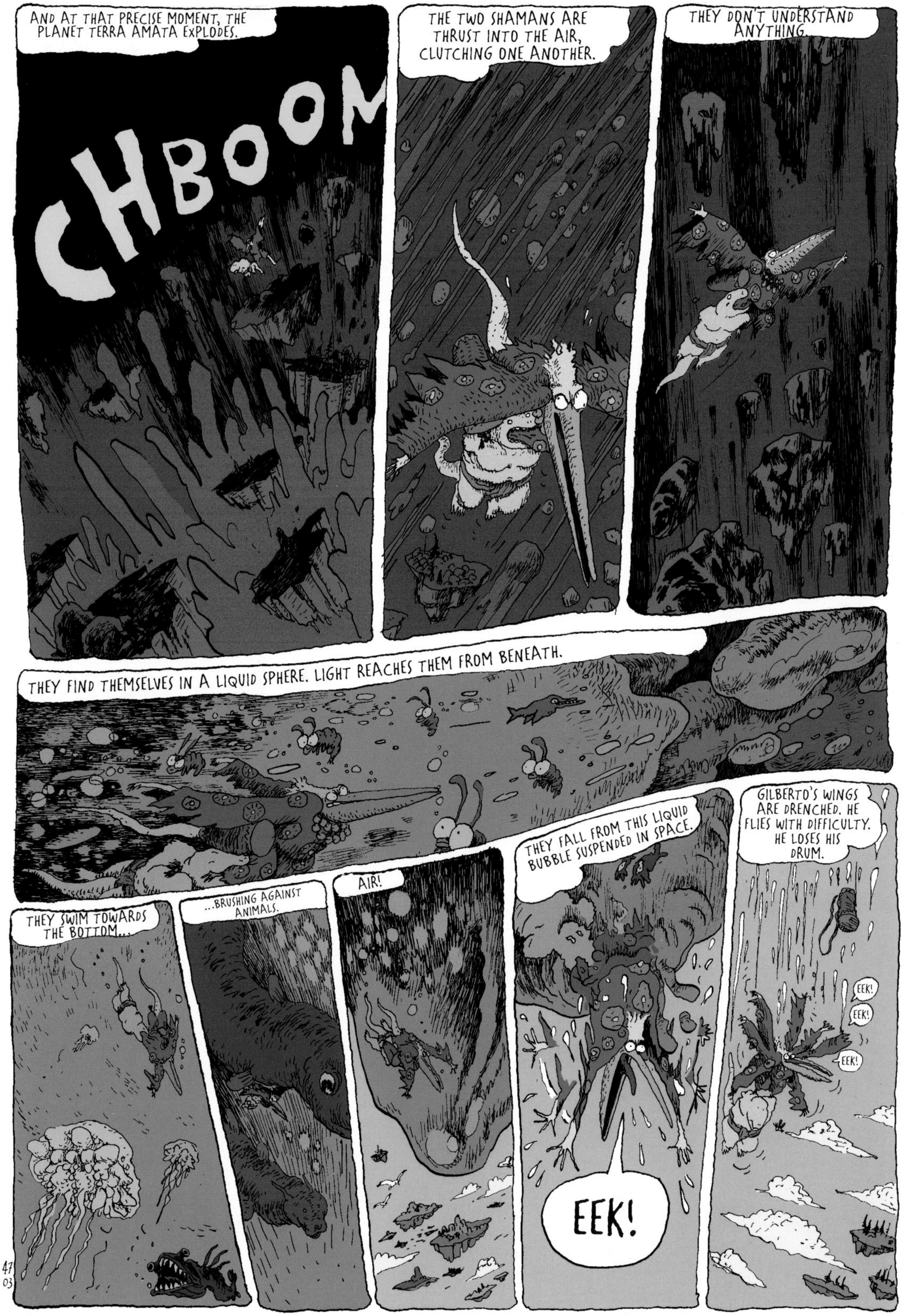
AND AT THAT PRECISE MOMENT, THE PLANET TERRA AMATA EXPLODES.
CHBOOM
THE TWO SHAMANS ARE THRUST INTO THE AIR, CLUTCHING ONE ANOTHER.
THEY DON'T UNDERSTAND ANYTHING.
THEY FIND THEMSELVES IN A LIQUID SPHERE. LIGHT REACHES THEM FROM BENEATH.
THEY SWIM TOWARDS THE BOTTOM...
...BRUSHING AGAINST ANIMALS.
AIR!
THEY FALL FROM THIS LIQUID BUBBLE SUSPENDED IN SPACE.
EEK!
GILBERTO'S WINGS ARE DRENCHED. HE FLIES WITH DIFFICULTY. HE LOSES HIS DRUM.
EEK!
EEK!
EEK!
47
03

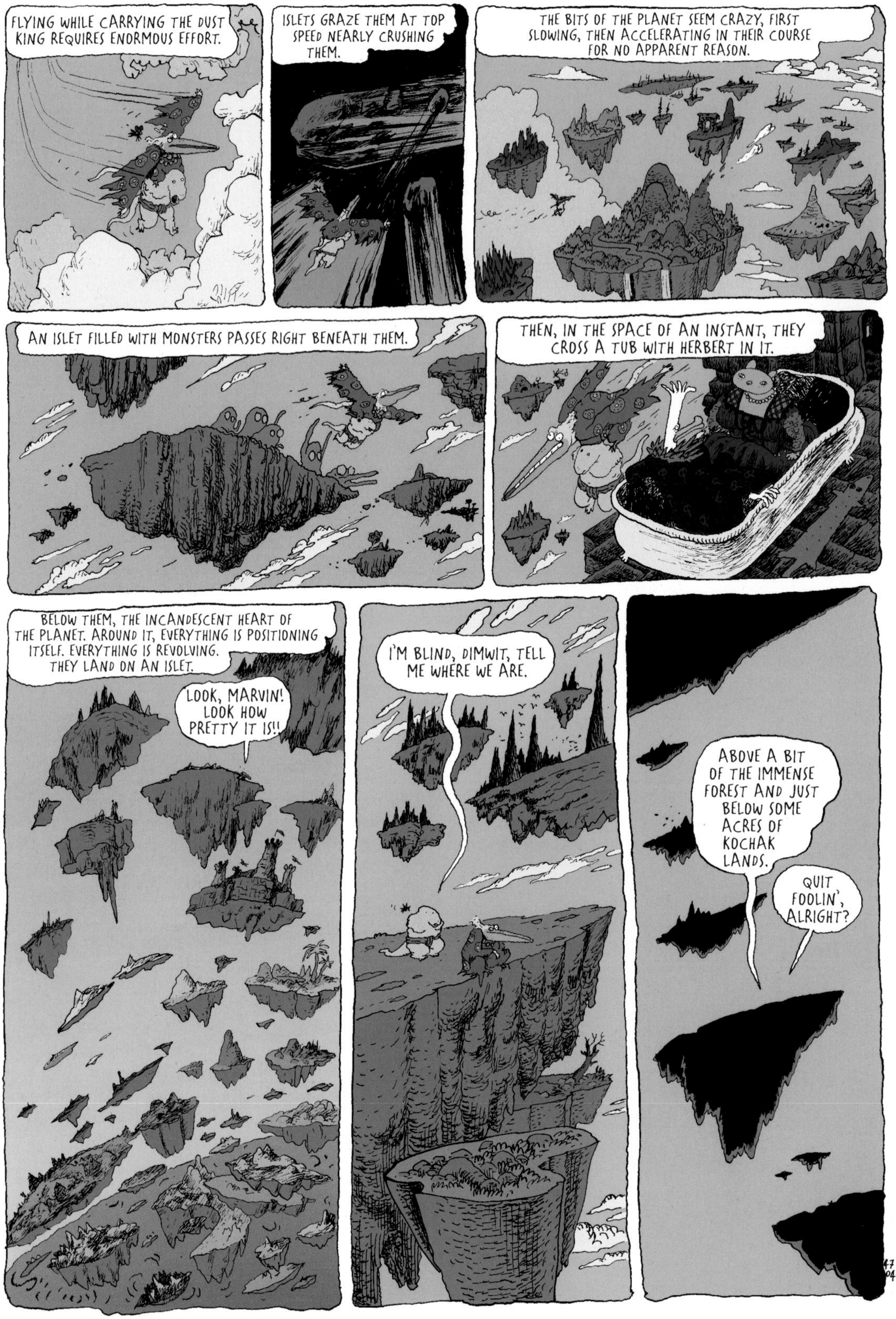
FLYING WHILE CARRYING THE DUST KING REQUIRES ENORMOUS EFFORT.
ISLETS GRAZE THEM AT TOP SPEED NEARLY CRUSHING THEM.
THE BITS OF THE PLANET SEEM CRAZY, FIRST SLOWING, THEN ACCELERATING IN THEIR COURSE FOR NO APPARENT REASON.
AN ISLET FILLED WITH MONSTERS PASSES RIGHT BENEATH THEM.
THEN, IN THE SPACE OF AN INSTANT, THEY CROSS A TUB WITH HERBERT IN IT.
BELOW THEM, THE INCANDESCENT HEART OF THE PLANET. AROUND IT, EVERYTHING IS POSITIONING ITSELF. EVERYTHING IS REVOLVING. THEY LAND ON AN ISLET.
LOOK, MARVIN! LOOK HOW PRETTY IT IS!!
I'M BLIND, DIMWIT, TELL ME WHERE WE ARE.
ABOVE A BIT OF THE IMMENSE FOREST AND JUST BELOW SOME ACRES OF KOCHAK LANDS.
QUIT FOOLIN', ALRIGHT?

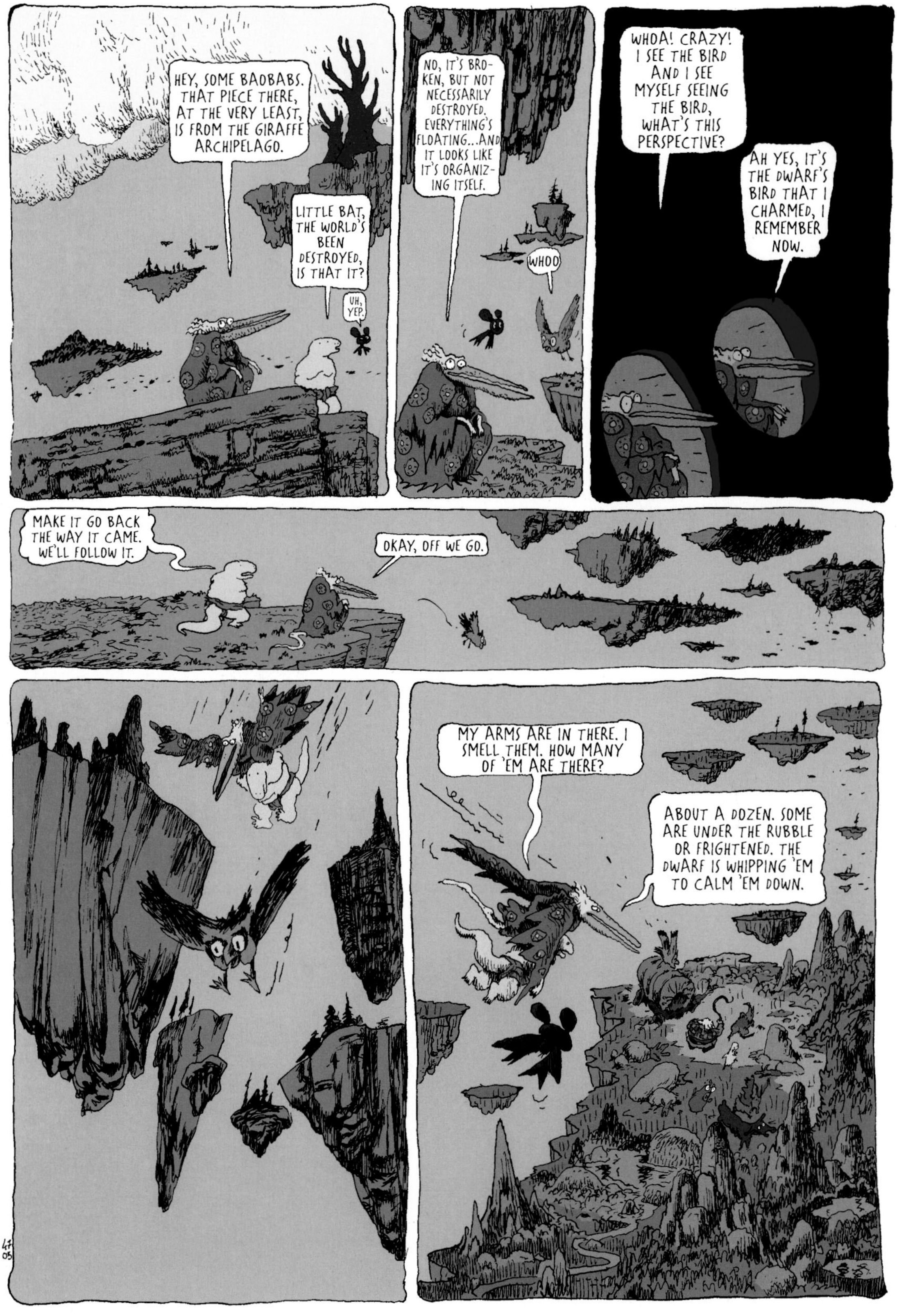
HEY, SOME BAOBABS. THAT PIECE THERE, AT THE VERY LEAST, IS FROM THE GIRAFFE ARCHIPELAGO.
LITTLE BAT, THE WORLD'S BEEN DESTROYED, IS THAT IT?
UH, YEP.
NO, IT'S BROKEN, BUT NOT NECESSARILY DESTROYED. EVERYTHING'S FLOATING...AND IT LOOKS LIKE IT'S ORGANIZING ITSELF.
WHOO
WHOA! CRAZY! I SEE THE BIRD AND I SEE MYSELF SEEING THE BIRD, WHAT'S THIS PERSPECTIVE?
AH YES, IT'S THE DWARF'S BIRD THAT I CHARMED, I REMEMBER NOW.
MAKE IT GO BACK THE WAY IT CAME. WE'LL FOLLOW IT.
OKAY, OFF WE GO.
MY ARMS ARE IN THERE. I SMELL THEM. HOW MANY OF 'EM ARE THERE?
ABOUT A DOZEN. SOME ARE UNDER THE RUBBLE OR FRIGHTENED. THE DWARF IS WHIPPING 'EM TO CALM 'EM DOWN.
47
05

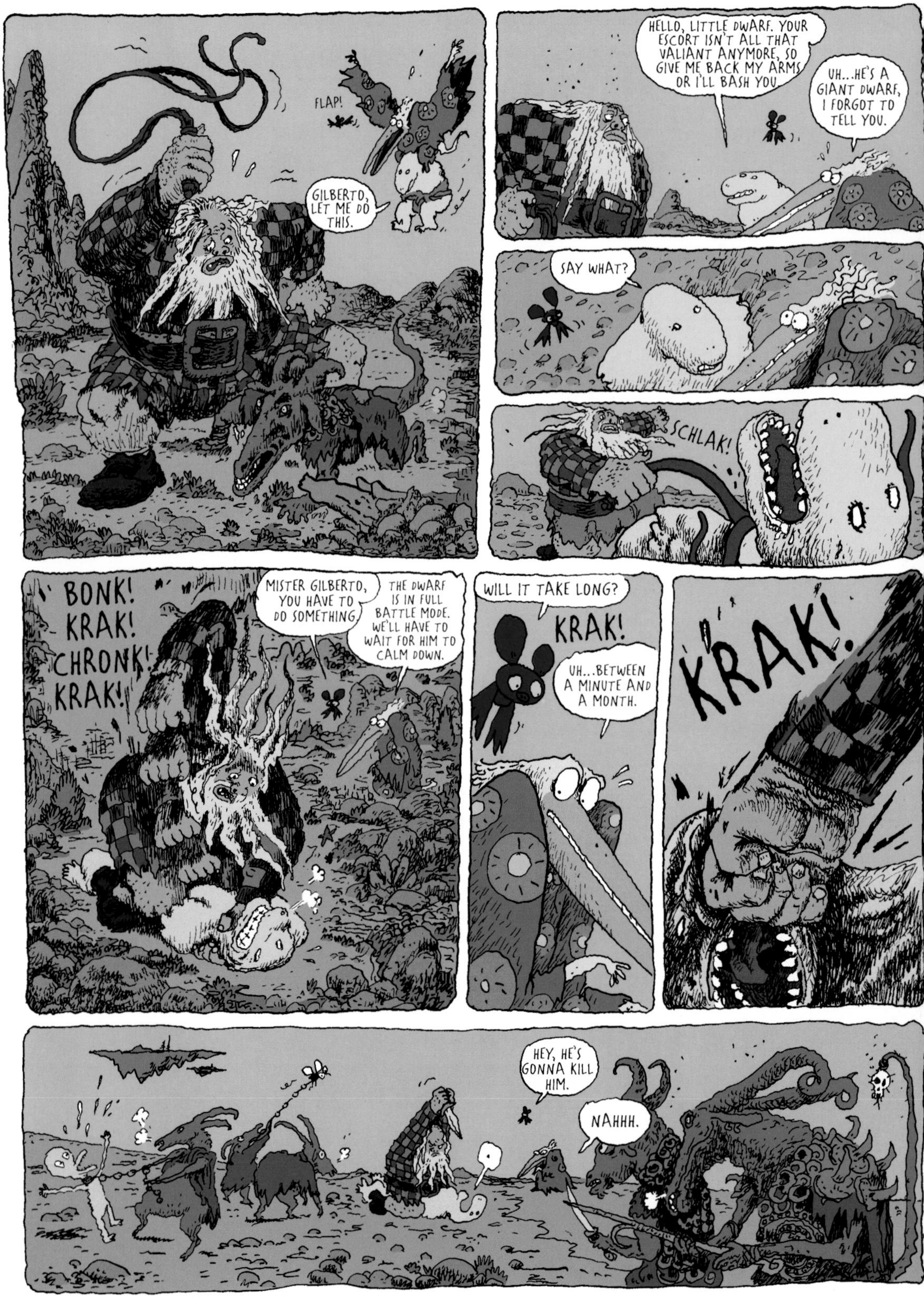
FLAP!
GILBERTO, LET ME DO THIS.
HELLO, LITTLE DWARF. YOUR ESCORT ISN'T ALL THAT VALIANT ANYMORE, SO GIVE ME BACK MY ARMS OR I'LL BASH YOU.
UH...HE'S A GIANT DWARF, I FORGOT TO TELL YOU.
SAY WHAT?
SCHLAK!
BONK! KRAK! CHRONK! KRAK!
MISTER GILBERTO, YOU HAVE TO DO SOMETHING.
THE DWARF IS IN FULL BATTLE MODE. WE'LL HAVE TO WAIT FOR HIM TO CALM DOWN.
WILL IT TAKE LONG?
KRAK!
UH...BETWEEN A MINUTE AND A MONTH.
KRAK!
HEY, HE'S GONNA KILL HIM.
NAHHH.

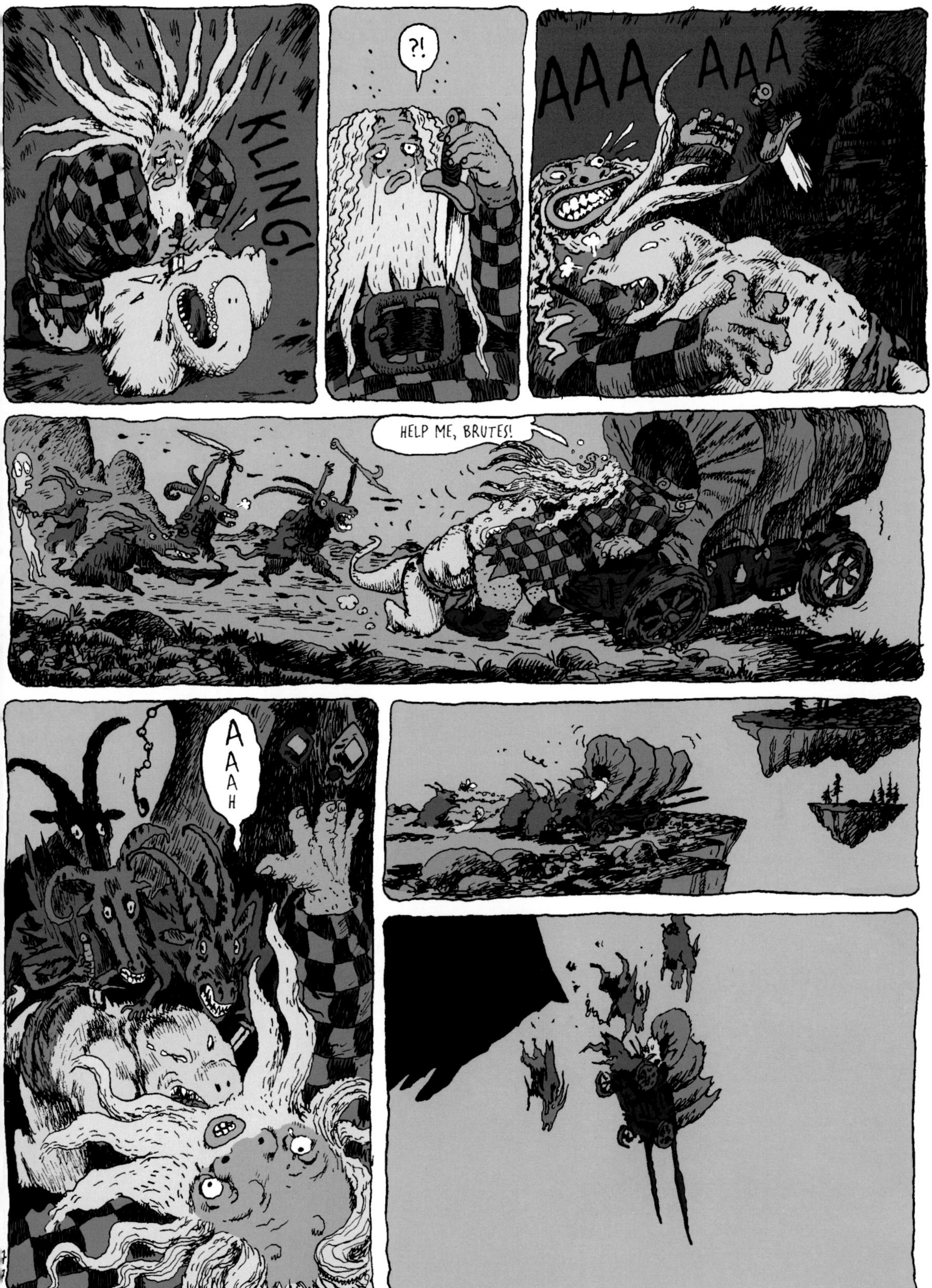
KLING!
?!
AAA AAA
HELP ME, BRUTES!
A
A
A
H

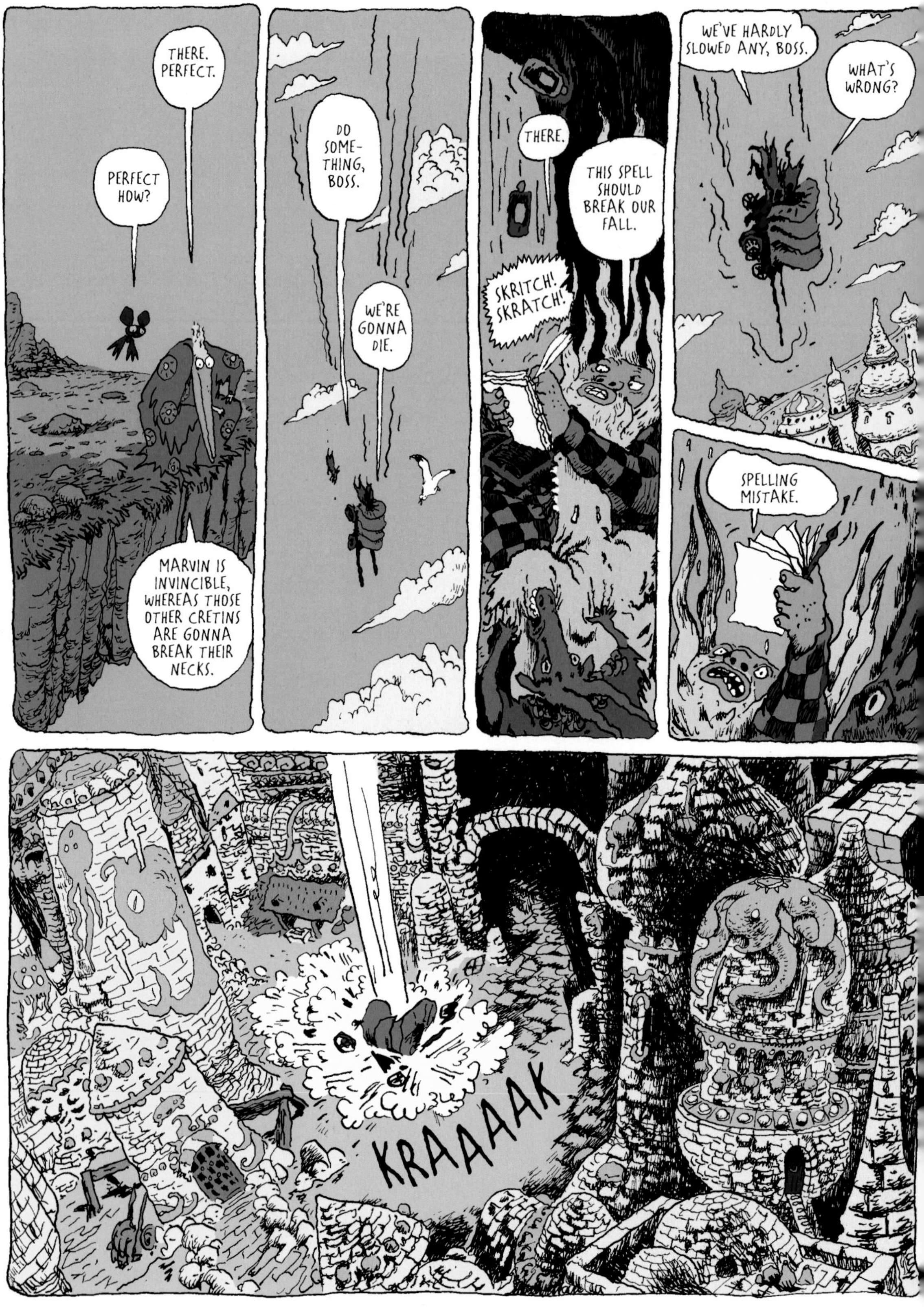
THERE. PERFECT.
PERFECT HOW?
MARVIN IS INVINCIBLE, WHEREAS THOSE OTHER CRETINS ARE GONNA BREAK THEIR NECKS.
DO SOMETHING, BOSS.
WE'RE GONNA DIE.
THERE.
THIS SPELL SHOULD BREAK OUR FALL.
SKRITCH! SKRATCH!
WE'VE HARDLY SLOWED ANY, BOSS.
WHAT'S WRONG?
SPELLING MISTAKE.
KRAAAAK

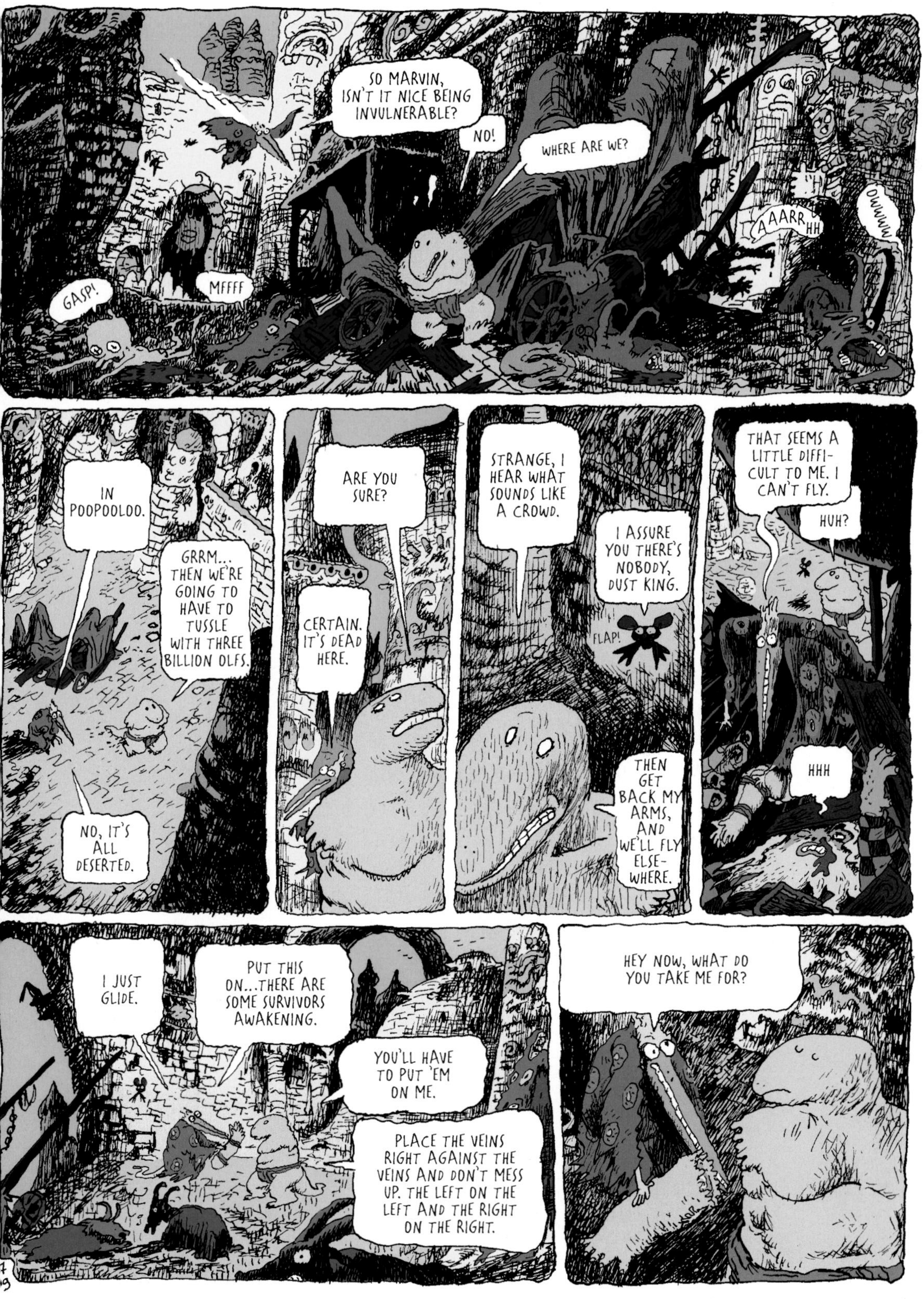

SO MARVIN, ISN'T IT NICE BEING INVULNERABLE?
NO!
WHERE ARE WE?
GASP!
MFFFF
AAARRHH
OWWWW
IN POOPOOLOO.
GRRM... THEN WE'RE GOING TO HAVE TO TUSSLE WITH THREE BILLION OLFS.
NO, IT'S ALL DESERTED.
ARE YOU SURE?
CERTAIN. IT'S DEAD HERE.
STRANGE, I HEAR WHAT SOUNDS LIKE A CROWD.
I ASSURE YOU THERE'S NOBODY, DUST KING.
FLAP!
THEN GET BACK MY ARMS, AND WE'LL FLY ELSEWHERE.
THAT SEEMS A LITTLE DIFFICULT TO ME. I CAN'T FLY.
HUH?
HHH
I JUST GLIDE.
PUT THIS ON...THERE ARE SOME SURVIVORS AWAKENING.
YOU'LL HAVE TO PUT 'EM ON ME.
PLACE THE VEINS RIGHT AGAINST THE VEINS AND DON'T MESS UP. THE LEFT ON THE LEFT AND THE RIGHT ON THE RIGHT.
HEY NOW, WHAT DO YOU TAKE ME FOR?

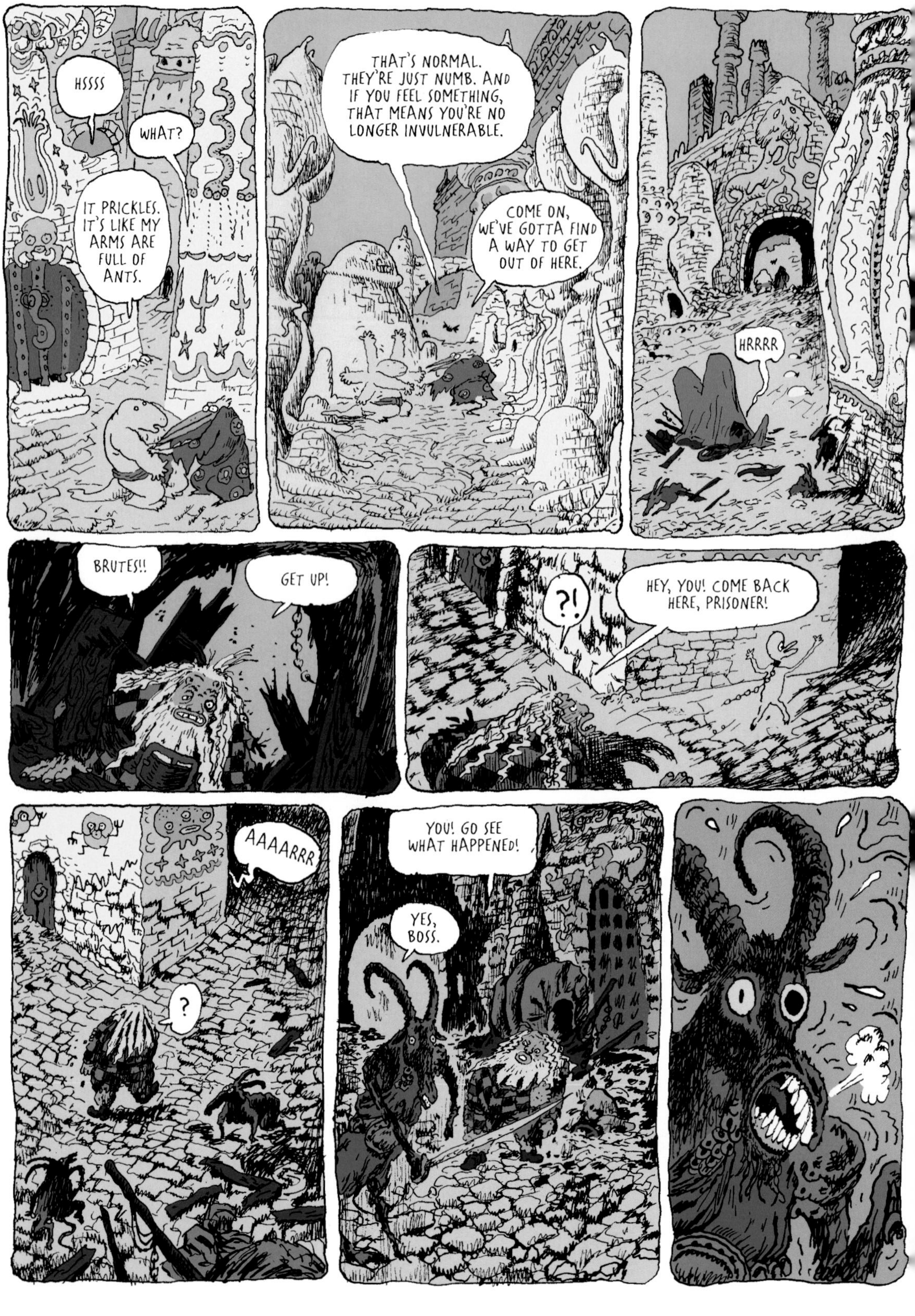

HSSSS
WHAT?
IT PRICKLES. IT'S LIKE MY ARMS ARE FULL OF ANTS.
THAT'S NORMAL. THEY'RE JUST NUMB. AND IF YOU FEEL SOMETHING, THAT MEANS YOU'RE NO LONGER INVULNERABLE.
COME ON, WE'VE GOTTA FIND A WAY TO GET OUT OF HERE.
HRRRR
BRUTES!!
GET UP!
?!
HEY, YOU! COME BACK HERE, PRISONER!
AAAARRR
?
YOU! GO SEE WHAT HAPPENED!
YES, BOSS.

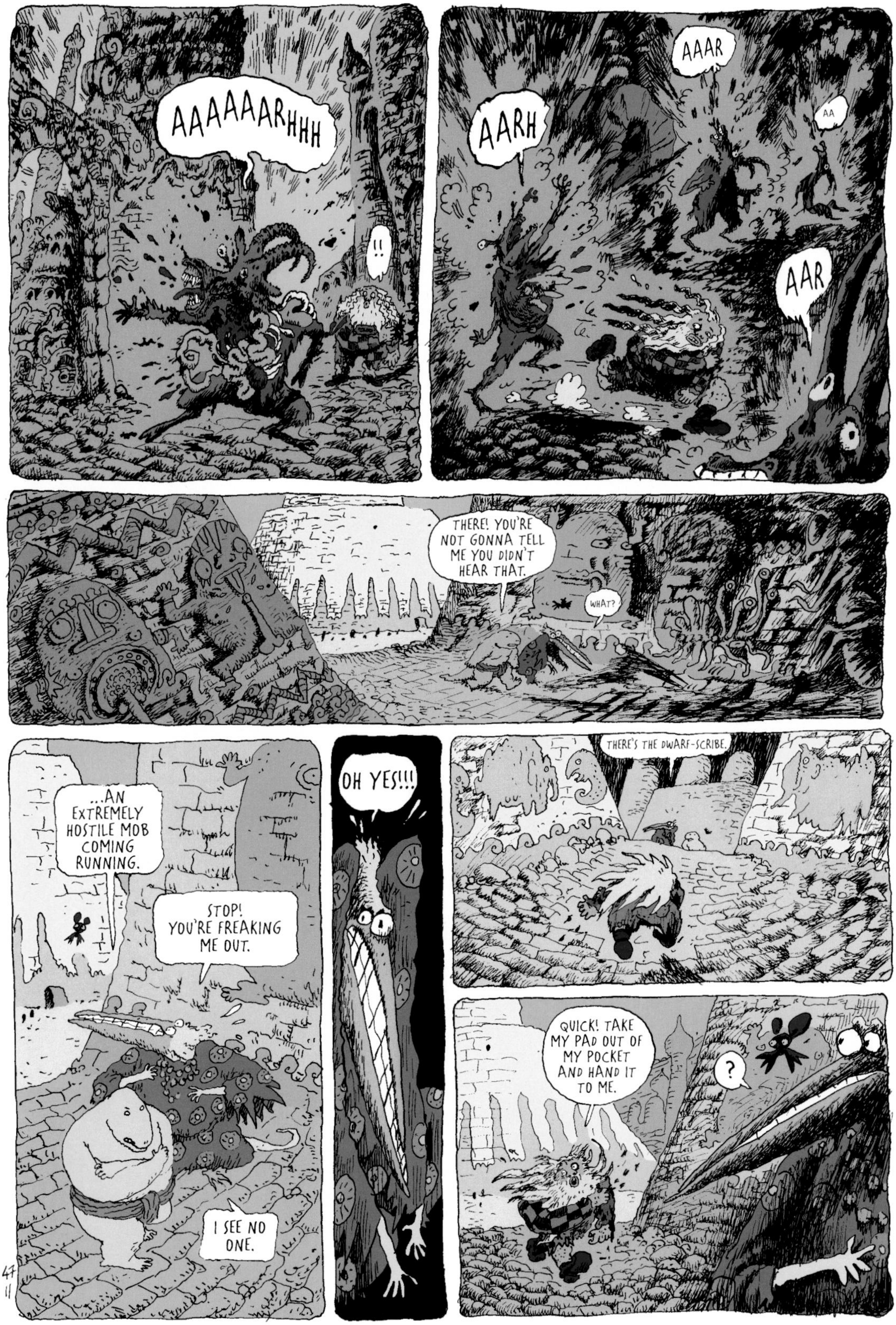
AAAAAARHHH
!!
AAAR
AARH
AA
AAR
THERE! YOU'RE NOT GONNA TELL ME YOU DIDN'T HEAR THAT.
WHAT?
...AN EXTREMELY HOSTILE MOB COMING RUNNING.
STOP! YOU'RE FREAKING ME OUT.
I SEE NO ONE.
OH YES!!!
THERE'S THE DWARF-SCRIBE.
QUICK! TAKE MY PAD OUT OF MY POCKET AND HAND IT TO ME.
?

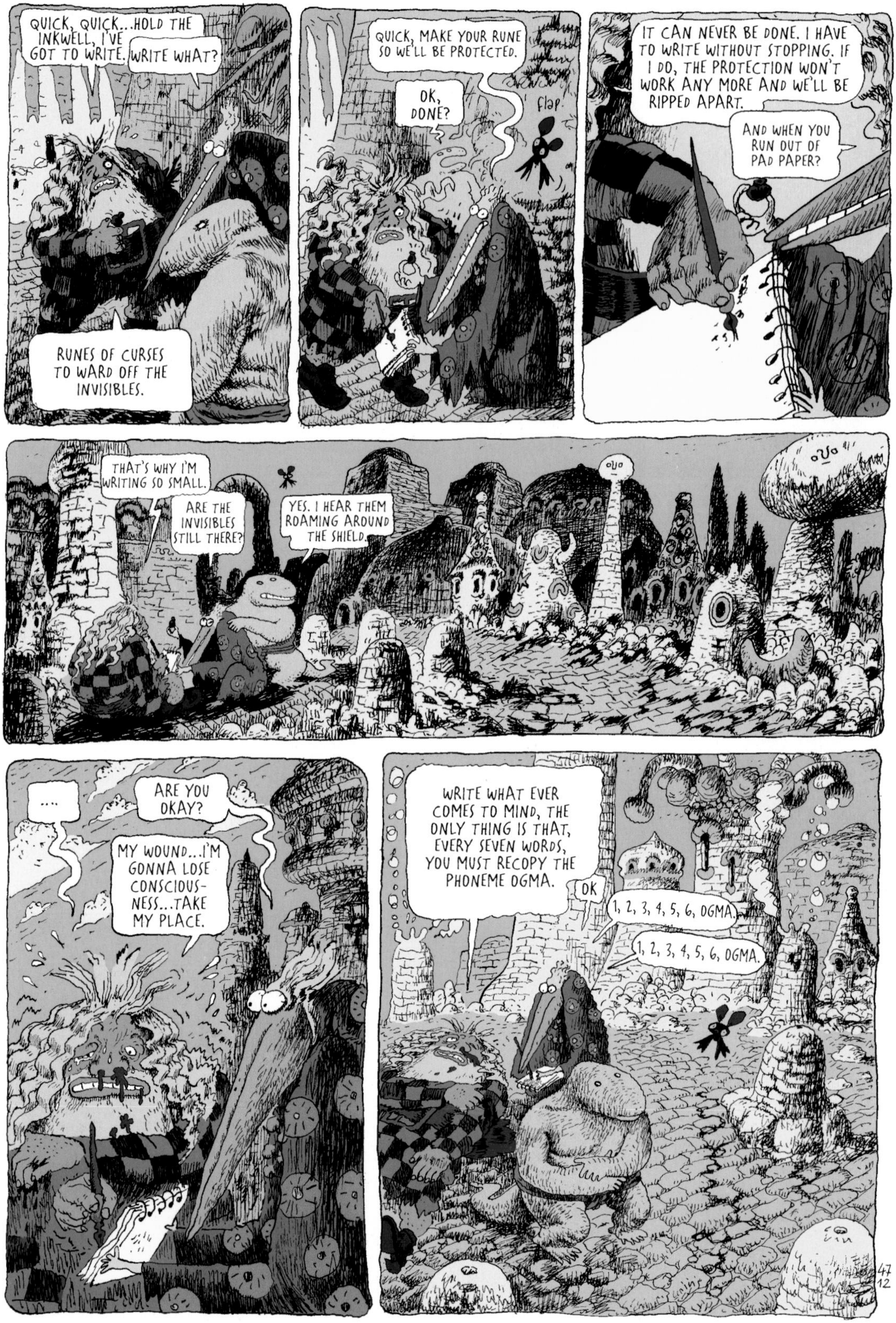
QUICK, QUICK...HOLD THE INKWELL, I'VE GOT TO WRITE.
WRITE WHAT?
RUNES OF CURSES TO WARD OFF THE INVISIBLES.
QUICK, MAKE YOUR RUNE SO WE'LL BE PROTECTED.
OK, DONE?
FLAP
IT CAN NEVER BE DONE. I HAVE TO WRITE WITHOUT STOPPING. IF I DO, THE PROTECTION WON'T WORK ANY MORE AND WE'LL BE RIPPED APART.
AND WHEN YOU RUN OUT OF PAD PAPER?
THAT'S WHY I'M WRITING SO SMALL.
ARE THE INVISIBLES STILL THERE?
YES. I HEAR THEM ROAMING AROUND THE SHIELD.
....
ARE YOU OKAY?
MY WOUND...I'M GONNA LOSE CONSCIOUS-NESS...TAKE MY PLACE.
WRITE WHAT EVER COMES TO MIND, THE ONLY THING IS THAT, EVERY SEVEN WORDS, YOU MUST RECOPY THE PHONEME OGMA.
OK
1, 2, 3, 4, 5, 6, OGMA.
1, 2, 3, 4, 5, 6, OGMA.

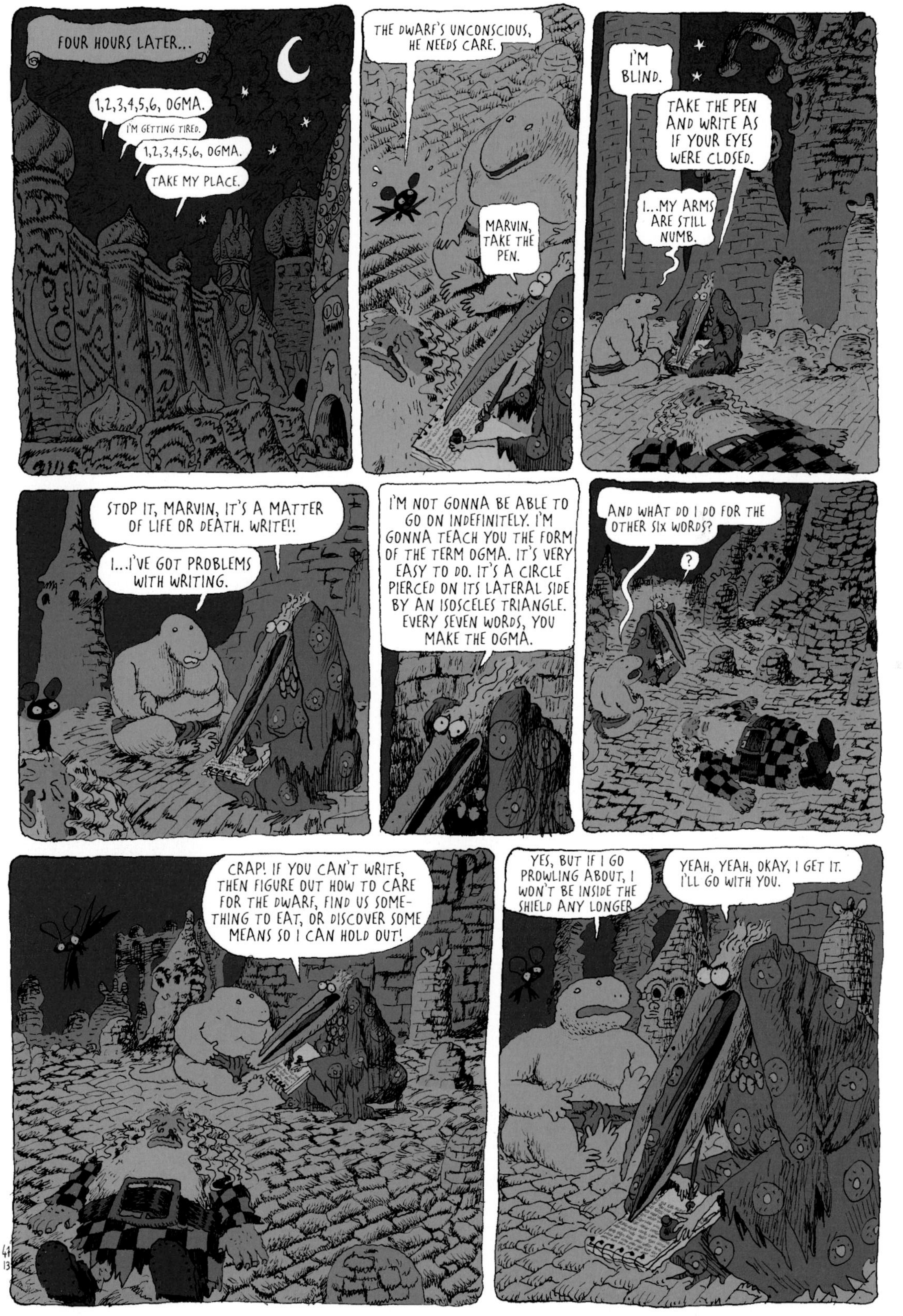
FOUR HOURS LATER...
1,2,3,4,5,6, OGMA.
I'M GETTING TIRED.
1,2,3,4,5,6, OGMA.
TAKE MY PLACE.
THE DWARF'S UNCONSCIOUS, HE NEEDS CARE.
MARVIN, TAKE THE PEN.
I'M BLIND.
TAKE THE PEN AND WRITE AS IF YOUR EYES WERE CLOSED.
I...MY ARMS ARE STILL NUMB.
STOP IT, MARVIN, IT'S A MATTER OF LIFE OR DEATH. WRITE!!
I...I'VE GOT PROBLEMS WITH WRITING.
I'M NOT GONNA BE ABLE TO GO ON INDEFINITELY. I'M GONNA TEACH YOU THE FORM OF THE TERM OGMA. IT'S VERY EASY TO DO. IT'S A CIRCLE PIERCED ON ITS LATERAL SIDE BY AN ISOSCELES TRIANGLE. EVERY SEVEN WORDS, YOU MAKE THE OGMA.
AND WHAT DO I DO FOR THE OTHER SIX WORDS?
?
CRAP! IF YOU CAN'T WRITE, THEN FIGURE OUT HOW TO CARE FOR THE DWARF, FIND US SOMETHING TO EAT, OR DISCOVER SOME MEANS SO I CAN HOLD OUT!
YES, BUT IF I GO PROWLING ABOUT, I WON'T BE INSIDE THE SHIELD ANY LONGER
YEAH, YEAH, OKAY, I GET IT. I'LL GO WITH YOU.

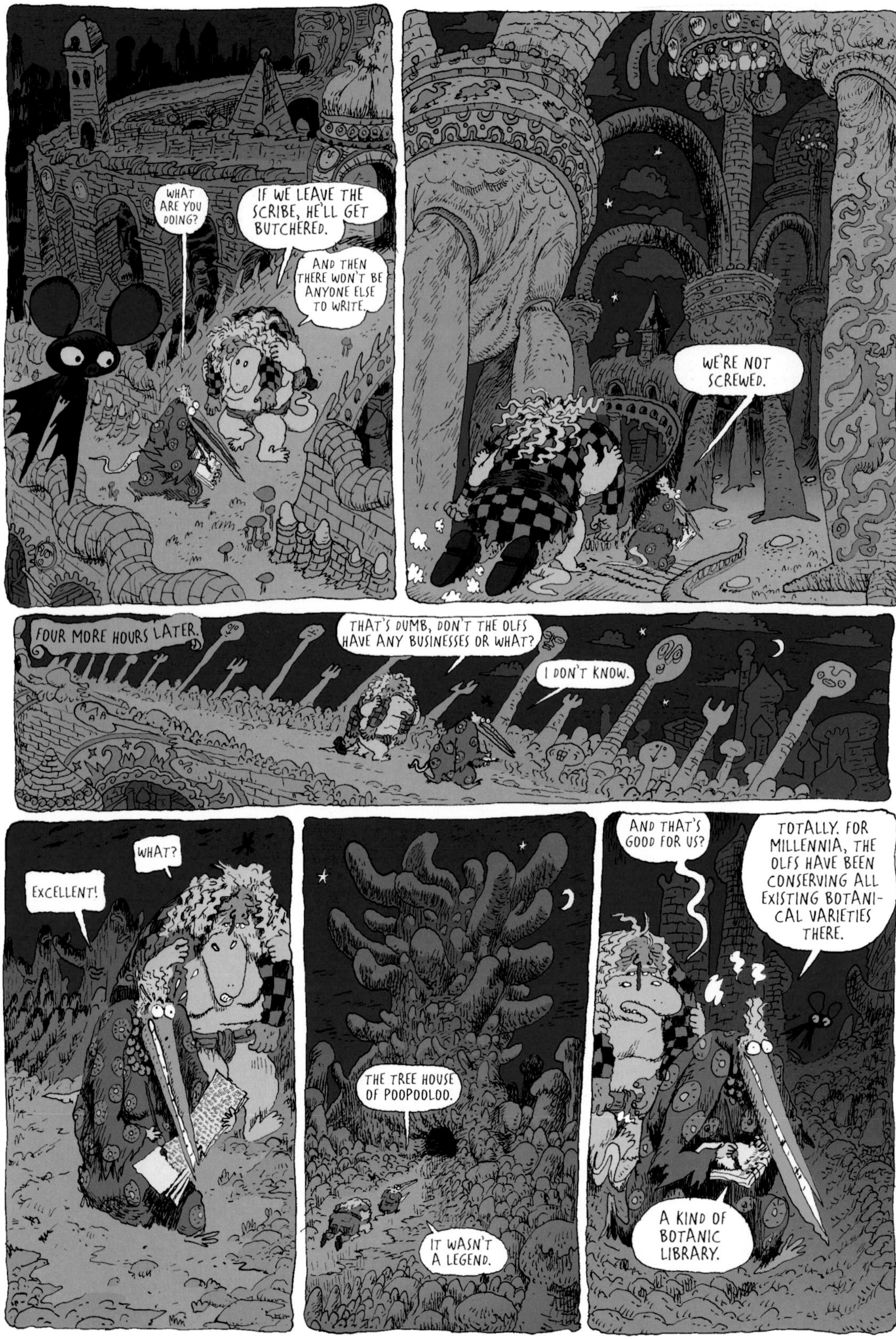
WHAT ARE YOU DOING?
IF WE LEAVE THE SCRIBE, HE'LL GET BUTCHERED.
AND THEN THERE WON'T BE ANYONE ELSE TO WRITE.
WE'RE NOT SCREWED.
FOUR MORE HOURS LATER.
THAT'S DUMB, DON'T THE OLFS HAVE ANY BUSINESSES OR WHAT?
I DON'T KNOW.
EXCELLENT!
WHAT?
THE TREE HOUSE OF POOPOOLOO.
IT WASN'T A LEGEND.
AND THAT'S GOOD FOR US?
TOTALLY. FOR MILLENNIA, THE OLFS HAVE BEEN CONSERVING ALL EXISTING BOTANICAL VARIETIES THERE.
A KIND OF BOTANIC LIBRARY.

WHEN I WAS A TEENAGER ON THE WHITE ISLAND, THERE WERE LOTS OF OLD JUNKIES WHO DREAMT OF THIS EL DORADO.

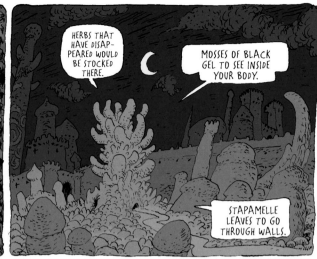

HERBS THAT HAVE DISAPPEARED WOULD BE STOCKED THERE.

MOSSES OF BLACK GEL TO SEE INSIDE YOUR BODY.

STAPAMELLE LEAVES TO GO THROUGH WALLS.

POLLEN FROM PURPLE ACACIAS TO MULTIPLY OUR NEURONS BY FIVE FOR TWENTY FOUR HOURS.

LICHENS OF CALIDURYS TO TELEPORT.

YEAH, BUT DON'T FORGET TO WRITE THE RUNES ALL THE SAME.

IT'S ALL HERE!

MARTYR FLOWERS!

THERE ARE MARTYR FLOWERS.

WHAT'S THAT FOR?

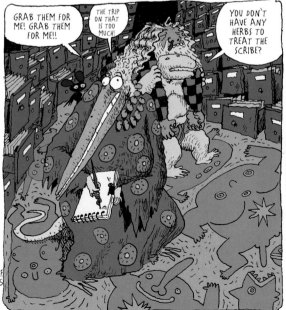

GRAB THEM FOR ME! GRAB THEM FOR ME!!

THE TRIP ON THAT IS TOO MUCH!

YOU DON'T HAVE ANY HERBS TO TREAT THE SCRIBE?

HERE! STICK THIS ON HIS WOUND.

WHOAA!! BULBS OF VEGETAL LEMMING.

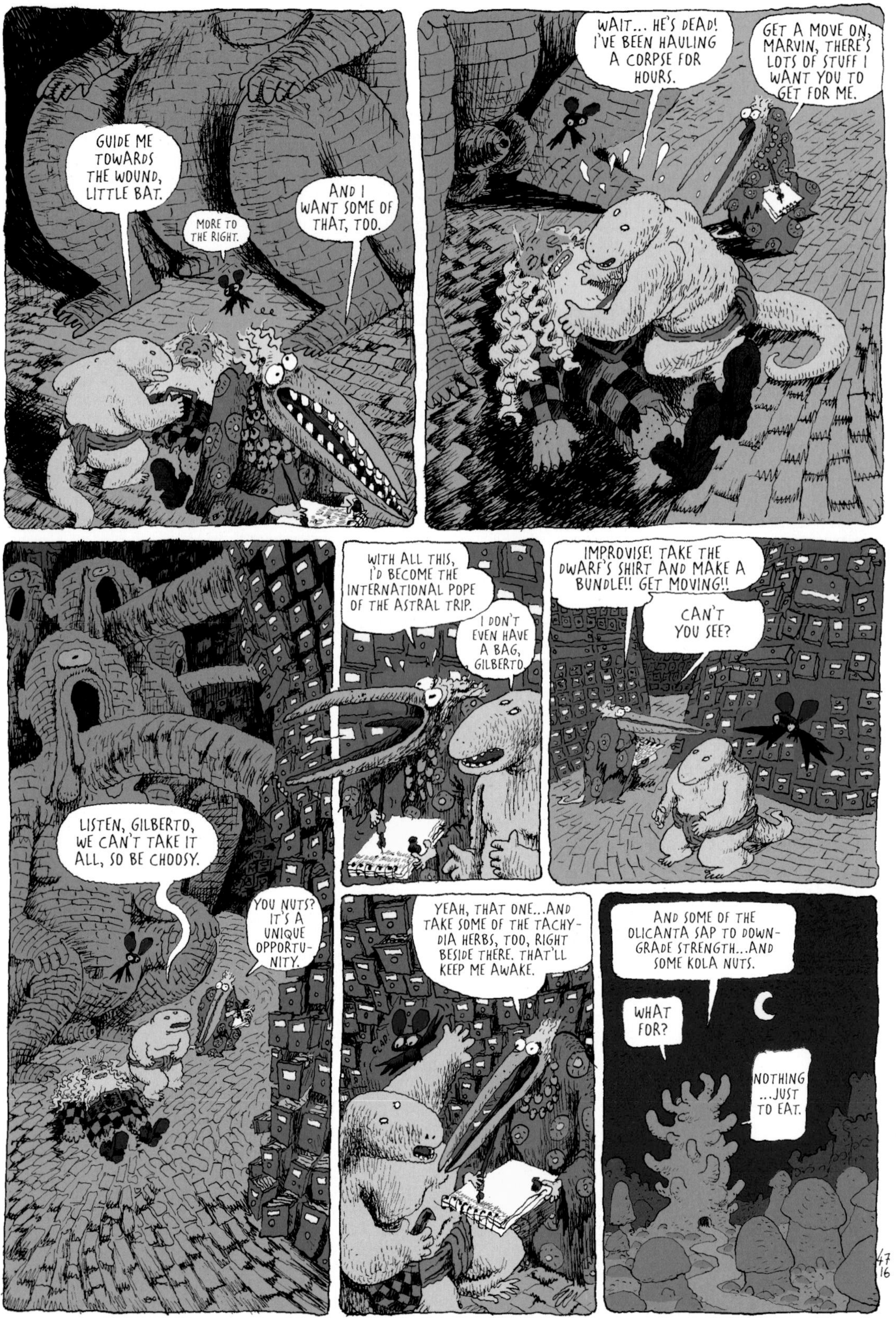

GUIDE ME TOWARDS THE WOUND, LITTLE BAT.
MORE TO THE RIGHT.
AND I WANT SOME OF THAT, TOO.
WAIT... HE'S DEAD! I'VE BEEN HAULING A CORPSE FOR HOURS.
GET A MOVE ON, MARVIN, THERE'S LOTS OF STUFF I WANT YOU TO GET FOR ME.
LISTEN, GILBERTO, WE CAN'T TAKE IT ALL, SO BE CHOOSY.
YOU NUTS? IT'S A UNIQUE OPPORTUNITY.
WITH ALL THIS, I'D BECOME THE INTERNATIONAL POPE OF THE ASTRAL TRIP.
I DON'T EVEN HAVE A BAG, GILBERTO.
IMPROVISE! TAKE THE DWARF'S SHIRT AND MAKE A BUNDLE!! GET MOVING!!
CAN'T YOU SEE?
YEAH, THAT ONE...AND TAKE SOME OF THE TACHYDIA HERBS, TOO, RIGHT BESIDE THERE. THAT'LL KEEP ME AWAKE.
FLAP!
AND SOME OF THE OLICANTA SAP TO DOWNGRADE STRENGTH...AND SOME KOLA NUTS.
WHAT FOR?
NOTHING ...JUST TO EAT.

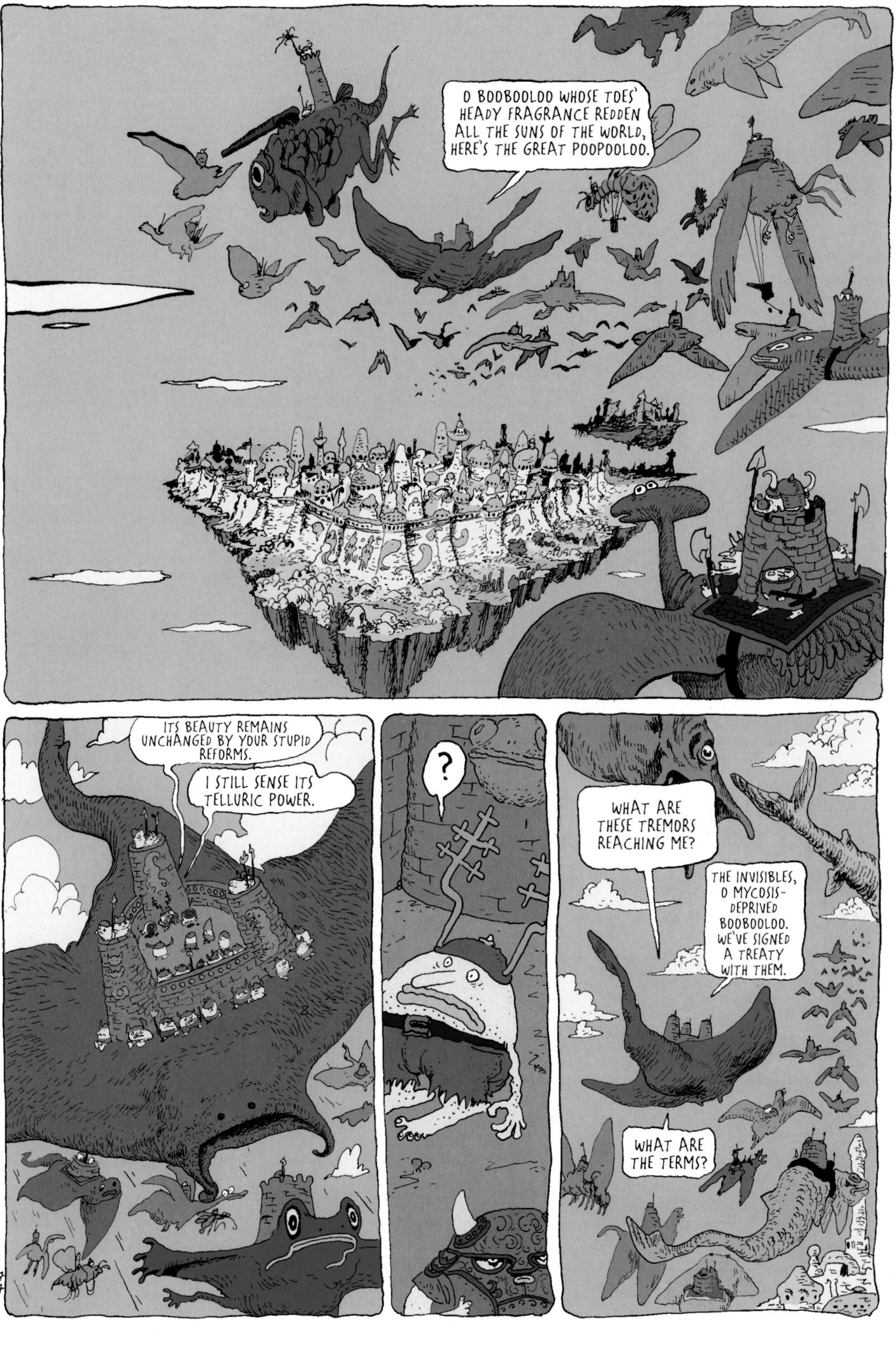
O BOOBOOLOO WHOSE TOES' HEADY FRAGRANCE REDDEN ALL THE SUNS OF THE WORLD, HERE'S THE GREAT POOPOOLOO.
ITS BEAUTY REMAINS UNCHANGED BY YOUR STUPID REFORMS.
I STILL SENSE ITS TELLURIC POWER.
?
WHAT ARE THESE TREMORS REACHING ME?
THE INVISIBLES, O MYCOSIS-DEPRIVED BOOBOOLOO. WE'VE SIGNED A TREATY WITH THEM.
WHAT ARE THE TERMS?

THEY OCCUPY ALL THE SPACES OF POOPOOLOO WE DON'T USE.

MEANING?

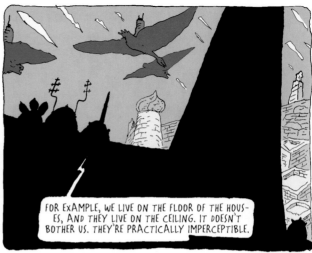

FOR EXAMPLE, WE LIVE ON THE FLOOR OF THE HOUSES, AND THEY LIVE ON THE CEILING. IT DOESN'T BOTHER US. THEY'RE PRACTICALLY IMPERCEPTIBLE.

WHAT'S THE INTEREST OF THIS TREATY FOR US?

THEY PROTECT THE CITY; THEY'RE BLOOD-THIRSTY KILLERS.

OK, THAT'S GOOD.

YES, THANKS TO THESE INVISIBLES, WE CAN COMPLETELY DESERT THE CITY AND BE CERTAIN THAT THERE WON'T BE ANY INTRUDERS.

AND THOSE TWO DICK-HEADS THERE ON THE SQUARE, WHAT'S THAT?

MARVIN.

YES.

UH...I THINK THE TWO BILLION OLFS ARE RETURNING.

47
18

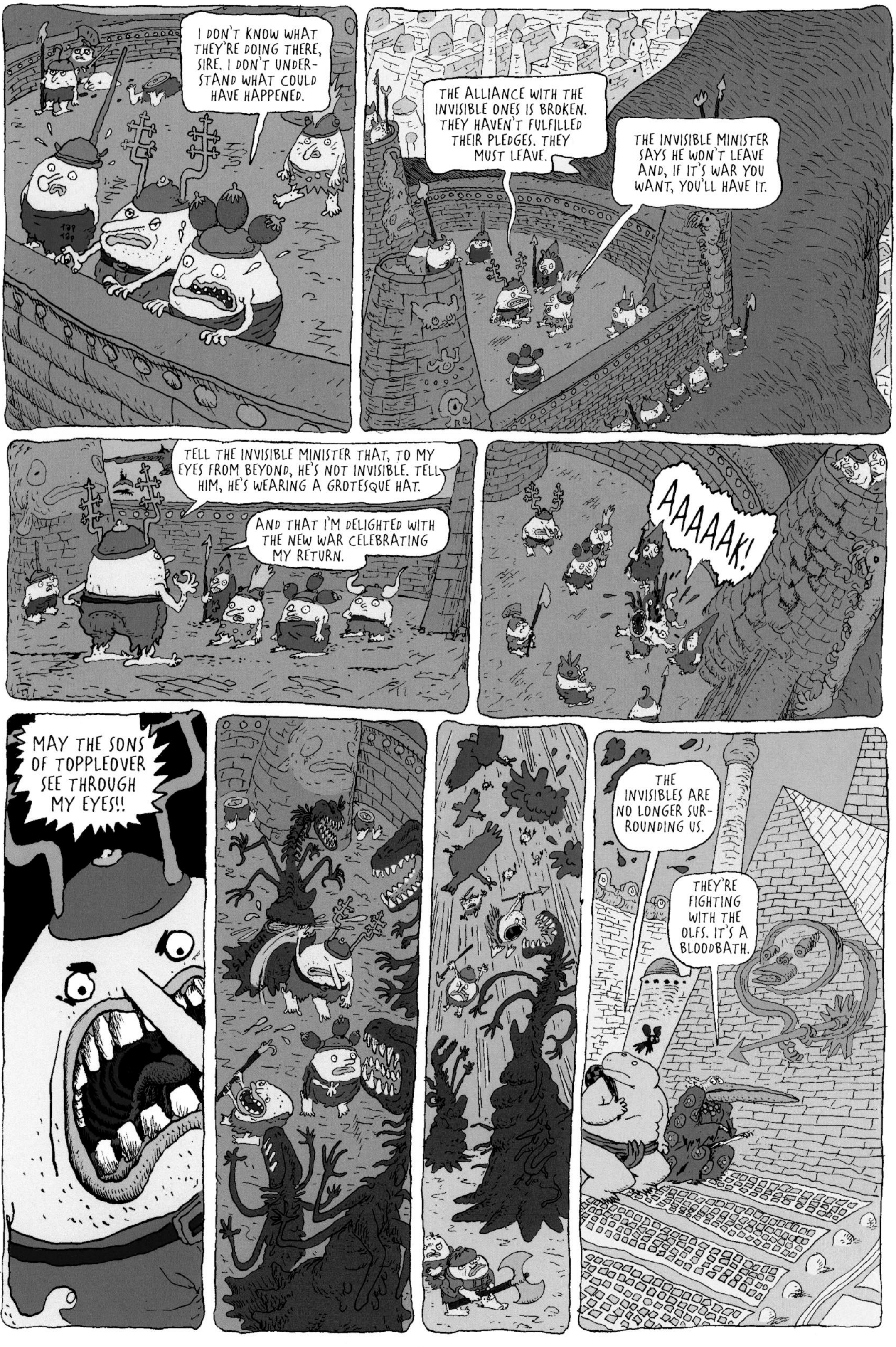
I DON'T KNOW WHAT THEY'RE DOING THERE, SIRE. I DON'T UNDERSTAND WHAT COULD HAVE HAPPENED.
THE ALLIANCE WITH THE INVISIBLE ONES IS BROKEN. THEY HAVEN'T FULFILLED THEIR PLEDGES. THEY MUST LEAVE.
THE INVISIBLE MINISTER SAYS HE WON'T LEAVE AND, IF IT'S WAR YOU WANT, YOU'LL HAVE IT.
TELL THE INVISIBLE MINISTER THAT, TO MY EYES FROM BEYOND, HE'S NOT INVISIBLE. TELL HIM, HE'S WEARING A GROTESQUE HAT.
AND THAT I'M DELIGHTED WITH THE NEW WAR CELEBRATING MY RETURN.
AAAAAK!
MAY THE SONS OF TOPPLEOVER SEE THROUGH MY EYES!!
SLATCH!
THE INVISIBLES ARE NO LONGER SURROUNDING US.
THEY'RE FIGHTING WITH THE OLFS. IT'S A BLOODBATH.

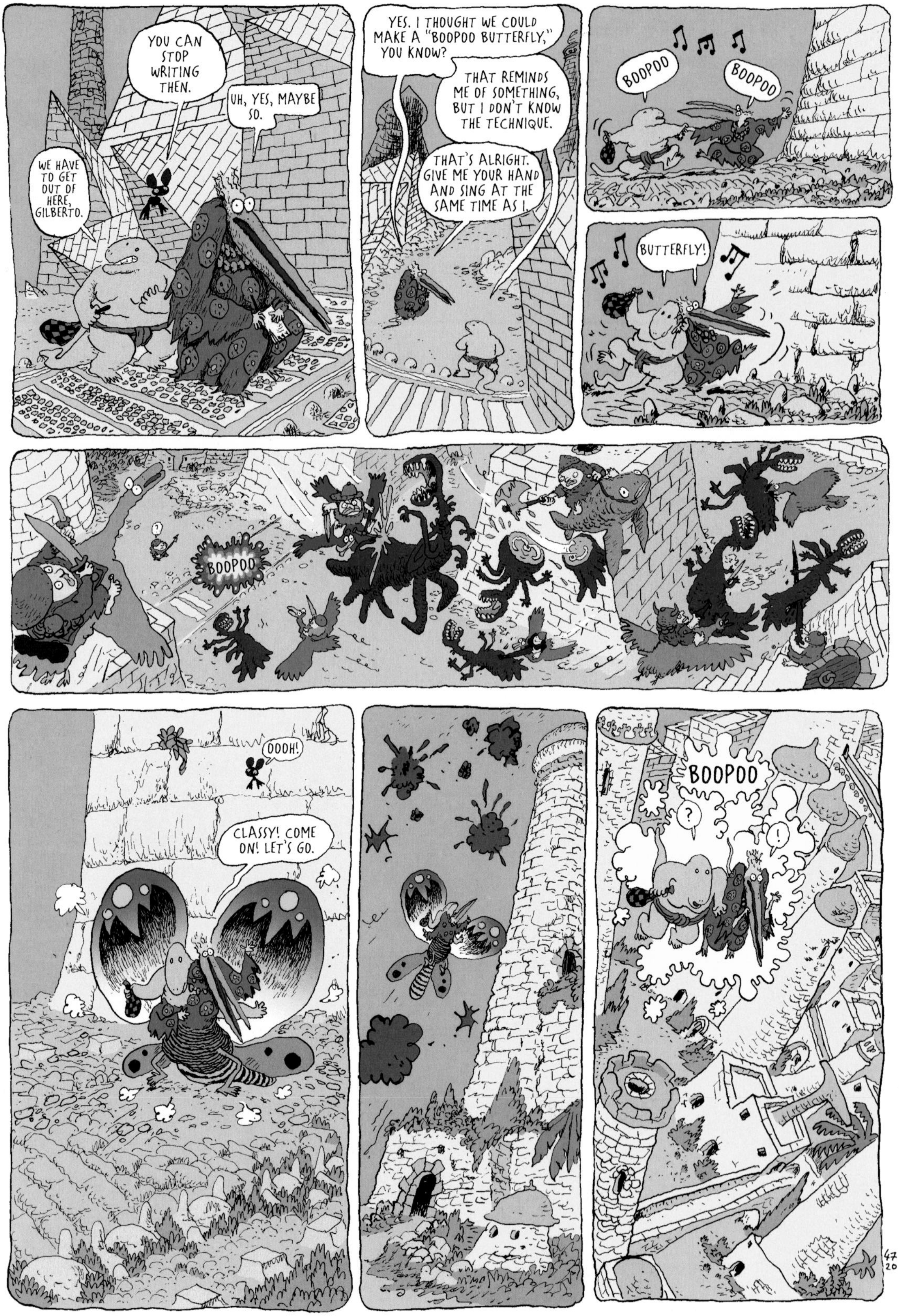
YOU CAN STOP WRITING THEN.
UH, YES, MAYBE SO.
WE HAVE TO GET OUT OF HERE, GILBERTO.
YES. I THOUGHT WE COULD MAKE A "BOOPOO BUTTERFLY," YOU KNOW?
THAT REMINDS ME OF SOMETHING, BUT I DON'T KNOW THE TECHNIQUE.
THAT'S ALRIGHT. GIVE ME YOUR HAND AND SING AT THE SAME TIME AS I.
BOOPOO
BOOPOO
BUTTERFLY!
BOOPOO
OOOH!
CLASSY! COME ON! LET'S GO.
BOOPOO
?
!

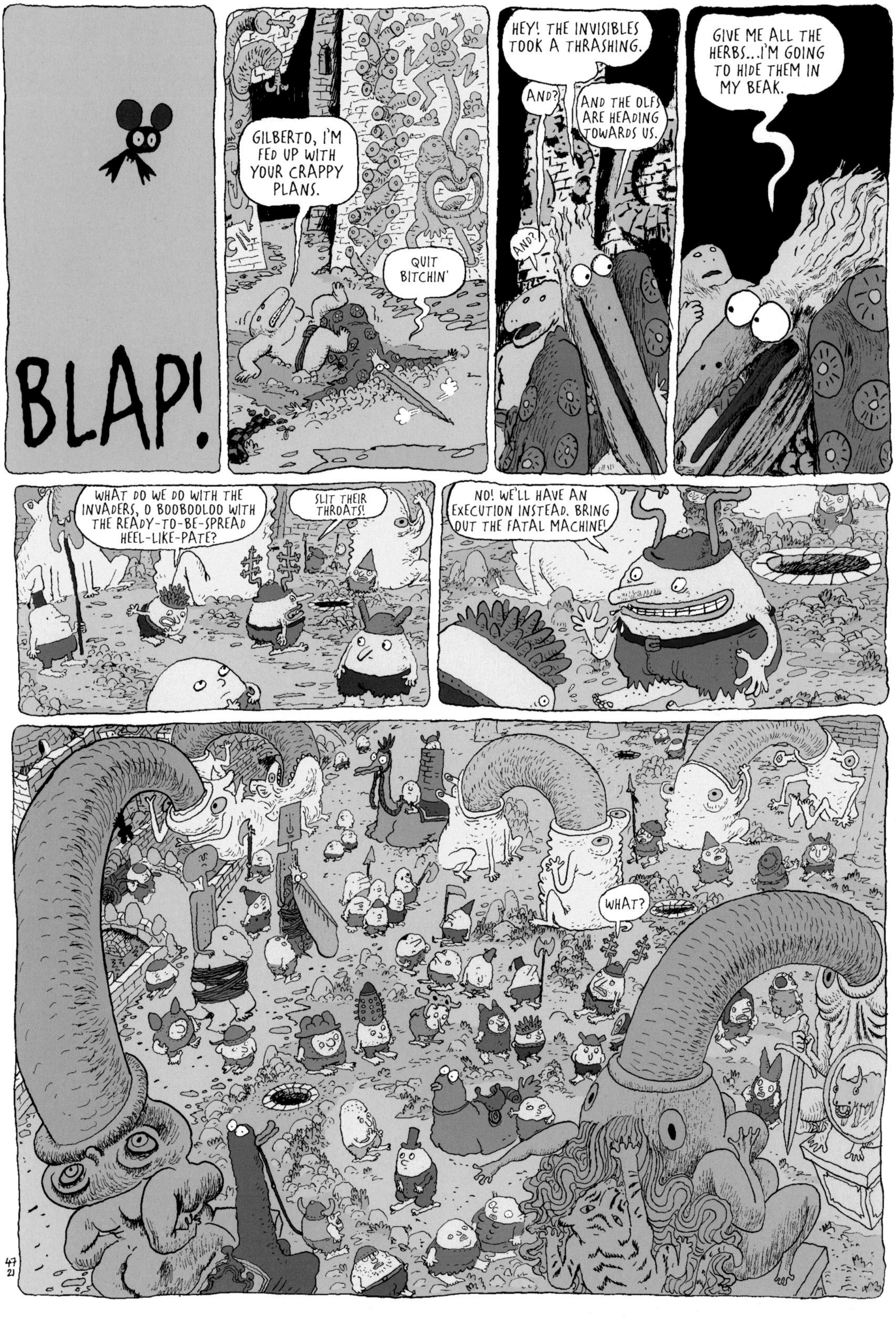
BLAP!
GILBERTO, I'M FED UP WITH YOUR CRAPPY PLANS.
QUIT BITCHIN'
HEY! THE INVISIBLES TOOK A THRASHING.
AND?
AND THE OLFS ARE HEADING TOWARDS US.
AND?
GIVE ME ALL THE HERBS...I'M GOING TO HIDE THEM IN MY BEAK.
WHAT DO WE DO WITH THE INVADERS, O BOOBOOLOO WITH THE READY-TO-BE-SPREAD HEEL-LIKE-PATE?
SLIT THEIR THROATS!
NO! WE'LL HAVE AN EXECUTION INSTEAD. BRING OUT THE FATAL MACHINE!
WHAT?

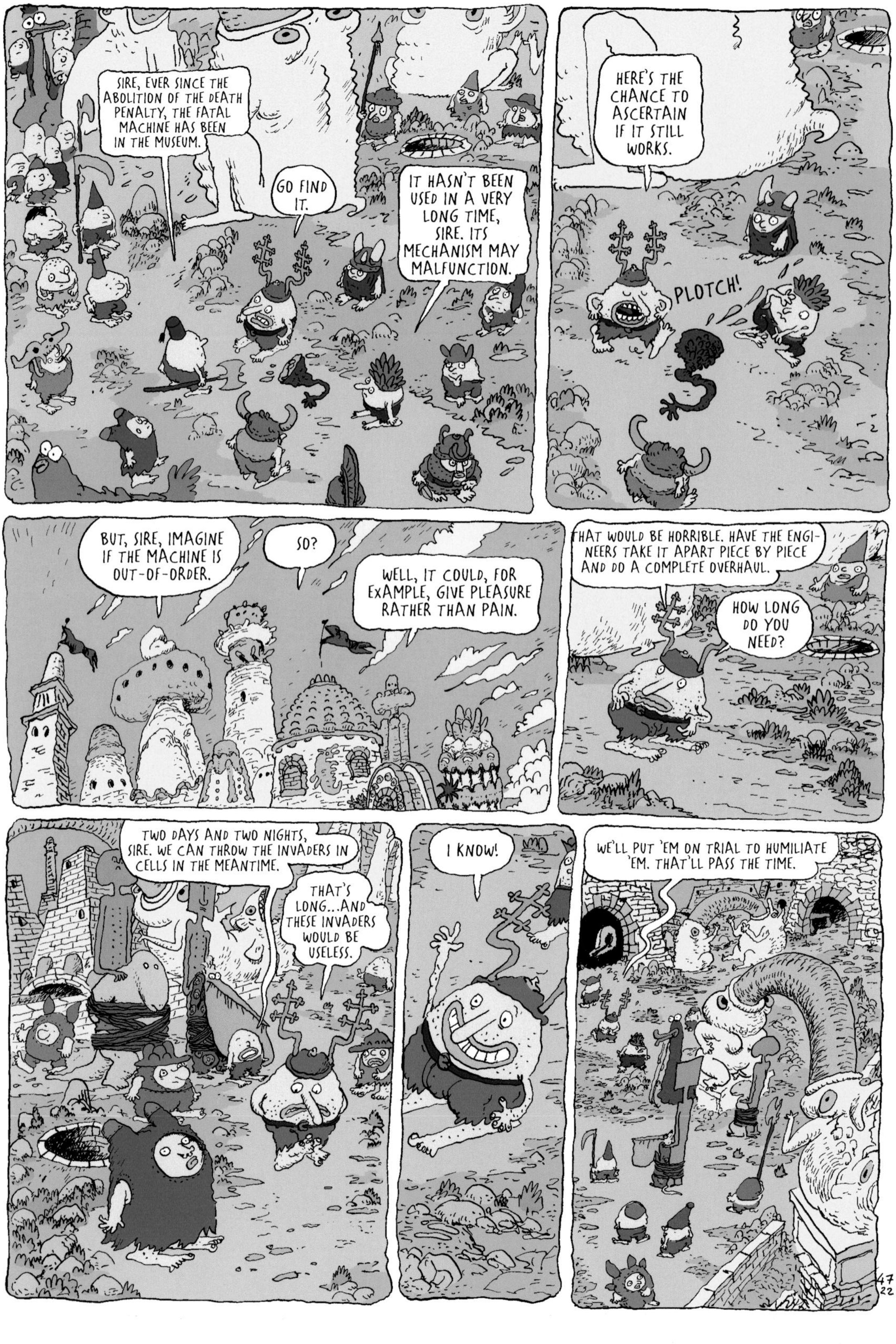
SIRE, EVER SINCE THE ABOLITION OF THE DEATH PENALTY, THE FATAL MACHINE HAS BEEN IN THE MUSEUM.
GO FIND IT.
IT HASN'T BEEN USED IN A VERY LONG TIME, SIRE. ITS MECHANISM MAY MALFUNCTION.
HERE'S THE CHANCE TO ASCERTAIN IF IT STILL WORKS.
PLOTCH!
BUT, SIRE, IMAGINE IF THE MACHINE IS OUT-OF-ORDER.
SO?
WELL, IT COULD, FOR EXAMPLE, GIVE PLEASURE RATHER THAN PAIN.
THAT WOULD BE HORRIBLE. HAVE THE ENGINEERS TAKE IT APART PIECE BY PIECE AND DO A COMPLETE OVERHAUL.
HOW LONG DO YOU NEED?
TWO DAYS AND TWO NIGHTS, SIRE. WE CAN THROW THE INVADERS IN CELLS IN THE MEANTIME.
THAT'S LONG...AND THESE INVADERS WOULD BE USELESS.
I KNOW!
WE'LL PUT 'EM ON TRIAL TO HUMILIATE 'EM. THAT'LL PASS THE TIME.

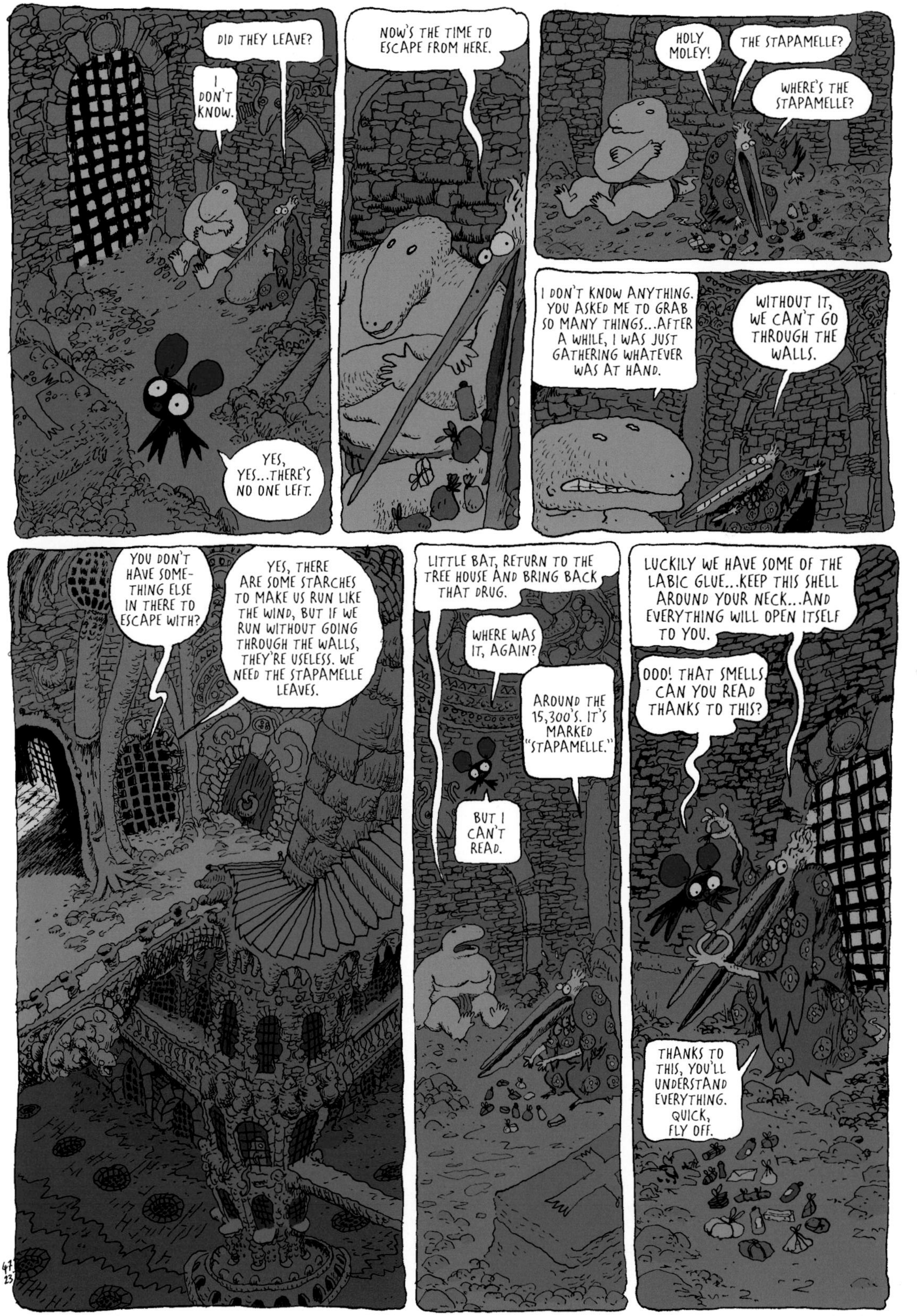

DID THEY LEAVE?
I DON'T KNOW.
YES, YES...THERE'S NO ONE LEFT.
NOW'S THE TIME TO ESCAPE FROM HERE.
HOLY MOLEY!
THE STAPAMELLE?
WHERE'S THE STAPAMELLE?
I DON'T KNOW ANYTHING. YOU ASKED ME TO GRAB SO MANY THINGS...AFTER A WHILE, I WAS JUST GATHERING WHATEVER WAS AT HAND.
WITHOUT IT, WE CAN'T GO THROUGH THE WALLS.
YOU DON'T HAVE SOMETHING ELSE IN THERE TO ESCAPE WITH?
YES, THERE ARE SOME STARCHES TO MAKE US RUN LIKE THE WIND, BUT IF WE RUN WITHOUT GOING THROUGH THE WALLS, THEY'RE USELESS. WE NEED THE STAPAMELLE LEAVES.
LITTLE BAT, RETURN TO THE TREE HOUSE AND BRING BACK THAT DRUG.
WHERE WAS IT, AGAIN?
AROUND THE 15,300'S. IT'S MARKED "STAPAMELLE."
BUT I CAN'T READ.
LUCKILY WE HAVE SOME OF THE LABIC GLUE...KEEP THIS SHELL AROUND YOUR NECK...AND EVERYTHING WILL OPEN ITSELF TO YOU.
OOO! THAT SMELLS. CAN YOU READ THANKS TO THIS?
THANKS TO THIS, YOU'LL UNDERSTAND EVERYTHING. QUICK, FLY OFF.
47
23

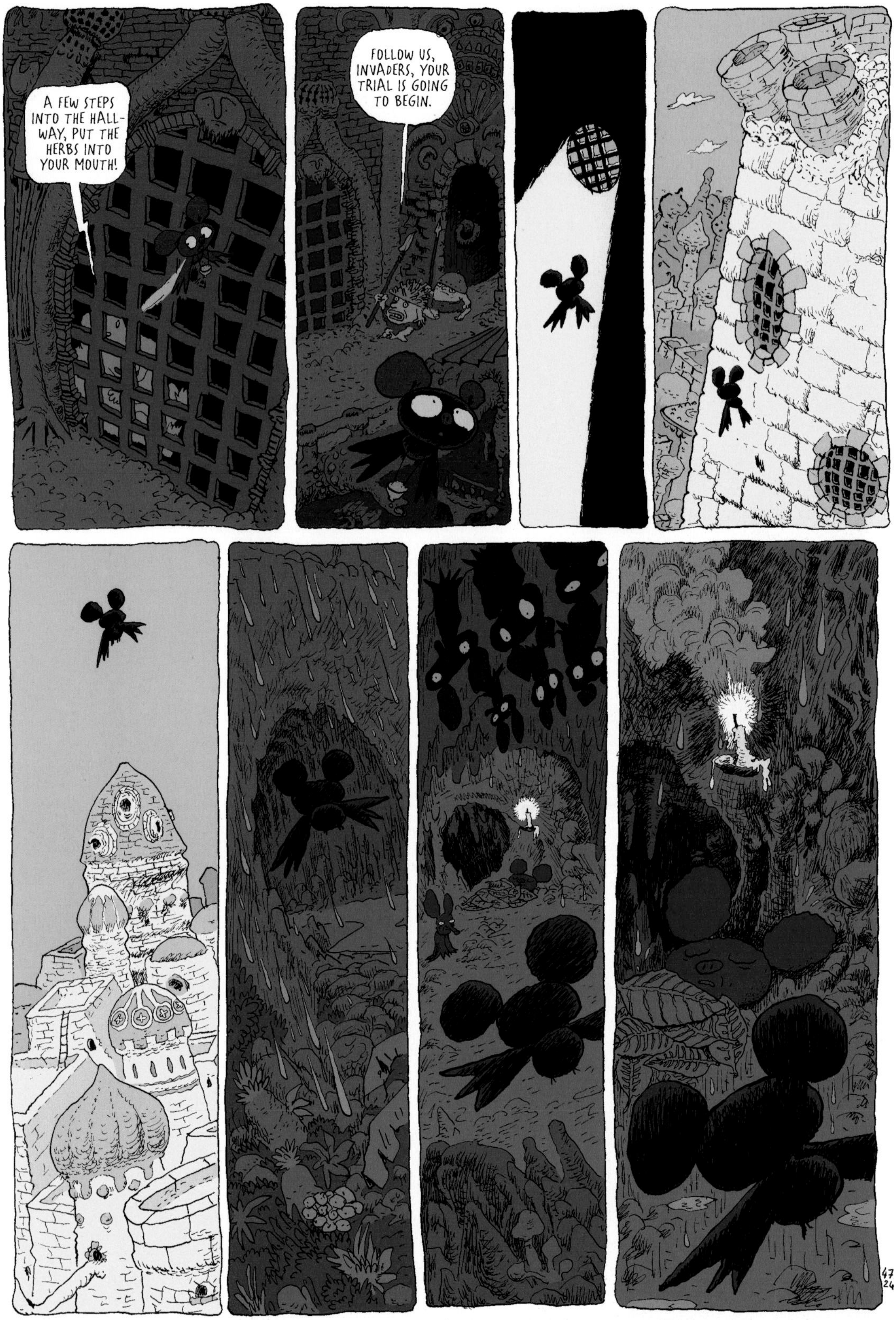
A FEW STEPS INTO THE HALL-WAY, PUT THE HERBS INTO YOUR MOUTH!
FOLLOW US, INVADERS, YOUR TRIAL IS GOING TO BEGIN.

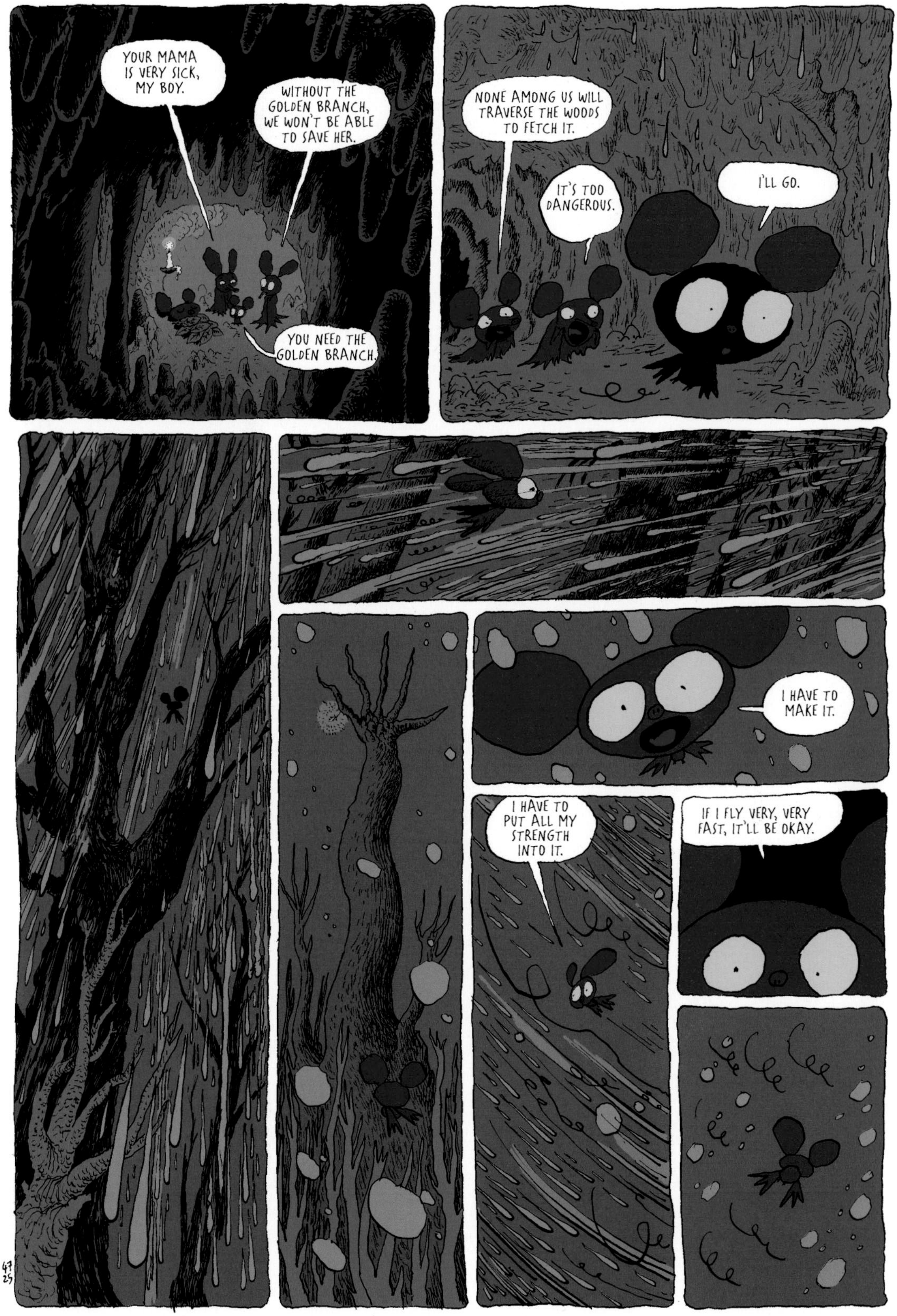
YOUR MAMA IS VERY SICK, MY BOY.
WITHOUT THE GOLDEN BRANCH, WE WON'T BE ABLE TO SAVE HER.
YOU NEED THE GOLDEN BRANCH.
NONE AMONG US WILL TRAVERSE THE WOODS TO FETCH IT.
IT'S TOO DANGEROUS.
I'LL GO.
I HAVE TO MAKE IT.
I HAVE TO PUT ALL MY STRENGTH INTO IT.
IF I FLY VERY, VERY FAST, IT'LL BE OKAY.

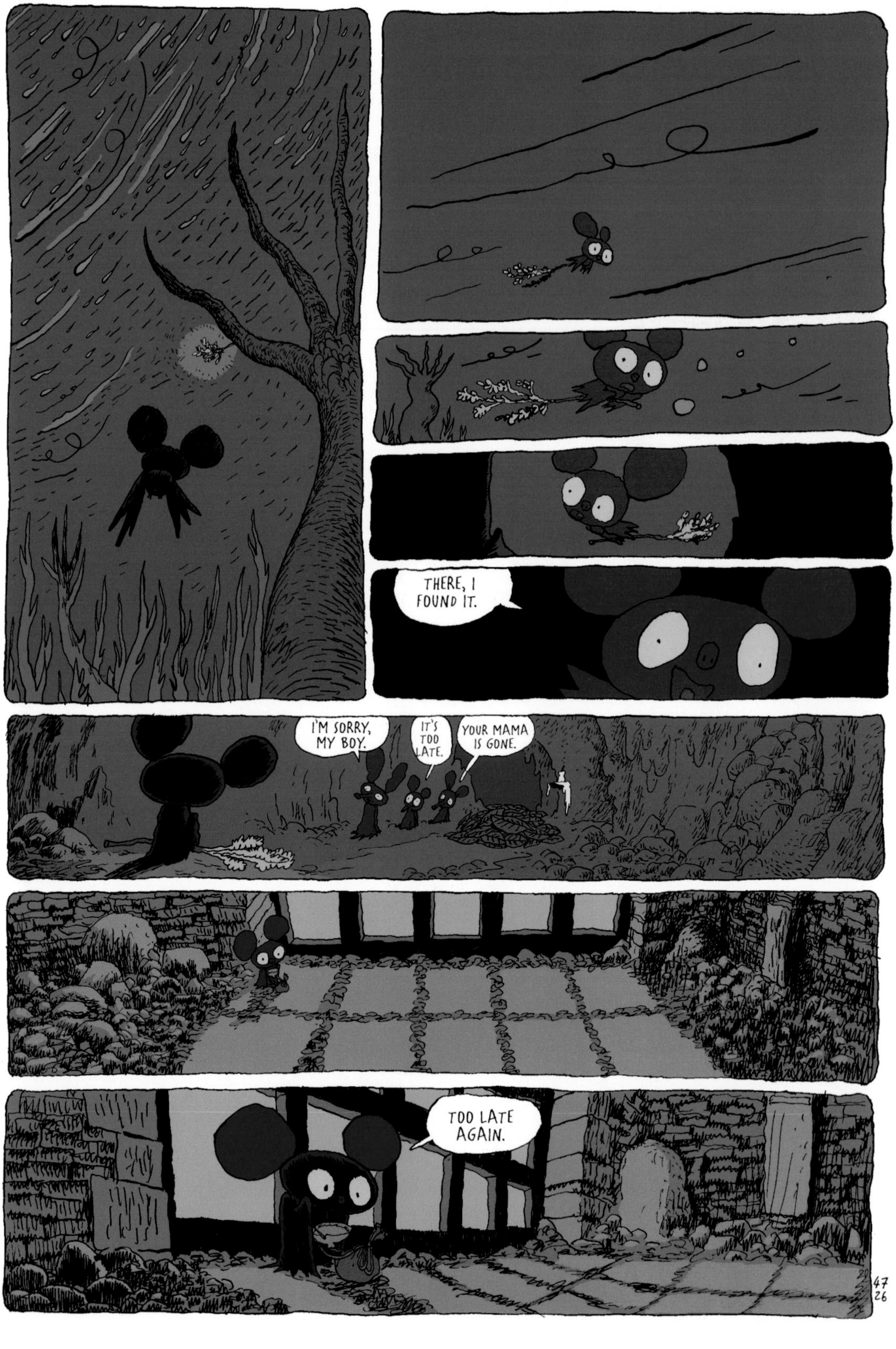
THERE, I FOUND IT.
I'M SORRY, MY BOY.
IT'S TOO LATE.
YOUR MAMA IS GONE.
TOO LATE AGAIN.

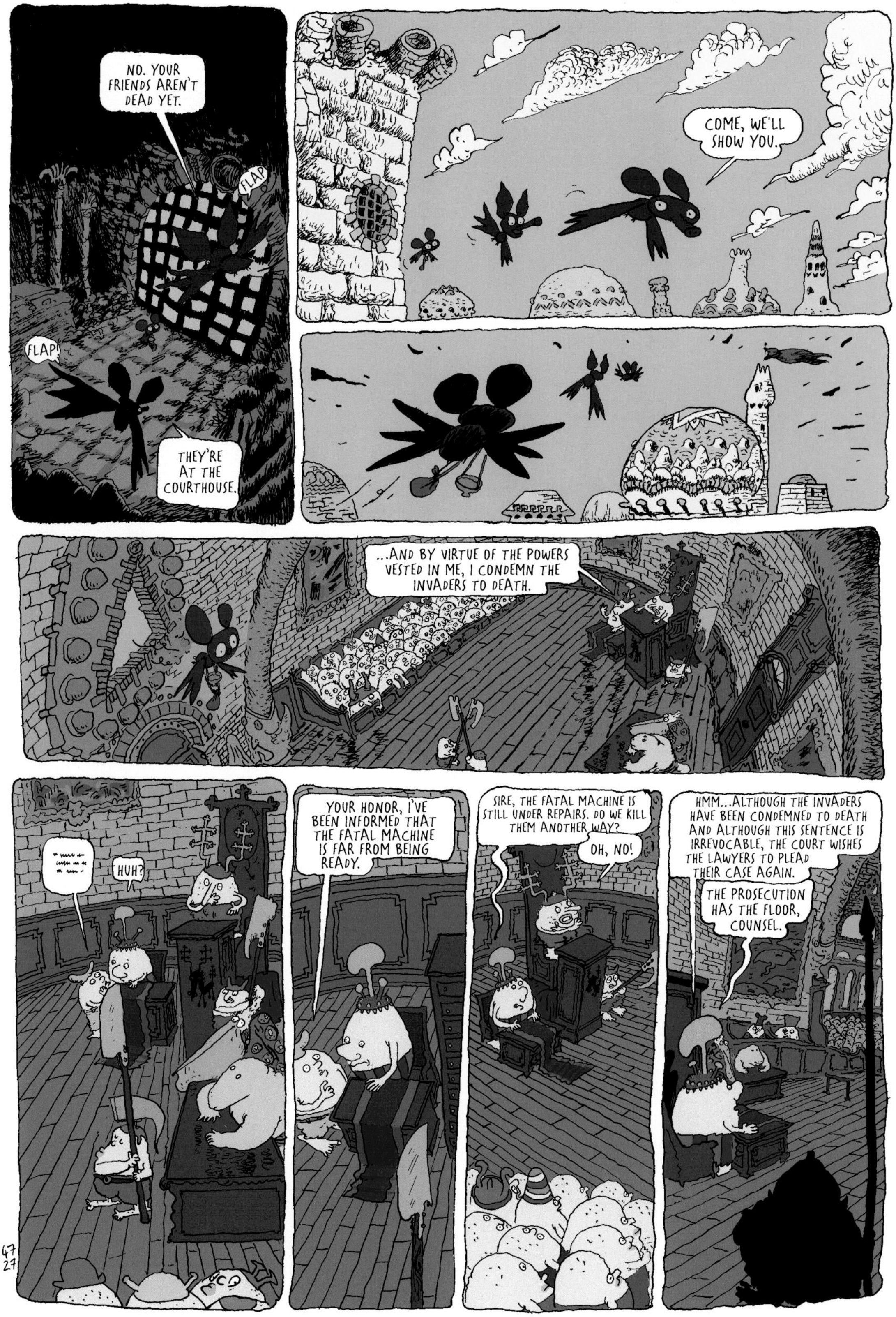
NO. YOUR FRIENDS AREN'T DEAD YET.
FLAP!
FLAP!
THEY'RE AT THE COURTHOUSE.
COME, WE'LL SHOW YOU.
...AND BY VIRTUE OF THE POWERS VESTED IN ME, I CONDEMN THE INVADERS TO DEATH.
HUH?
YOUR HONOR, I'VE BEEN INFORMED THAT THE FATAL MACHINE IS FAR FROM BEING READY.
SIRE, THE FATAL MACHINE IS STILL UNDER REPAIRS. DO WE KILL THEM ANOTHER WAY?
OH, NO!
HMM...ALTHOUGH THE INVADERS HAVE BEEN CONDEMNED TO DEATH AND ALTHOUGH THIS SENTENCE IS IRREVOCABLE, THE COURT WISHES THE LAWYERS TO PLEAD THEIR CASE AGAIN.
THE PROSECUTION HAS THE FLOOR, COUNSEL.

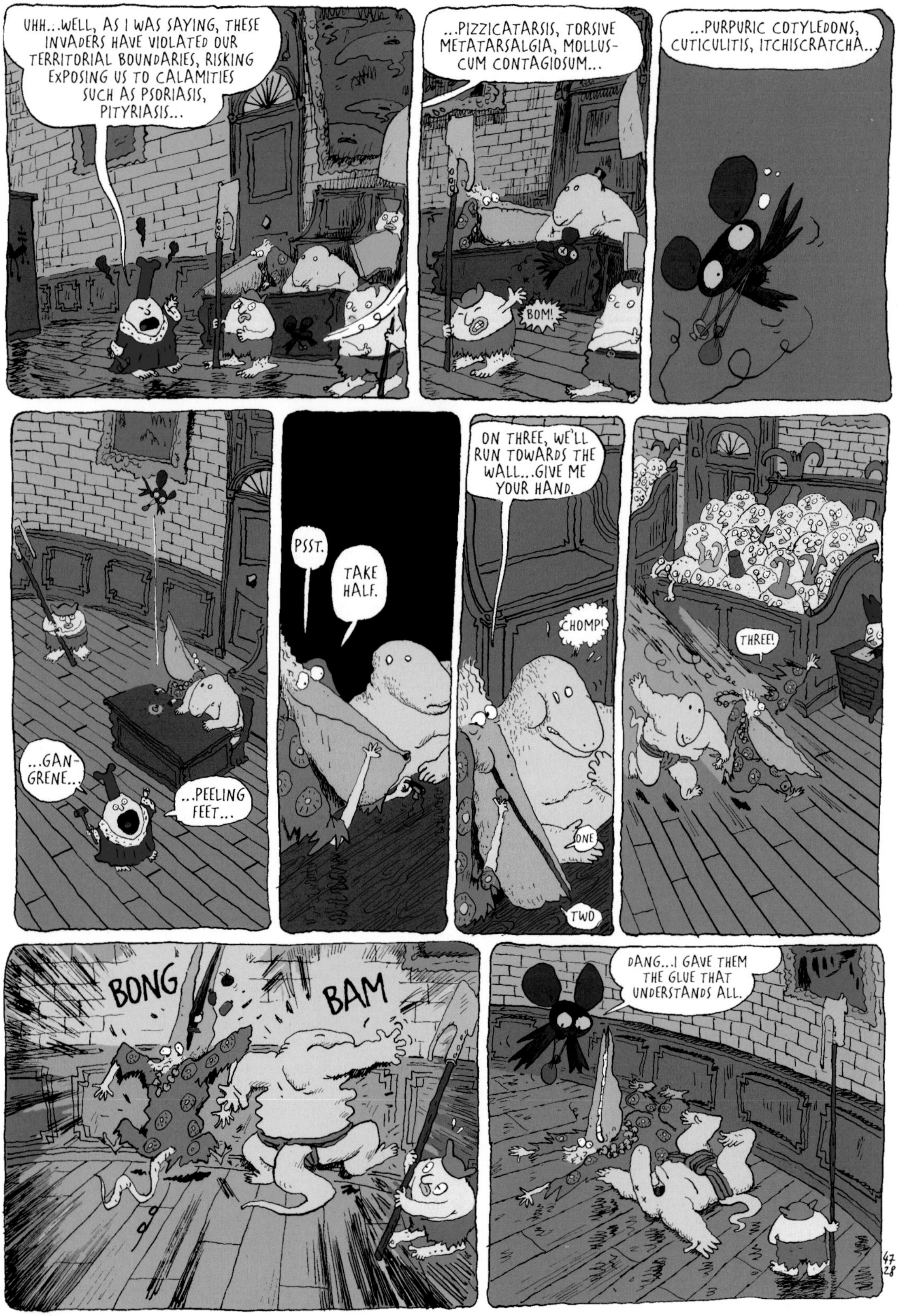
UHH...WELL, AS I WAS SAYING, THESE INVADERS HAVE VIOLATED OUR TERRITORIAL BOUNDARIES, RISKING EXPOSING US TO CALAMITIES SUCH AS PSORIASIS, PITYRIASIS...
...PIZZICATARSIS, TORSIVE METATARSALGIA, MOLLUSCUM CONTAGIOSUM...
BOM!
...PURPURIC COTYLEDONS, CUTICULITIS, ITCHISCRATCHA...
...GAN-GRENE...
...PEELING FEET...
PSST.
TAKE HALF.
ON THREE, WE'LL RUN TOWARDS THE WALL...GIVE ME YOUR HAND.
CHOMP!
ONE
TWO
THREE!
BONG
BAM
DANG...I GAVE THEM THE GLUE THAT UNDERSTANDS ALL.
47
28

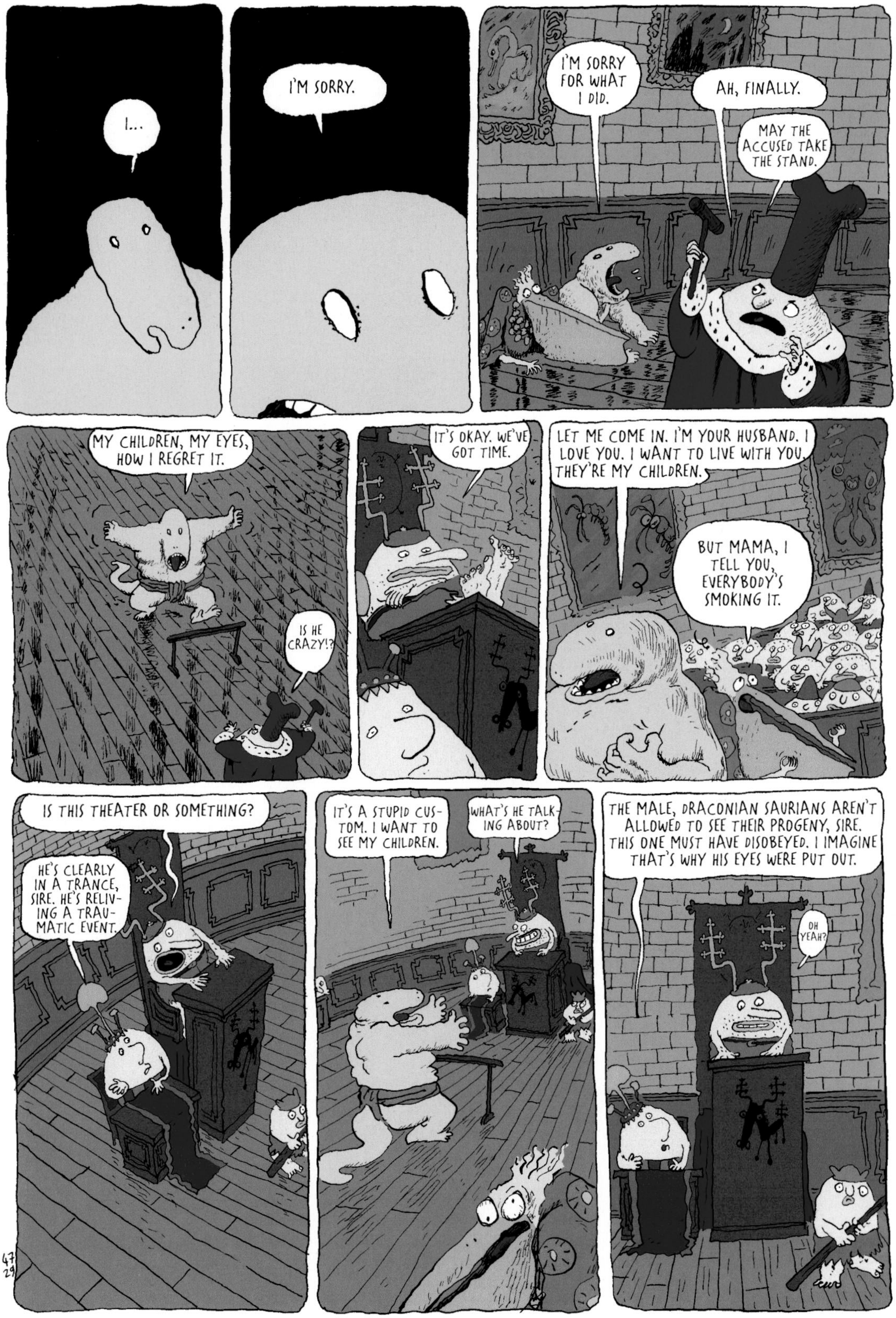
I...
I'M SORRY.
I'M SORRY FOR WHAT I DID.
AH, FINALLY.
MAY THE ACCUSED TAKE THE STAND.
MY CHILDREN, MY EYES, HOW I REGRET IT.
IS HE CRAZY!?
IT'S OKAY. WE'VE GOT TIME.
LET ME COME IN. I'M YOUR HUSBAND. I LOVE YOU. I WANT TO LIVE WITH YOU. THEY'RE MY CHILDREN.
BUT MAMA, I TELL YOU, EVERYBODY'S SMOKING IT.
IS THIS THEATER OR SOMETHING?
HE'S CLEARLY IN A TRANCE, SIRE. HE'S RELIVING A TRAUMATIC EVENT.
IT'S A STUPID CUSTOM. I WANT TO SEE MY CHILDREN.
WHAT'S HE TALKING ABOUT?
THE MALE, DRACONIAN SAURIANS AREN'T ALLOWED TO SEE THEIR PROGENY, SIRE. THIS ONE MUST HAVE DISOBEYED. I IMAGINE THAT'S WHY HIS EYES WERE PUT OUT.
OH YEAH?

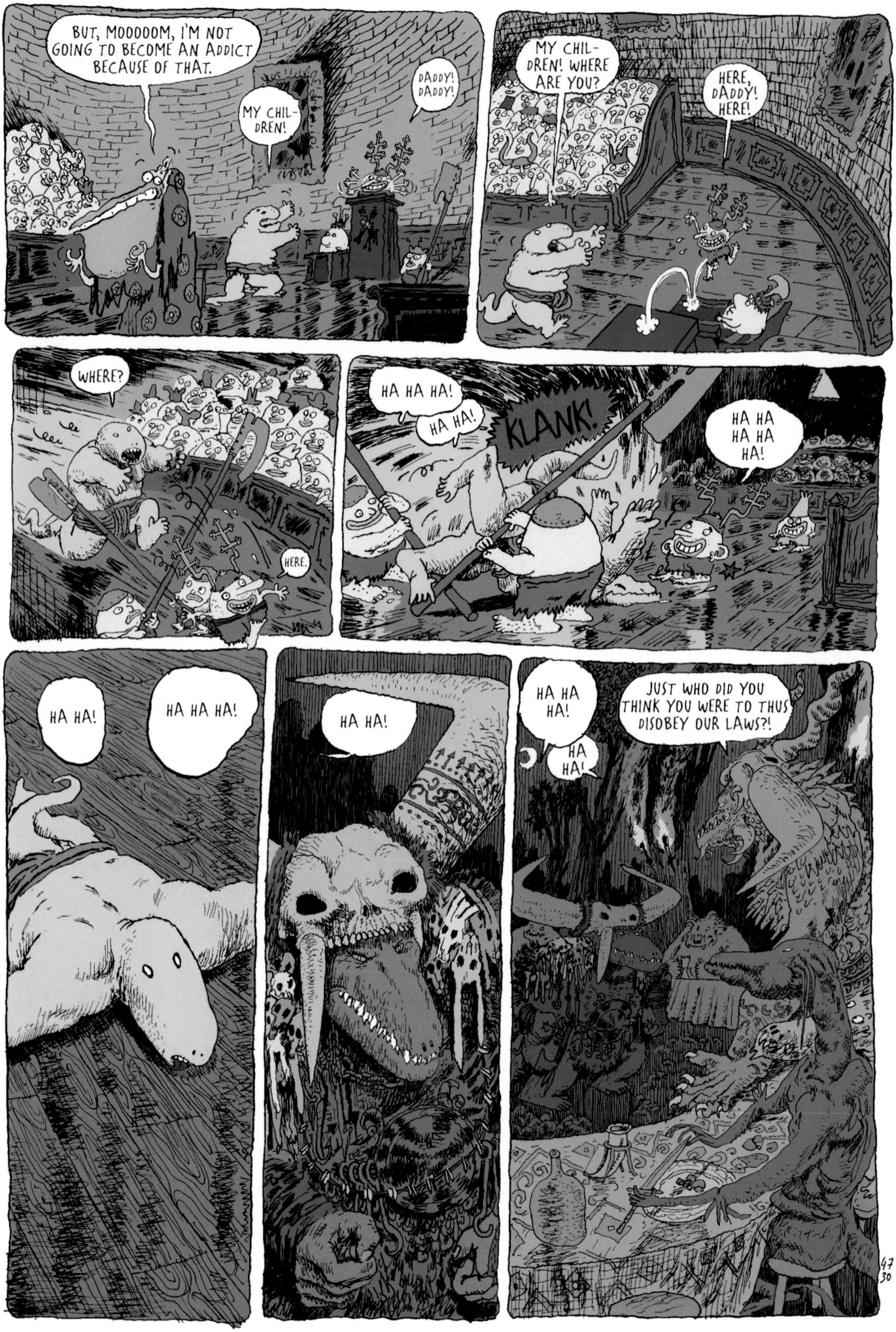

BUT, MOOOOOM, I'M NOT GOING TO BECOME AN ADDICT BECAUSE OF THAT.
MY CHIL-DREN!
DADDY! DADDY!
MY CHIL-DREN! WHERE ARE YOU?
HERE, DADDY! HERE!
WHERE?
HERE.
HA HA HA!
HA HA!
KLANK!
HA HA HA HA HA!
HA HA!
HA HA HA!
HA HA!
HA HA HA!
HA HA!
JUST WHO DID YOU THINK YOU WERE TO THUS DISOBEY OUR LAWS?!

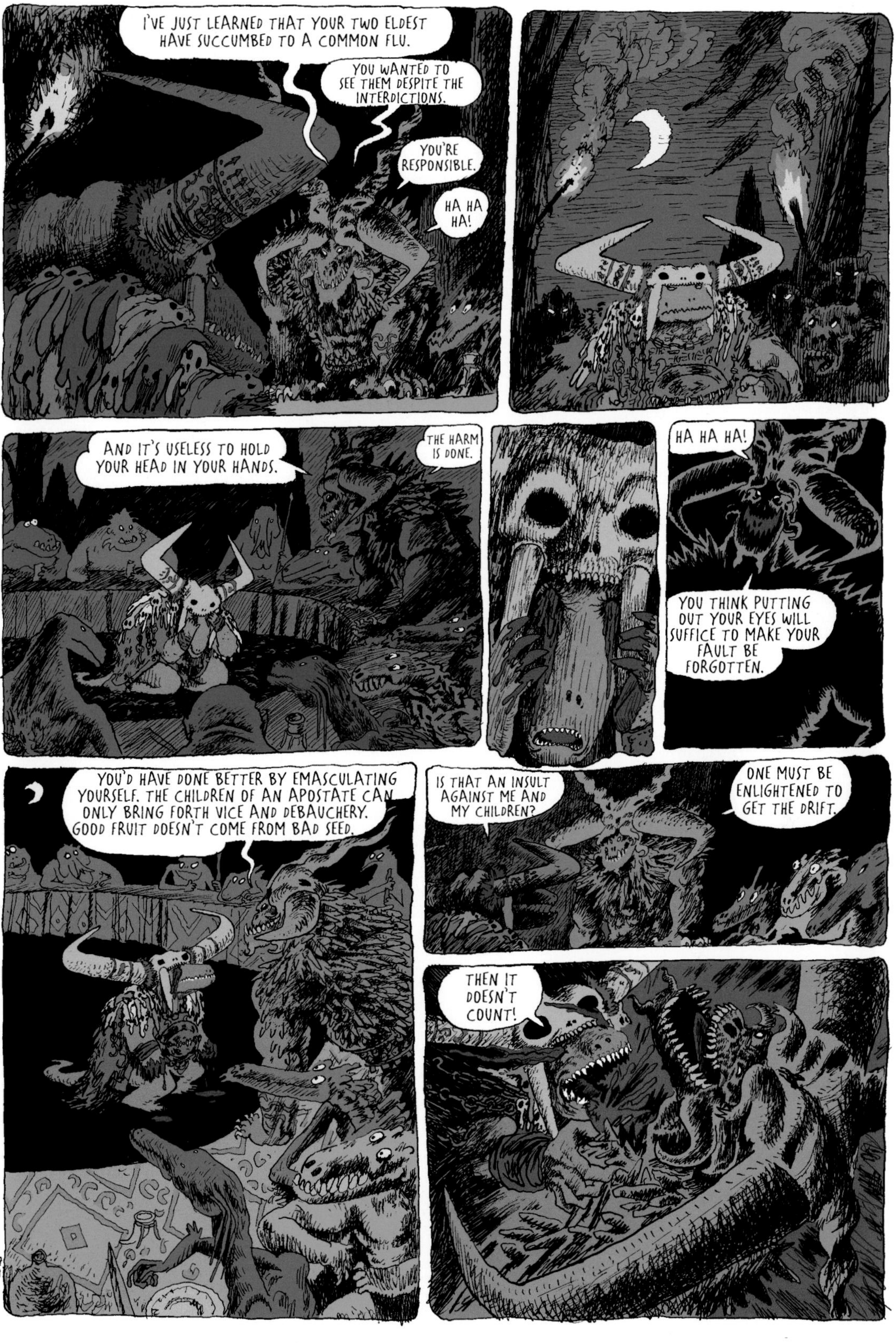

I'VE JUST LEARNED THAT YOUR TWO ELDEST HAVE SUCCUMBED TO A COMMON FLU.
YOU WANTED TO SEE THEM DESPITE THE INTERDICTIONS.
YOU'RE RESPONSIBLE.
HA HA HA!
AND IT'S USELESS TO HOLD YOUR HEAD IN YOUR HANDS.
THE HARM IS DONE.
HA HA HA!
YOU THINK PUTTING OUT YOUR EYES WILL SUFFICE TO MAKE YOUR FAULT BE FORGOTTEN.
YOU'D HAVE DONE BETTER BY EMASCULATING YOURSELF. THE CHILDREN OF AN APOSTATE CAN ONLY BRING FORTH VICE AND DEBAUCHERY. GOOD FRUIT DOESN'T COME FROM BAD SEED.
IS THAT AN INSULT AGAINST ME AND MY CHILDREN?
ONE MUST BE ENLIGHTENED TO GET THE DRIFT.
THEN IT DOESN'T COUNT!

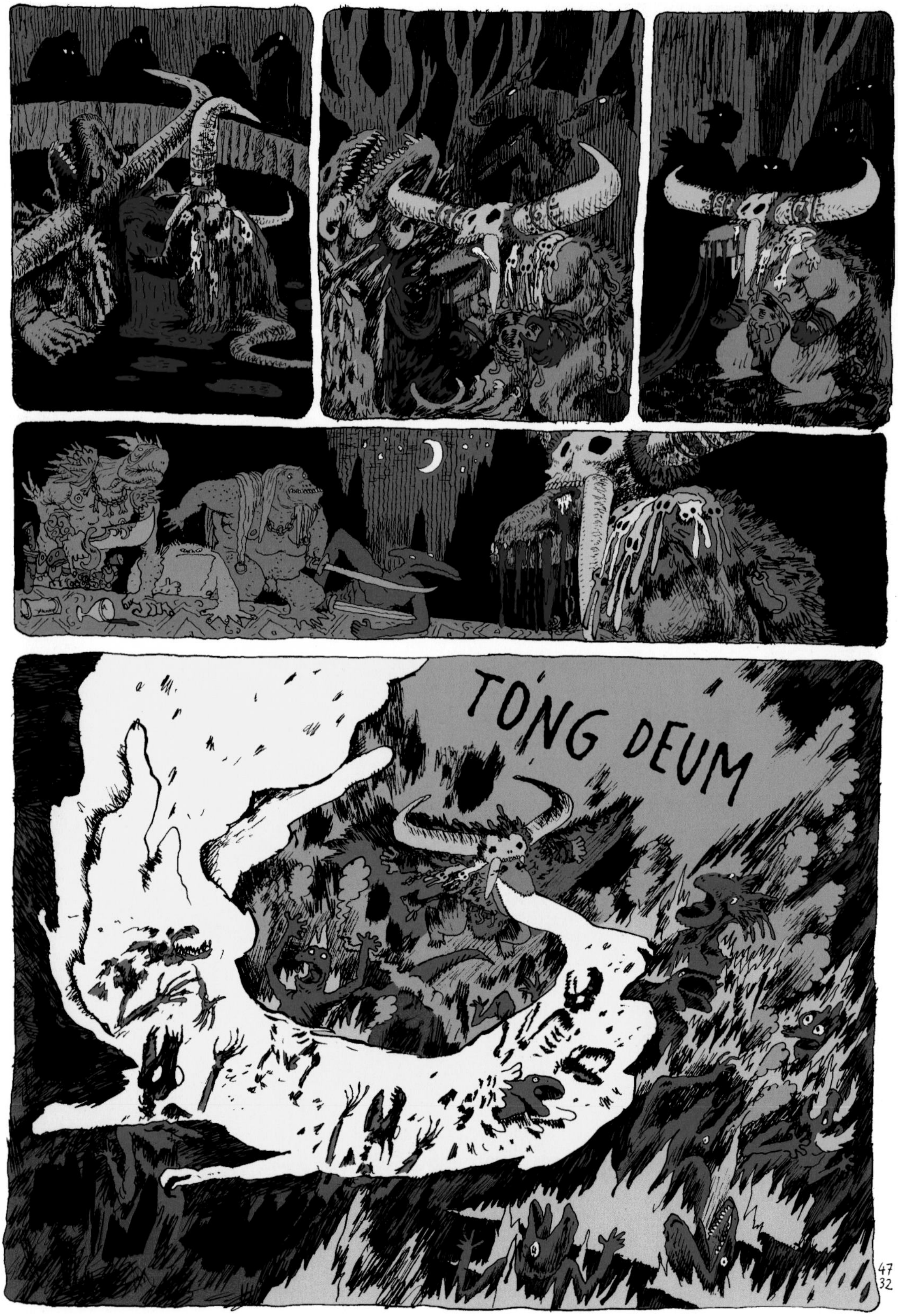
TONG DEUM

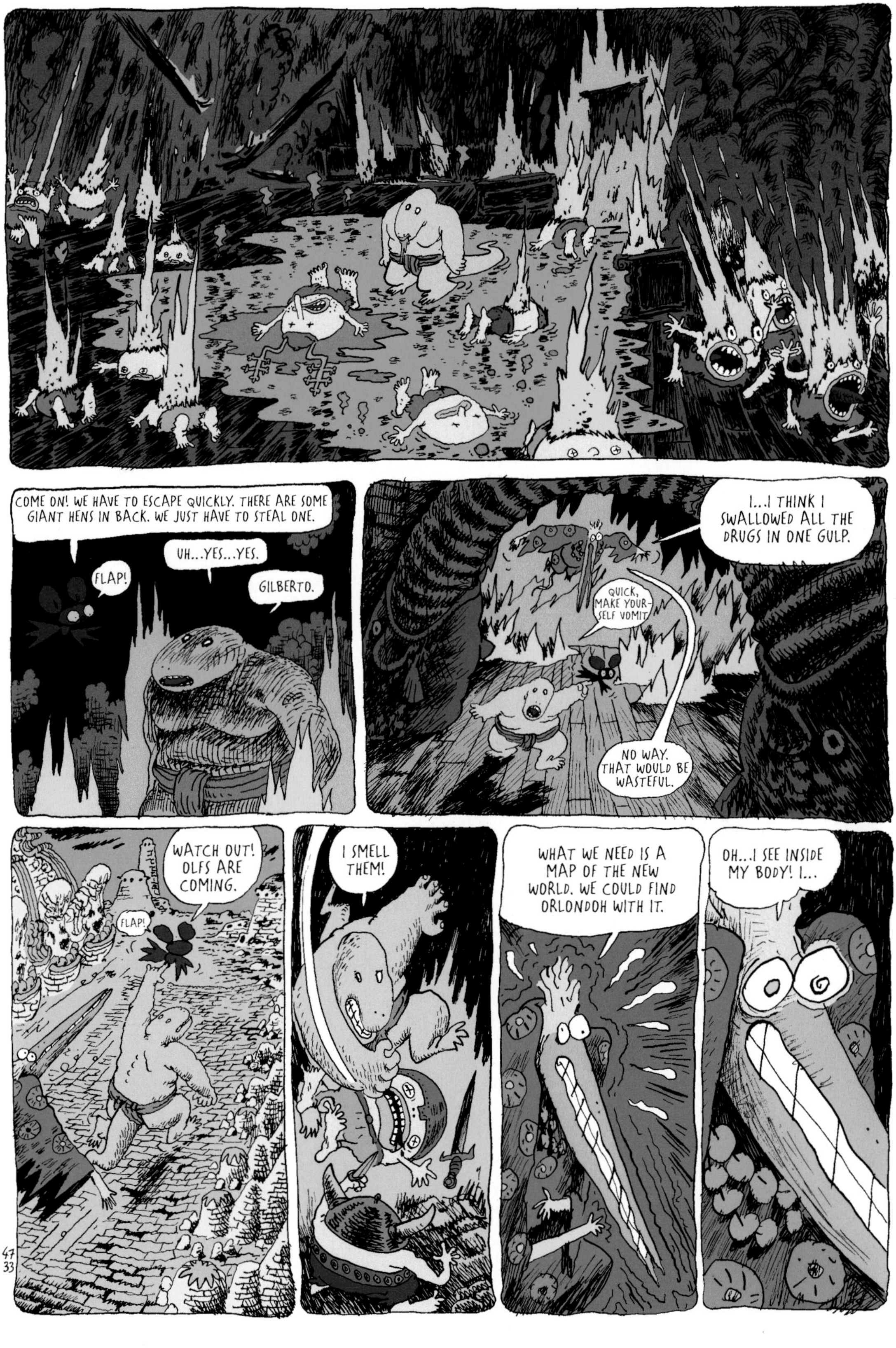
COME ON! WE HAVE TO ESCAPE QUICKLY. THERE ARE SOME GIANT HENS IN BACK. WE JUST HAVE TO STEAL ONE.
FLAP!
UH...YES...YES.
GILBERTO.
I...I THINK I SWALLOWED ALL THE DRUGS IN ONE GULP.
QUICK, MAKE YOURSELF VOMIT.
NO WAY. THAT WOULD BE WASTEFUL.
WATCH OUT! OLFS ARE COMING.
FLAP!
I SMELL THEM!
WHAT WE NEED IS A MAP OF THE NEW WORLD. WE COULD FIND ORLONDOH WITH IT.
OH...I SEE INSIDE MY BODY! I...

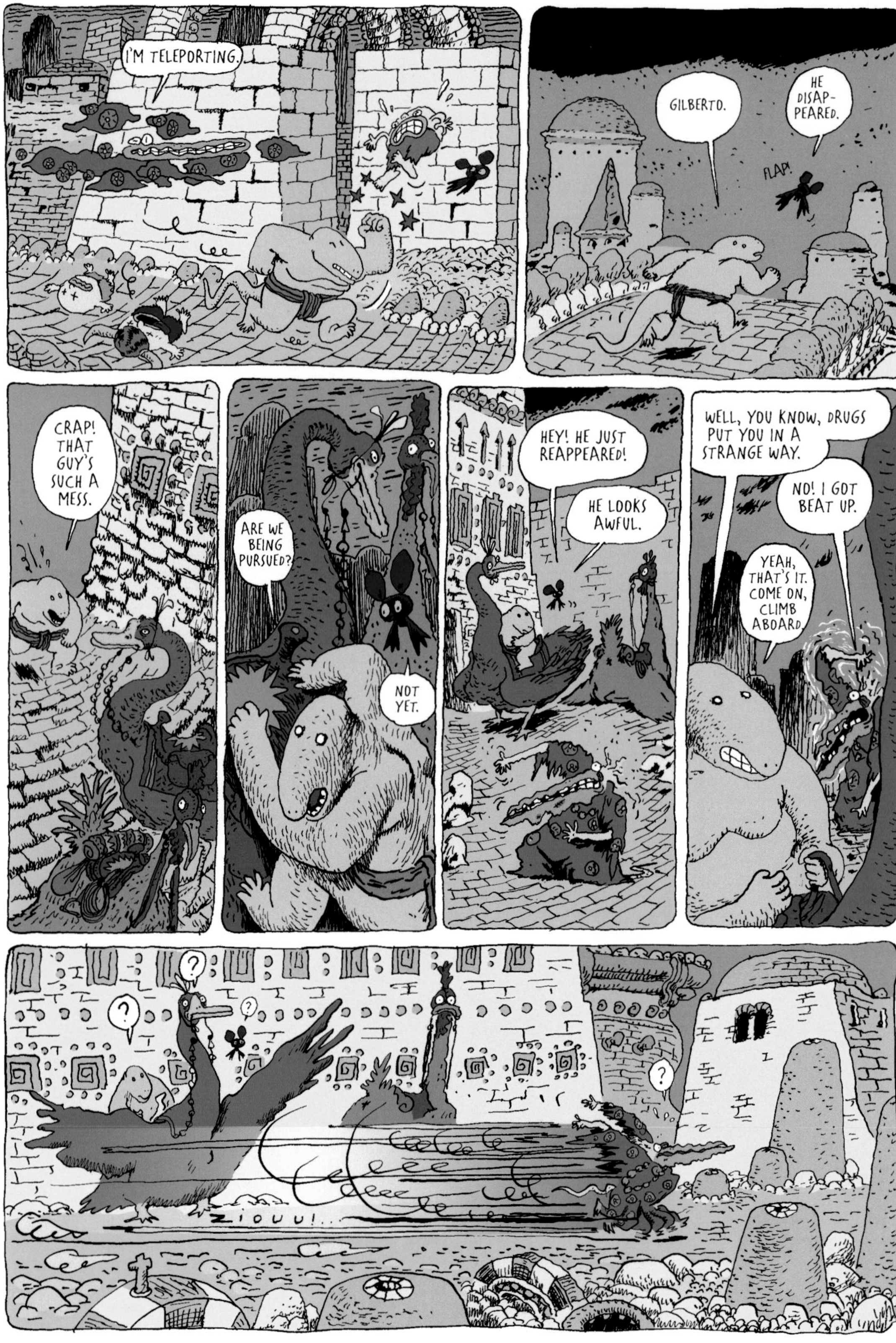
I'M TELEPORTING.
GILBERTO.
HE DISAP-PEARED.
FLAP!
CRAP! THAT GUY'S SUCH A MESS.
ARE WE BEING PURSUED?
NOT YET.
HEY! HE JUST REAPPEARED!
HE LOOKS AWFUL.
WELL, YOU KNOW, DRUGS PUT YOU IN A STRANGE WAY.
NO! I GOT BEAT UP.
YEAH, THAT'S IT. COME ON, CLIMB ABOARD.
?
?
?
?
ZIOUUU!

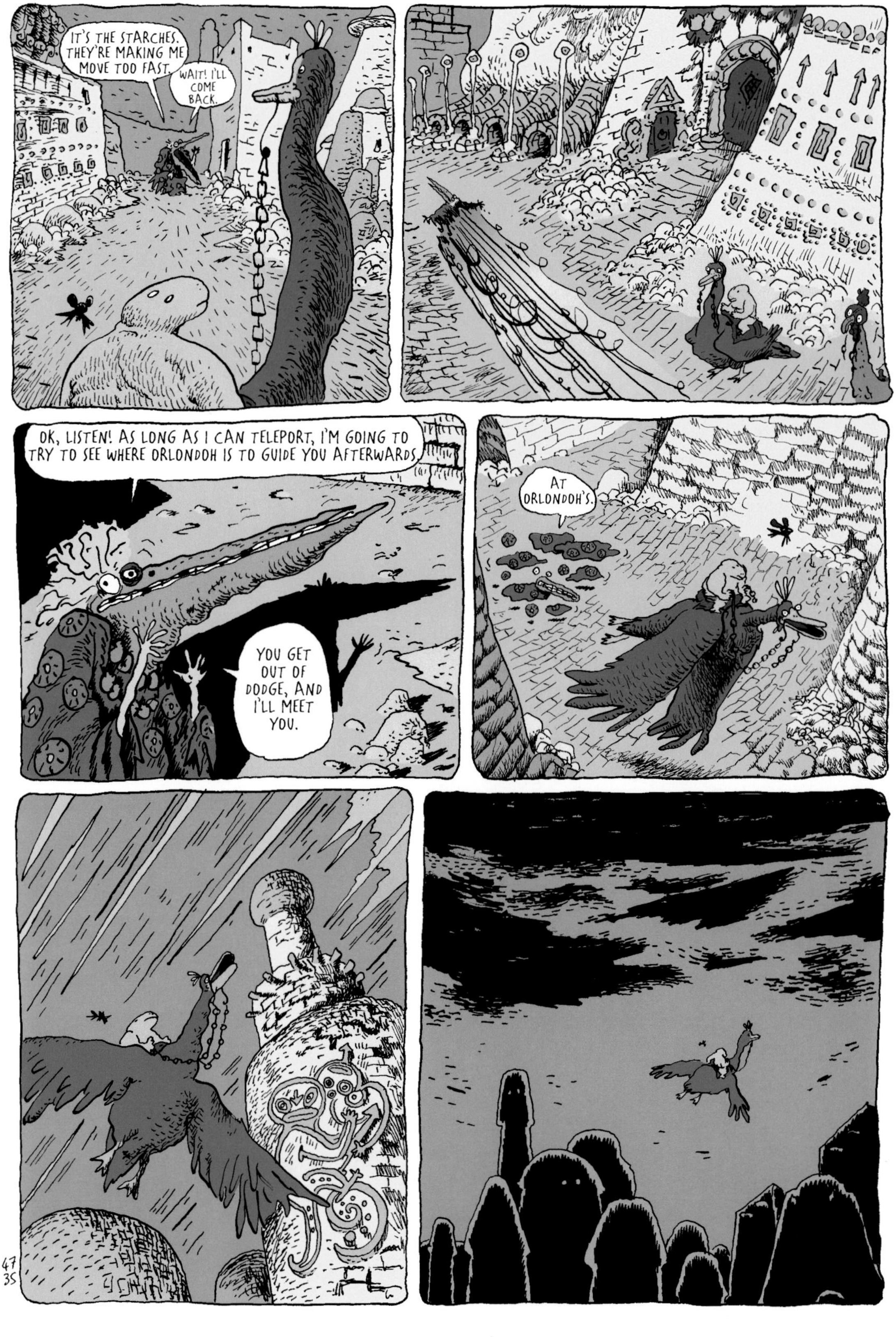
IT'S THE STARCHES. THEY'RE MAKING ME MOVE TOO FAST.
WAIT! I'LL COME BACK.
OK, LISTEN! AS LONG AS I CAN TELEPORT, I'M GOING TO TRY TO SEE WHERE ORLONDOH IS TO GUIDE YOU AFTERWARDS.
YOU GET OUT OF DODGE, AND I'LL MEET YOU.
AT ORLONDOH'S.

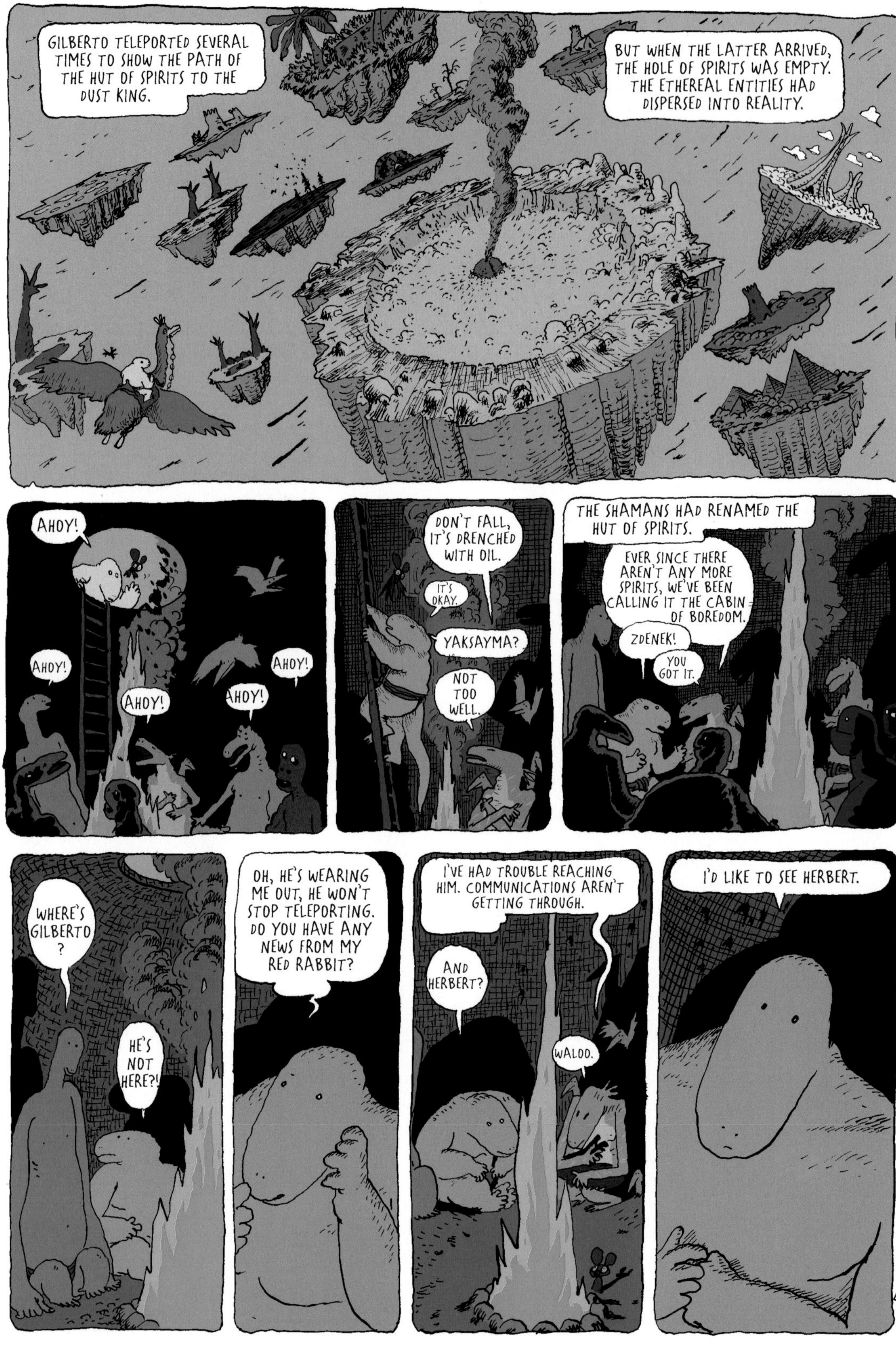
GILBERTO TELEPORTED SEVERAL TIMES TO SHOW THE PATH OF THE HUT OF SPIRITS TO THE DUST KING.
BUT WHEN THE LATTER ARRIVED, THE HOLE OF SPIRITS WAS EMPTY. THE ETHEREAL ENTITIES HAD DISPERSED INTO REALITY.
AHOY!
AHOY!
AHOY!
AHOY!
AHOY!
DON'T FALL, IT'S DRENCHED WITH OIL.
IT'S OKAY.
YAKSAYMA?
NOT TOO WELL.
THE SHAMANS HAD RENAMED THE HUT OF SPIRITS.
EVER SINCE THERE AREN'T ANY MORE SPIRITS, WE'VE BEEN CALLING IT THE CABIN OF BOREDOM.
ZDENEK!
YOU GOT IT.
WHERE'S GILBERTO ?
HE'S NOT HERE?!
OH, HE'S WEARING ME OUT, HE WON'T STOP TELEPORTING. DO YOU HAVE ANY NEWS FROM MY RED RABBIT?
I'VE HAD TROUBLE REACHING HIM. COMMUNICATIONS AREN'T GETTING THROUGH.
AND HERBERT?
WALOO.
I'D LIKE TO SEE HERBERT.

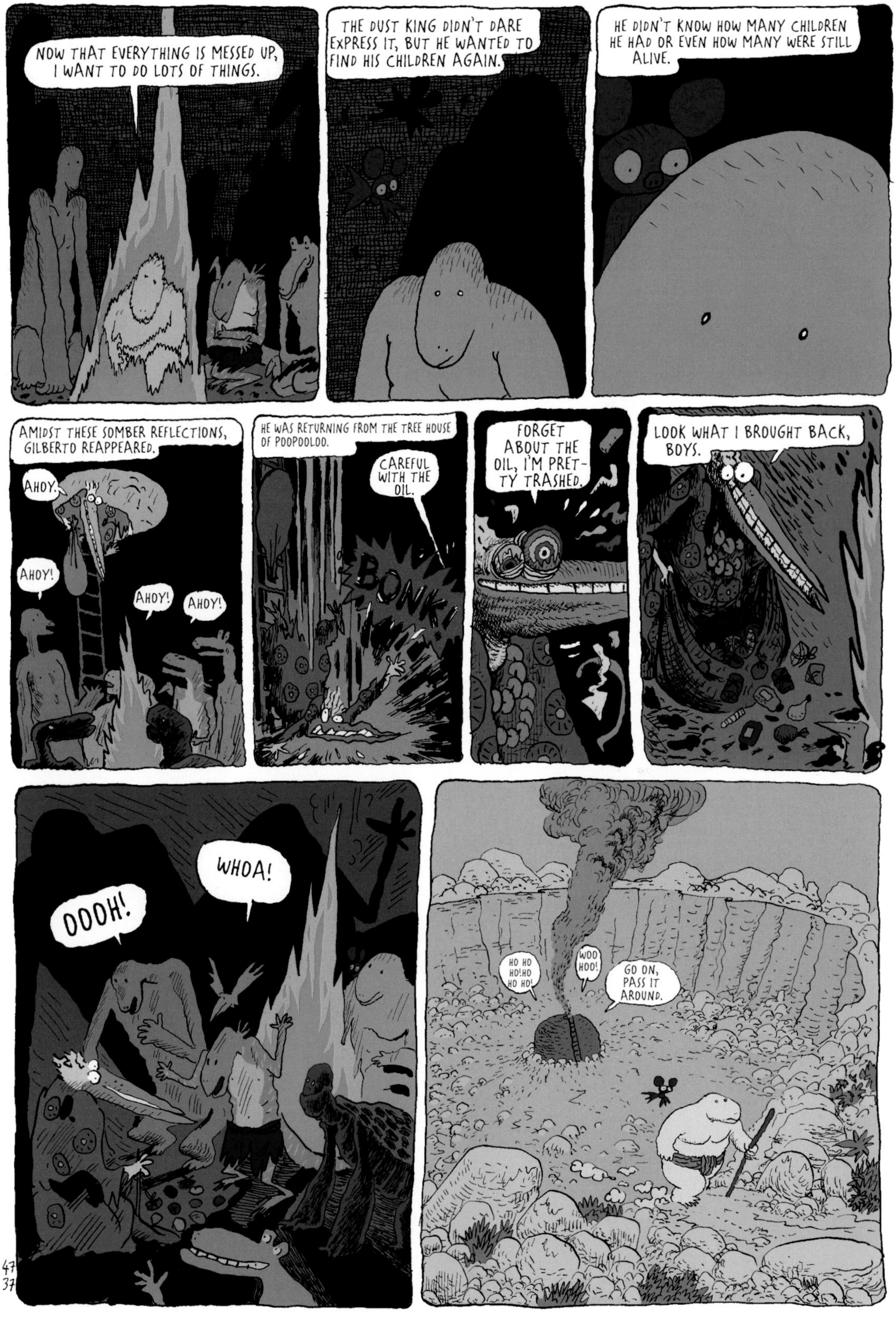

NOW THAT EVERYTHING IS MESSED UP, I WANT TO DO LOTS OF THINGS.
THE DUST KING DIDN'T DARE EXPRESS IT, BUT HE WANTED TO FIND HIS CHILDREN AGAIN.
HE DIDN'T KNOW HOW MANY CHILDREN HE HAD OR EVEN HOW MANY WERE STILL ALIVE.
AMIDST THESE SOMBER REFLECTIONS, GILBERTO REAPPEARED.
AHOY.
AHOY!
AHOY!
AHOY!
HE WAS RETURNING FROM THE TREE HOUSE OF POOPOOLOO.
CAREFUL WITH THE OIL.
BONK!
FORGET ABOUT THE OIL, I'M PRETTY TRASHED.
LOOK WHAT I BROUGHT BACK, BOYS.
WHOA!
OOOH!
HO HO HO! HO HO HO!
WOO HOO!
GO ON, PASS IT AROUND.

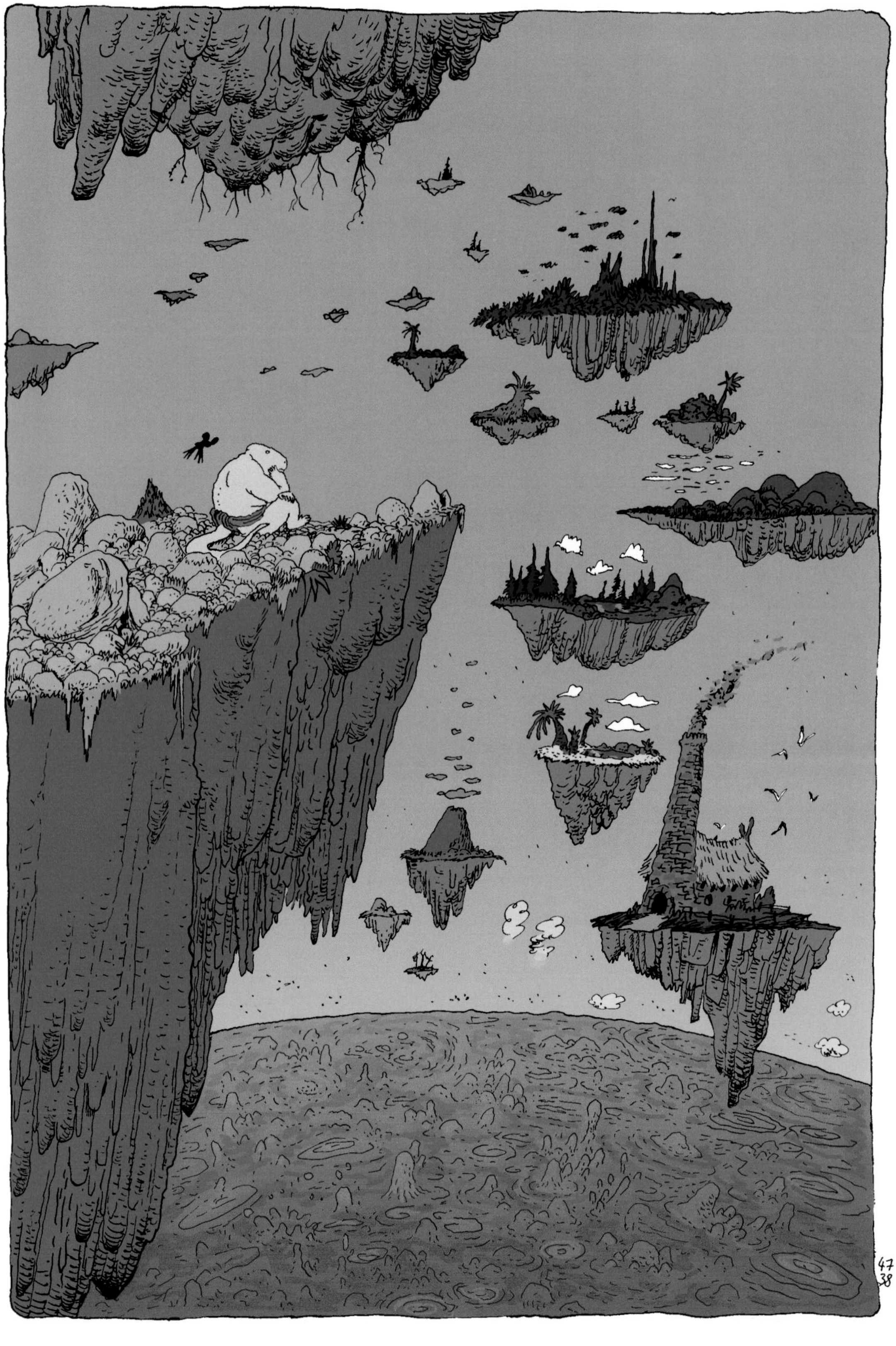

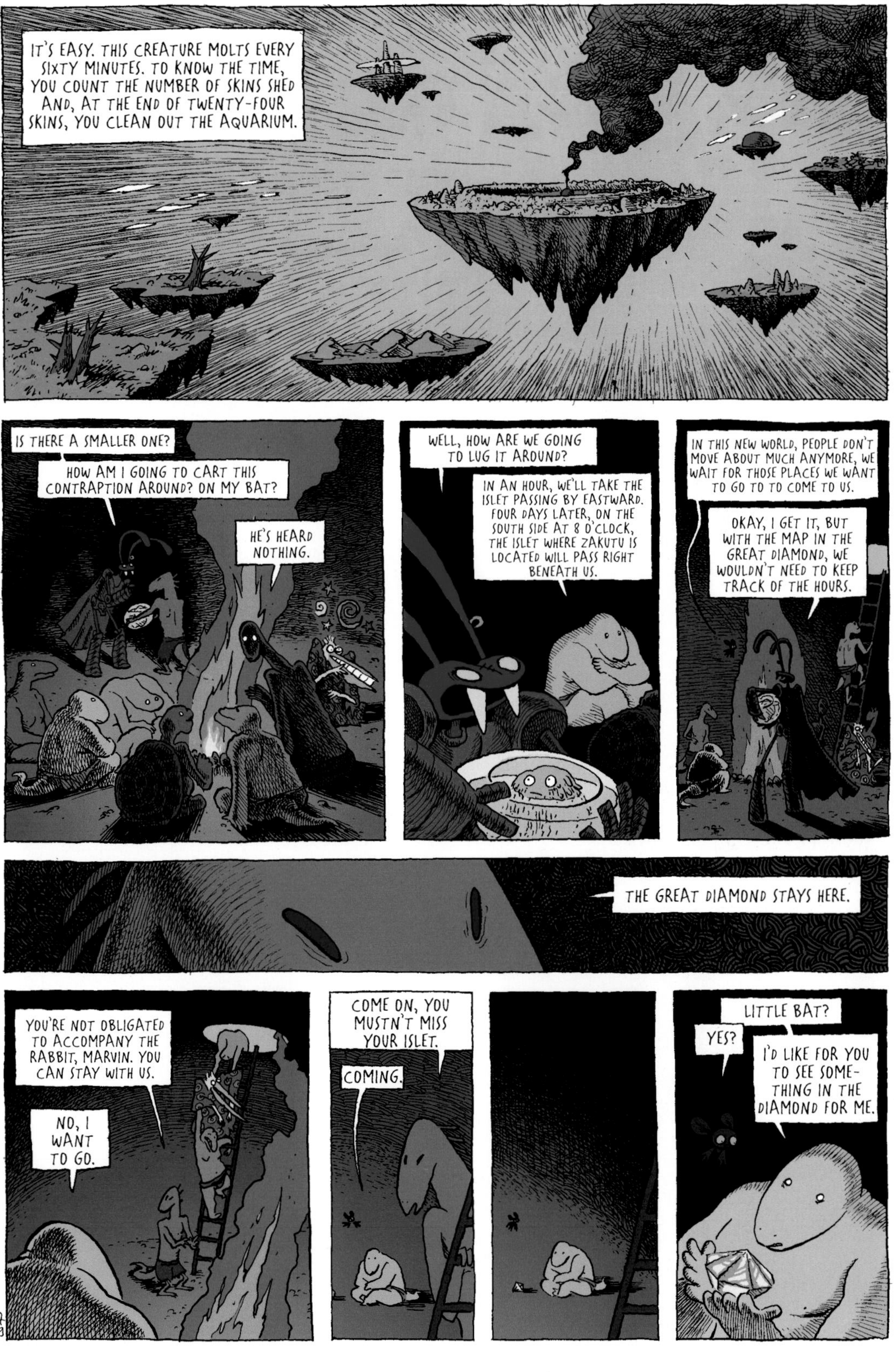
IT'S EASY. THIS CREATURE MOLTS EVERY SIXTY MINUTES. TO KNOW THE TIME, YOU COUNT THE NUMBER OF SKINS SHED AND, AT THE END OF TWENTY-FOUR SKINS, YOU CLEAN OUT THE AQUARIUM.
IS THERE A SMALLER ONE?
HOW AM I GOING TO CART THIS CONTRAPTION AROUND? ON MY BAT?
HE'S HEARD NOTHING.
WELL, HOW ARE WE GOING TO LUG IT AROUND?
IN AN HOUR, WE'LL TAKE THE ISLET PASSING BY EASTWARD. FOUR DAYS LATER, ON THE SOUTH SIDE AT 8 O'CLOCK, THE ISLET WHERE ZAKUTU IS LOCATED WILL PASS RIGHT BENEATH US.
IN THIS NEW WORLD, PEOPLE DON'T MOVE ABOUT MUCH ANYMORE, WE WAIT FOR THOSE PLACES WE WANT TO GO TO TO COME TO US.
OKAY, I GET IT, BUT WITH THE MAP IN THE GREAT DIAMOND, WE WOULDN'T NEED TO KEEP TRACK OF THE HOURS.
THE GREAT DIAMOND STAYS HERE.
YOU'RE NOT OBLIGATED TO ACCOMPANY THE RABBIT, MARVIN. YOU CAN STAY WITH US.
NO, I WANT TO GO.
COME ON, YOU MUSTN'T MISS YOUR ISLET.
COMING.
LITTLE BAT?
YES?
I'D LIKE FOR YOU TO SEE SOMETHING IN THE DIAMOND FOR ME.

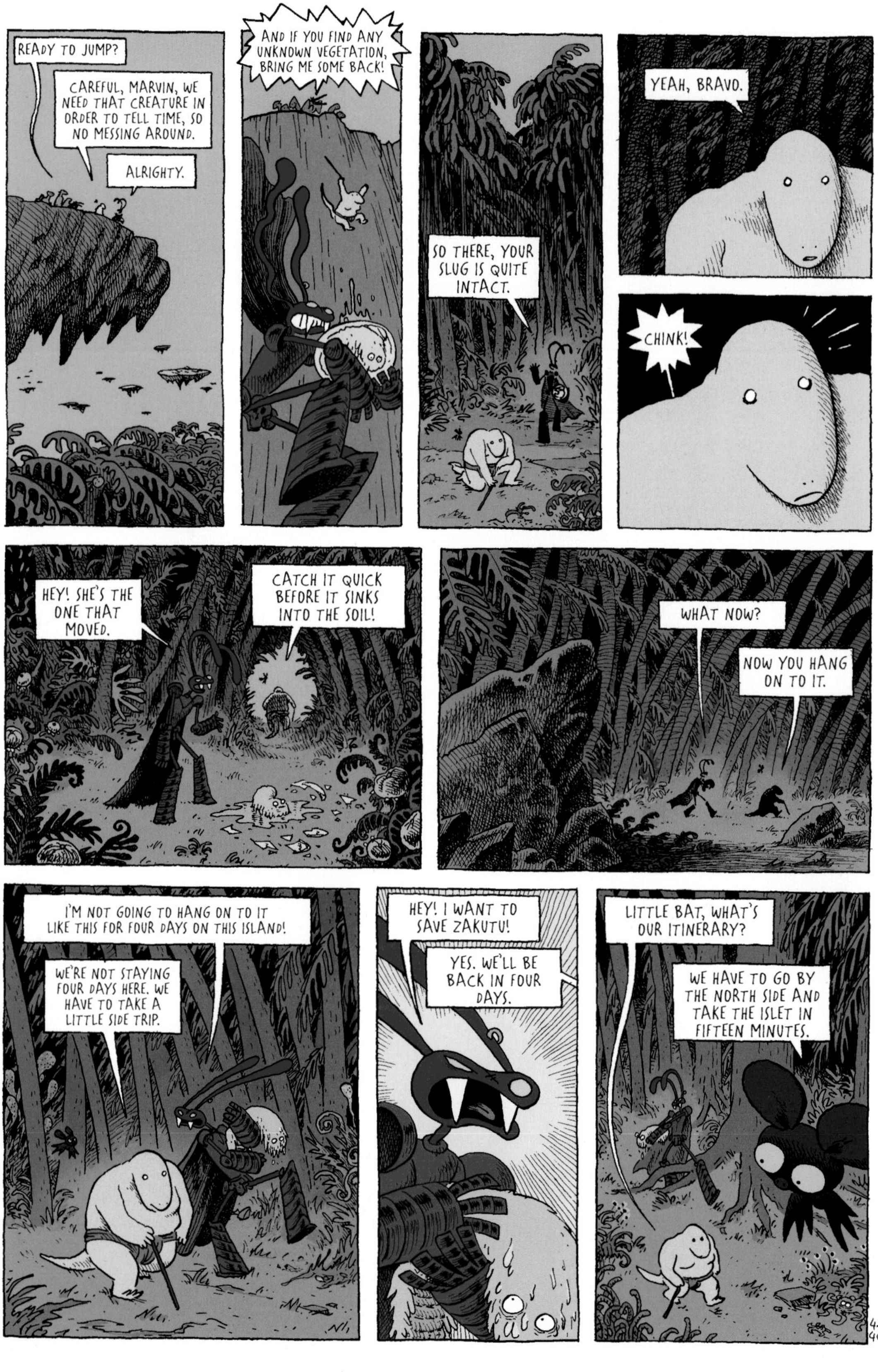
READY TO JUMP?
CAREFUL, MARVIN, WE NEED THAT CREATURE IN ORDER TO TELL TIME, SO NO MESSING AROUND.
ALRIGHTY.
AND IF YOU FIND ANY UNKNOWN VEGETATION, BRING ME SOME BACK!
SO THERE, YOUR SLUG IS QUITE INTACT.
YEAH, BRAVO.
CHINK!
HEY! SHE'S THE ONE THAT MOVED.
CATCH IT QUICK BEFORE IT SINKS INTO THE SOIL!
WHAT NOW?
NOW YOU HANG ON TO IT.
I'M NOT GOING TO HANG ON TO IT LIKE THIS FOR FOUR DAYS ON THIS ISLAND!
WE'RE NOT STAYING FOUR DAYS HERE. WE HAVE TO TAKE A LITTLE SIDE TRIP.
HEY! I WANT TO SAVE ZAKUTU!
YES. WE'LL BE BACK IN FOUR DAYS.
LITTLE BAT, WHAT'S OUR ITINERARY?
WE HAVE TO GO BY THE NORTH SIDE AND TAKE THE ISLET IN FIFTEEN MINUTES.

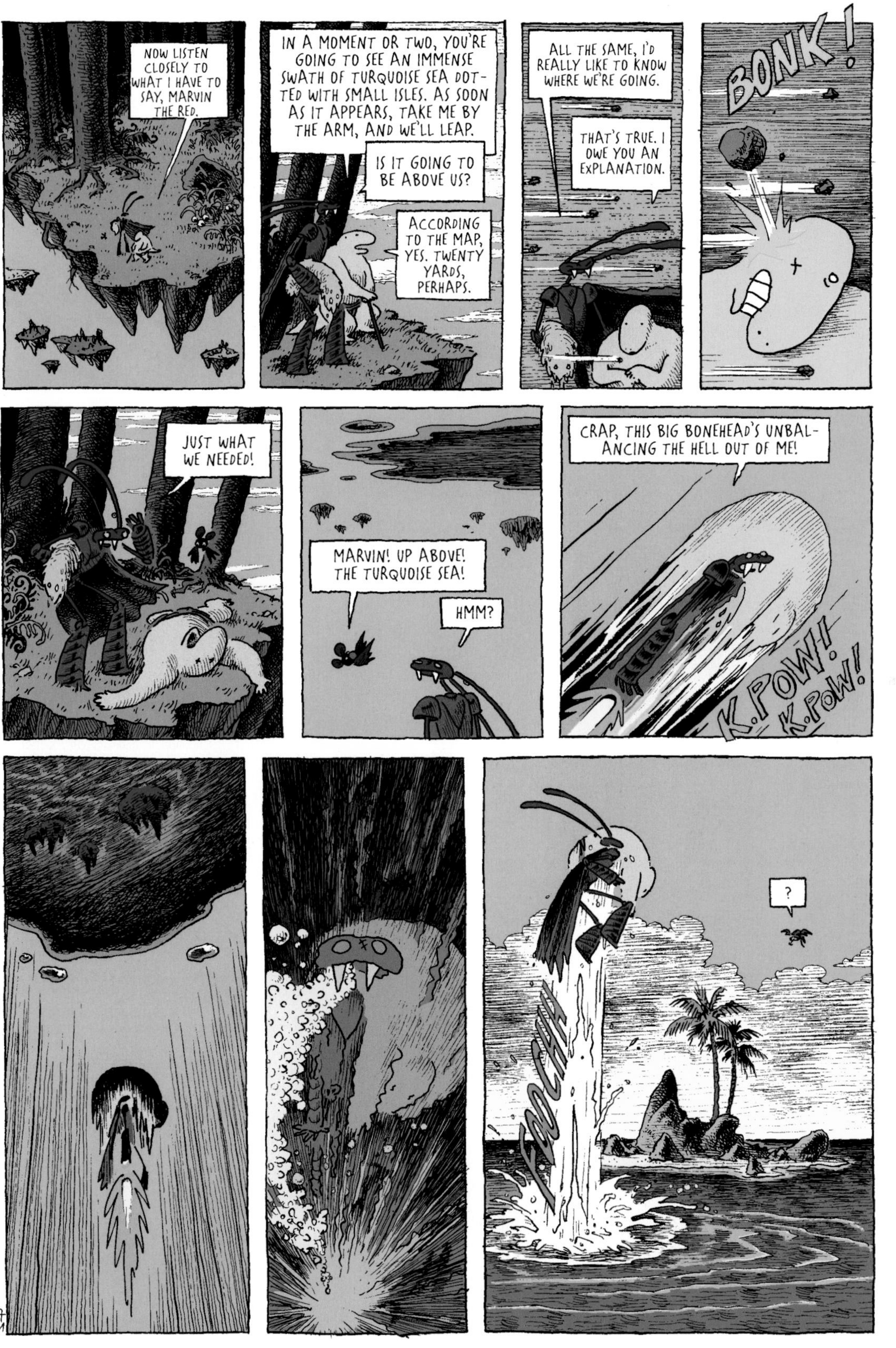
NOW LISTEN CLOSELY TO WHAT I HAVE TO SAY, MARVIN THE RED.
IN A MOMENT OR TWO, YOU'RE GOING TO SEE AN IMMENSE SWATH OF TURQUOISE SEA DOTTED WITH SMALL ISLES. AS SOON AS IT APPEARS, TAKE ME BY THE ARM, AND WE'LL LEAP.
IS IT GOING TO BE ABOVE US?
ACCORDING TO THE MAP, YES. TWENTY YARDS, PERHAPS.
ALL THE SAME, I'D REALLY LIKE TO KNOW WHERE WE'RE GOING.
THAT'S TRUE. I OWE YOU AN EXPLANATION.
BONK!
JUST WHAT WE NEEDED!
MARVIN! UP ABOVE! THE TURQUOISE SEA!
HMM?
CRAP, THIS BIG BONEHEAD'S UNBALANCING THE HELL OUT OF ME!
K.POW! K.POW!
FOOOCHH
?

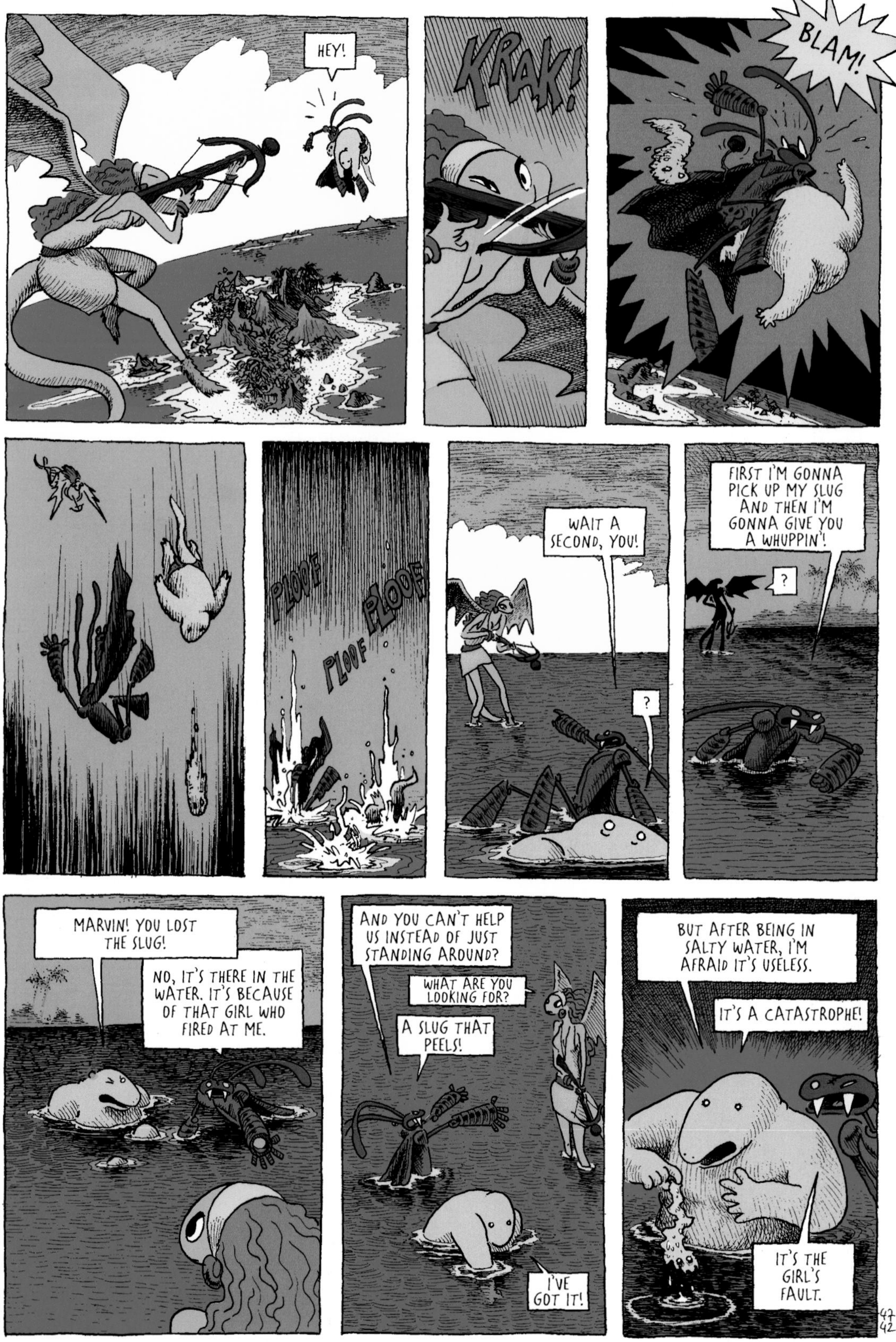
HEY!
KRAK!
BLAM!
PLOOF
PLOOF
PLOOF
WAIT A SECOND, YOU!
?
FIRST I'M GONNA PICK UP MY SLUG AND THEN I'M GONNA GIVE YOU A WHUPPIN'!
?
MARVIN! YOU LOST THE SLUG!
NO, IT'S THERE IN THE WATER. IT'S BECAUSE OF THAT GIRL WHO FIRED AT ME.
AND YOU CAN'T HELP US INSTEAD OF JUST STANDING AROUND?
WHAT ARE YOU LOOKING FOR?
A SLUG THAT PEELS!
I'VE GOT IT!
BUT AFTER BEING IN SALTY WATER, I'M AFRAID IT'S USELESS.
IT'S A CATASTROPHE!
IT'S THE GIRL'S FAULT.

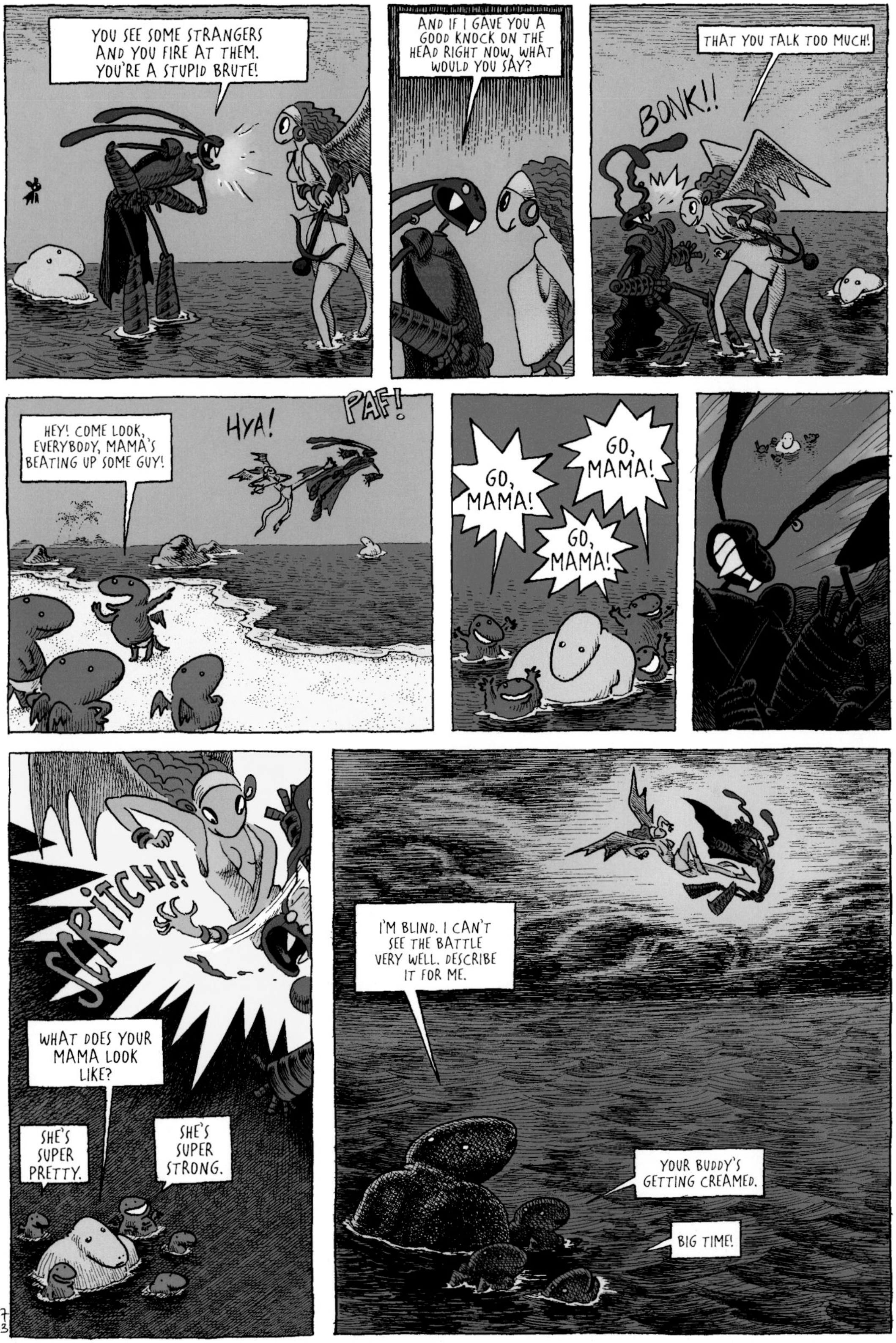
YOU SEE SOME STRANGERS AND YOU FIRE AT THEM. YOU'RE A STUPID BRUTE!
AND IF I GAVE YOU A GOOD KNOCK ON THE HEAD RIGHT NOW, WHAT WOULD YOU SAY?
THAT YOU TALK TOO MUCH!
BONK!!
HEY! COME LOOK, EVERYBODY, MAMA'S BEATING UP SOME GUY!
HYA!
PAF!
GO, MAMA!
GO, MAMA!
GO, MAMA!
SCRITCH!!
WHAT DOES YOUR MAMA LOOK LIKE?
SHE'S SUPER PRETTY.
SHE'S SUPER STRONG.
I'M BLIND. I CAN'T SEE THE BATTLE VERY WELL. DESCRIBE IT FOR ME.
YOUR BUDDY'S GETTING CREAMED.
BIG TIME!

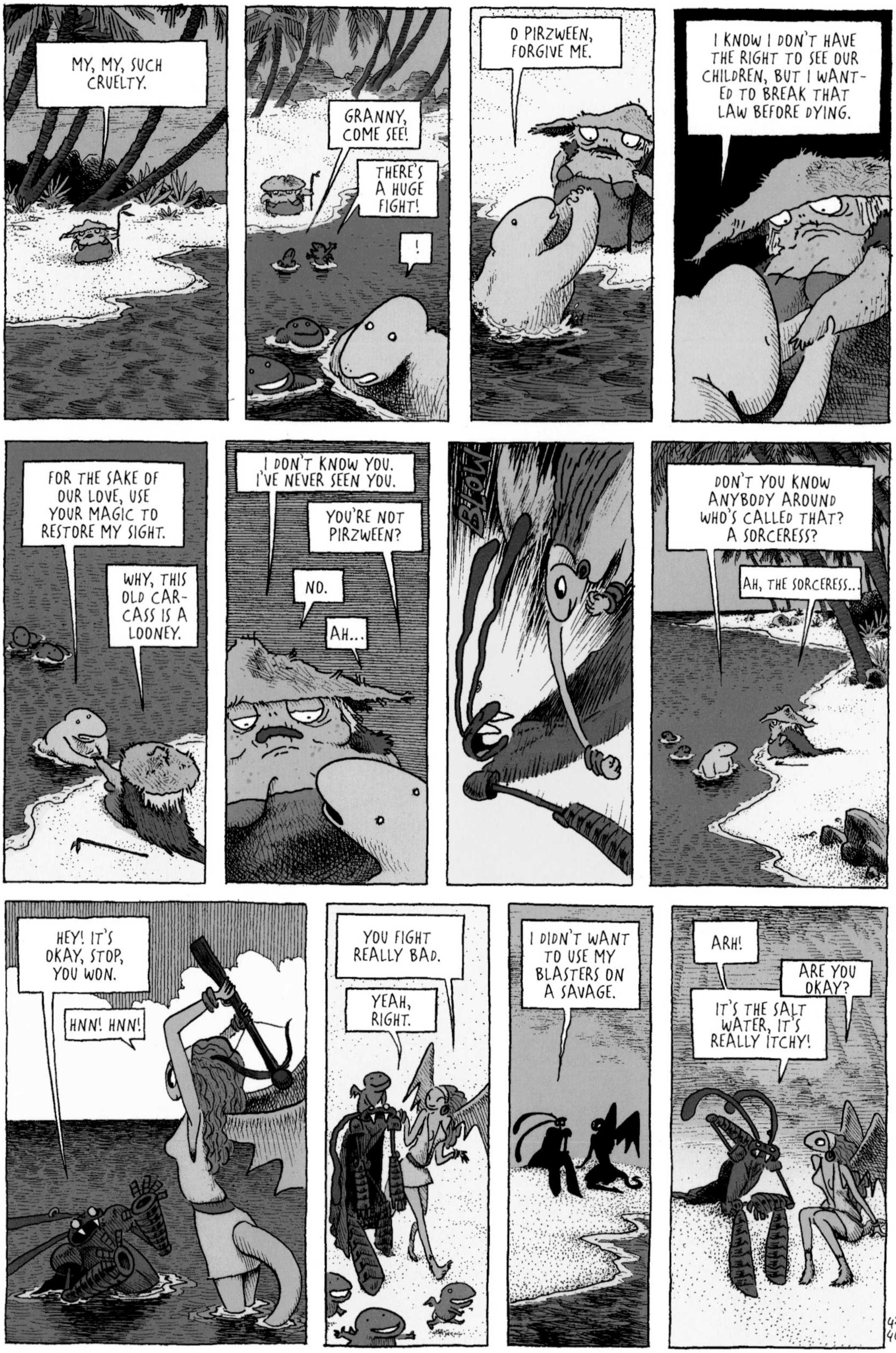
MY, MY, SUCH CRUELTY.
GRANNY, COME SEE!
THERE'S A HUGE FIGHT!
!
O PIRZWEEN, FORGIVE ME.
I KNOW I DON'T HAVE THE RIGHT TO SEE OUR CHILDREN, BUT I WANTED TO BREAK THAT LAW BEFORE DYING.
FOR THE SAKE OF OUR LOVE, USE YOUR MAGIC TO RESTORE MY SIGHT.
WHY, THIS OLD CARCASS IS A LOONEY.
I DON'T KNOW YOU. I'VE NEVER SEEN YOU.
YOU'RE NOT PIRZWEEN?
NO.
AH...
DON'T YOU KNOW ANYBODY AROUND WHO'S CALLED THAT? A SORCERESS?
AH, THE SORCERESS...
HEY! IT'S OKAY, STOP, YOU WON.
HNN! HNN!
YOU FIGHT REALLY BAD.
YEAH, RIGHT.
I DIDN'T WANT TO USE MY BLASTERS ON A SAVAGE.
ARH!
ARE YOU OKAY?
IT'S THE SALT WATER, IT'S REALLY ITCHY!

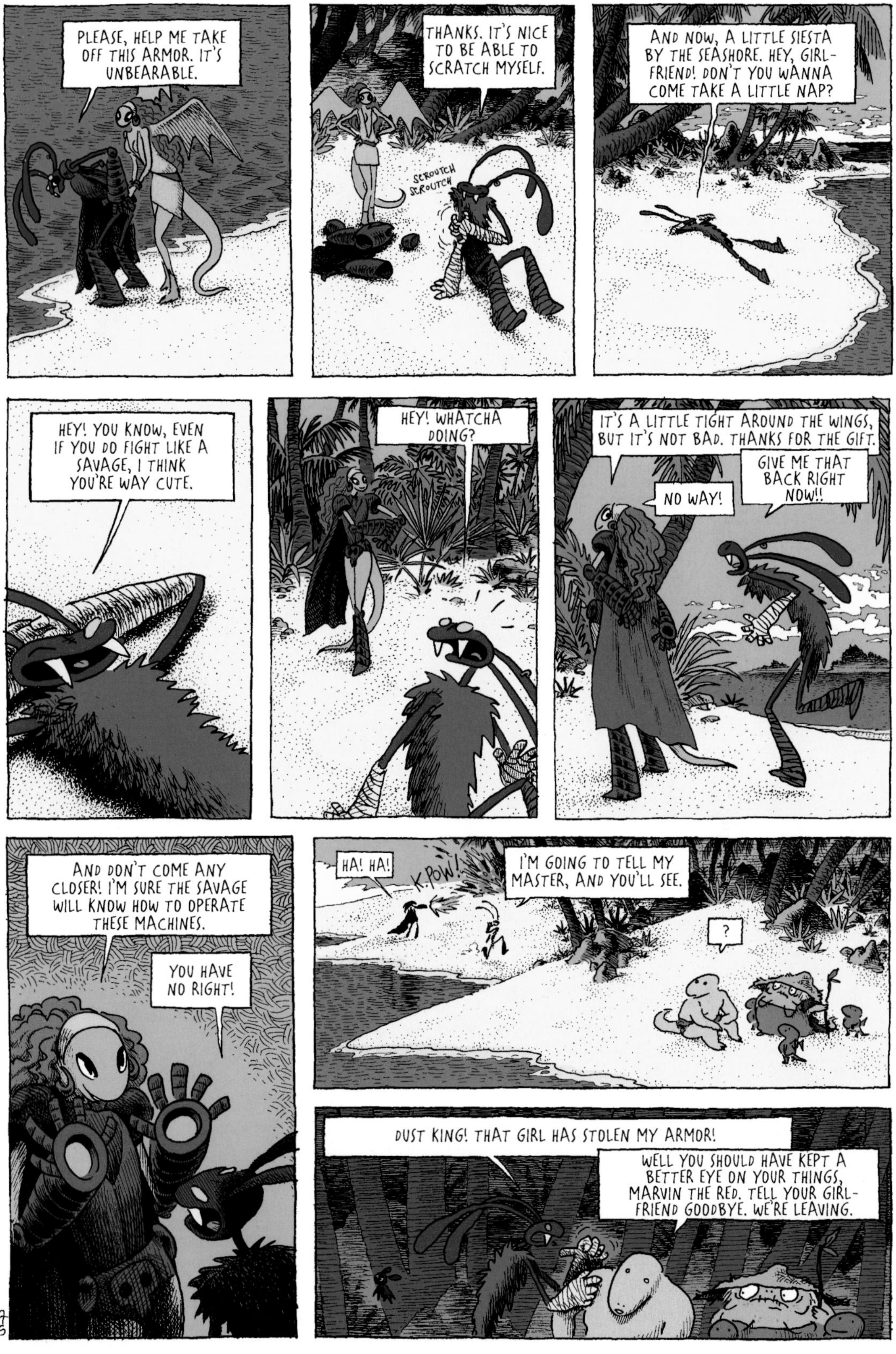
PLEASE, HELP ME TAKE OFF THIS ARMOR. IT'S UNBEARABLE.
THANKS. IT'S NICE TO BE ABLE TO SCRATCH MYSELF.
SCROUTCH SCROUTCH
AND NOW, A LITTLE SIESTA BY THE SEASHORE. HEY, GIRL-FRIEND! DON'T YOU WANNA COME TAKE A LITTLE NAP?
HEY! YOU KNOW, EVEN IF YOU DO FIGHT LIKE A SAVAGE, I THINK YOU'RE WAY CUTE.
HEY! WHATCHA DOING?
IT'S A LITTLE TIGHT AROUND THE WINGS, BUT IT'S NOT BAD. THANKS FOR THE GIFT.
NO WAY!
GIVE ME THAT BACK RIGHT NOW!!
AND DON'T COME ANY CLOSER! I'M SURE THE SAVAGE WILL KNOW HOW TO OPERATE THESE MACHINES.
YOU HAVE NO RIGHT!
HA! HA!
K.POW!
I'M GOING TO TELL MY MASTER, AND YOU'LL SEE.
?
DUST KING! THAT GIRL HAS STOLEN MY ARMOR!
WELL YOU SHOULD HAVE KEPT A BETTER EYE ON YOUR THINGS, MARVIN THE RED. TELL YOUR GIRL-FRIEND GOODBYE. WE'RE LEAVING.

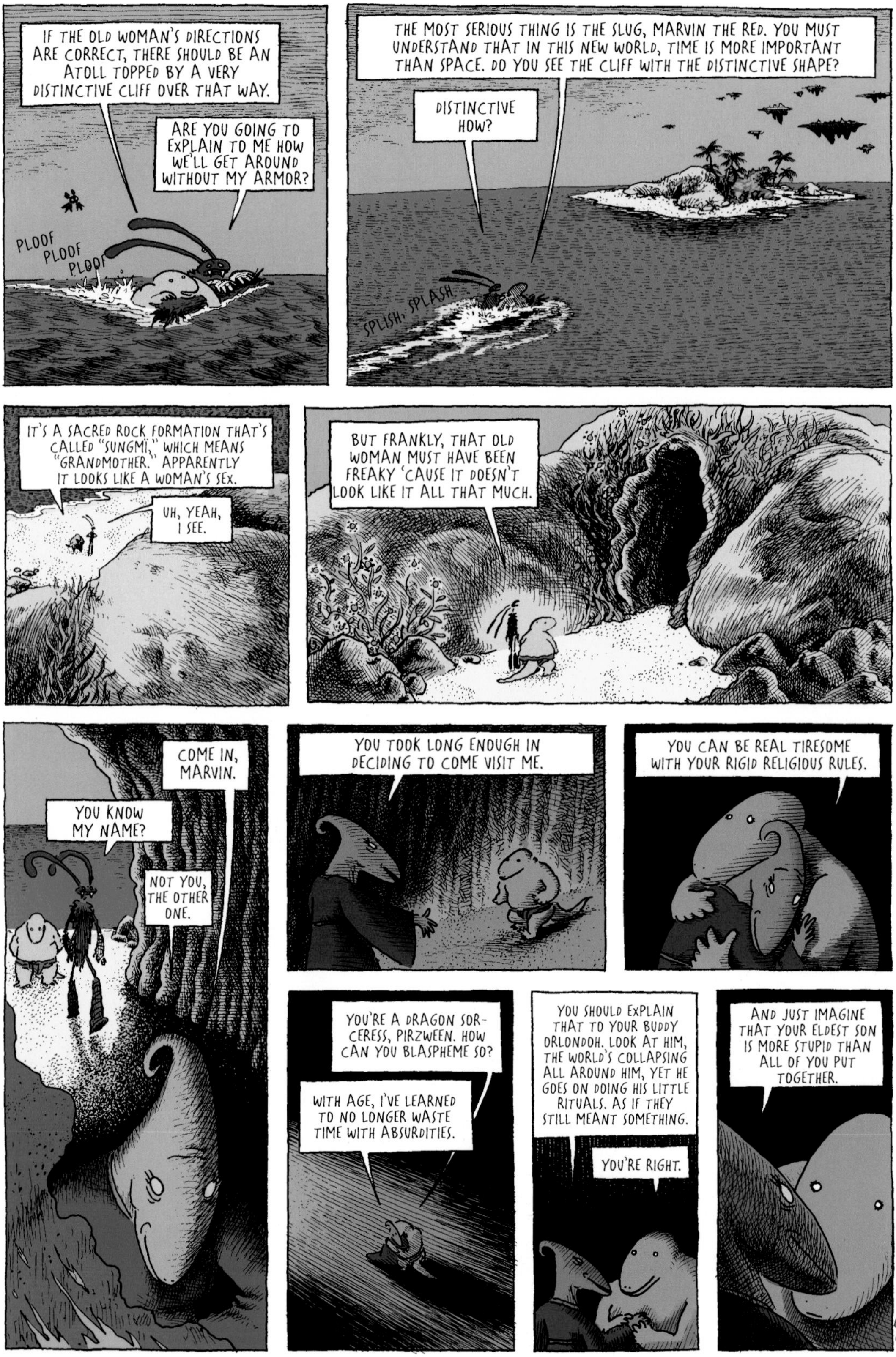
IF THE OLD WOMAN'S DIRECTIONS ARE CORRECT, THERE SHOULD BE AN ATOLL TOPPED BY A VERY DISTINCTIVE CLIFF OVER THAT WAY.
ARE YOU GOING TO EXPLAIN TO ME HOW WE'LL GET AROUND WITHOUT MY ARMOR?
PLOOF PLOOF PLOOF
THE MOST SERIOUS THING IS THE SLUG, MARVIN THE RED. YOU MUST UNDERSTAND THAT IN THIS NEW WORLD, TIME IS MORE IMPORTANT THAN SPACE. DO YOU SEE THE CLIFF WITH THE DISTINCTIVE SHAPE?
DISTINCTIVE HOW?
SPLISH, SPLASH
IT'S A SACRED ROCK FORMATION THAT'S CALLED "SUNGMI," WHICH MEANS "GRANDMOTHER." APPARENTLY IT LOOKS LIKE A WOMAN'S SEX.
UH, YEAH, I SEE.
BUT FRANKLY, THAT OLD WOMAN MUST HAVE BEEN FREAKY 'CAUSE IT DOESN'T LOOK LIKE IT ALL THAT MUCH.
COME IN, MARVIN.
YOU KNOW MY NAME?
NOT YOU, THE OTHER ONE.
YOU TOOK LONG ENOUGH IN DECIDING TO COME VISIT ME.
YOU CAN BE REAL TIRESOME WITH YOUR RIGID RELIGIOUS RULES.
YOU'RE A DRAGON SORCERESS, PIRZWEEN. HOW CAN YOU BLASPHEME SO?
WITH AGE, I'VE LEARNED TO NO LONGER WASTE TIME WITH ABSURDITIES.
YOU SHOULD EXPLAIN THAT TO YOUR BUDDY ORLONDOH. LOOK AT HIM, THE WORLD'S COLLAPSING ALL AROUND HIM, YET HE GOES ON DOING HIS LITTLE RITUALS. AS IF THEY STILL MEANT SOMETHING.
YOU'RE RIGHT.
AND JUST IMAGINE THAT YOUR ELDEST SON IS MORE STUPID THAN ALL OF YOU PUT TOGETHER.

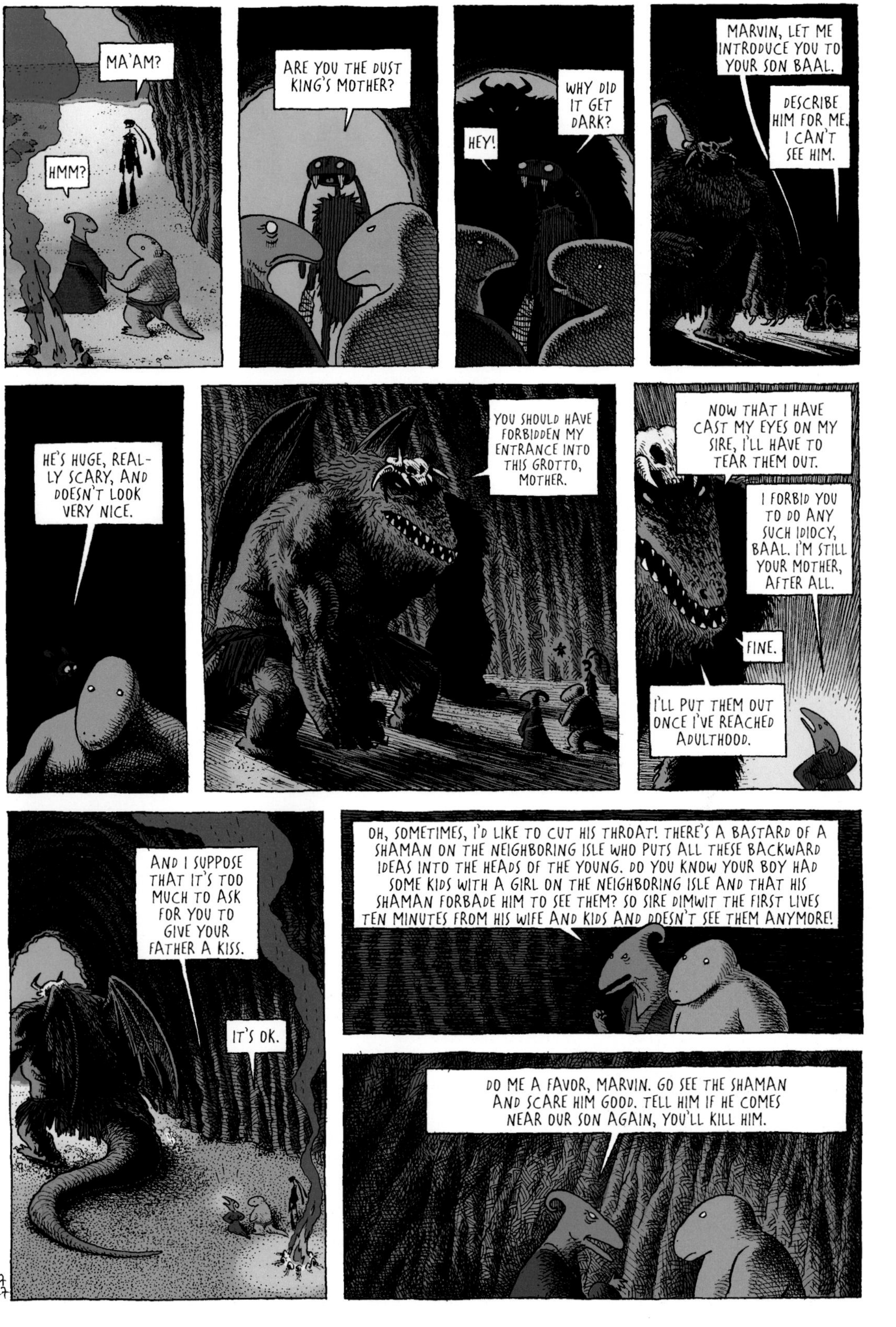
MA'AM?
HMM?
ARE YOU THE DUST KING'S MOTHER?
HEY!
WHY DID IT GET DARK?
MARVIN, LET ME INTRODUCE YOU TO YOUR SON BAAL.
DESCRIBE HIM FOR ME. I CAN'T SEE HIM.
HE'S HUGE, REAL-LY SCARY, AND DOESN'T LOOK VERY NICE.
YOU SHOULD HAVE FORBIDDEN MY ENTRANCE INTO THIS GROTTO, MOTHER.
NOW THAT I HAVE CAST MY EYES ON MY SIRE, I'LL HAVE TO TEAR THEM OUT.
I FORBID YOU TO DO ANY SUCH IDIOCY, BAAL. I'M STILL YOUR MOTHER, AFTER ALL.
FINE.
I'LL PUT THEM OUT ONCE I'VE REACHED ADULTHOOD.
AND I SUPPOSE THAT IT'S TOO MUCH TO ASK FOR YOU TO GIVE YOUR FATHER A KISS.
IT'S OK.
OH, SOMETIMES, I'D LIKE TO CUT HIS THROAT! THERE'S A BASTARD OF A SHAMAN ON THE NEIGHBORING ISLE WHO PUTS ALL THESE BACKWARD IDEAS INTO THE HEADS OF THE YOUNG. DO YOU KNOW YOUR BOY HAD SOME KIDS WITH A GIRL ON THE NEIGHBORING ISLE AND THAT HIS SHAMAN FORBADE HIM TO SEE THEM? SO SIRE DIMWIT THE FIRST LIVES TEN MINUTES FROM HIS WIFE AND KIDS AND DOESN'T SEE THEM ANYMORE!
DO ME A FAVOR, MARVIN. GO SEE THE SHAMAN AND SCARE HIM GOOD. TELL HIM IF HE COMES NEAR OUR SON AGAIN, YOU'LL KILL HIM.

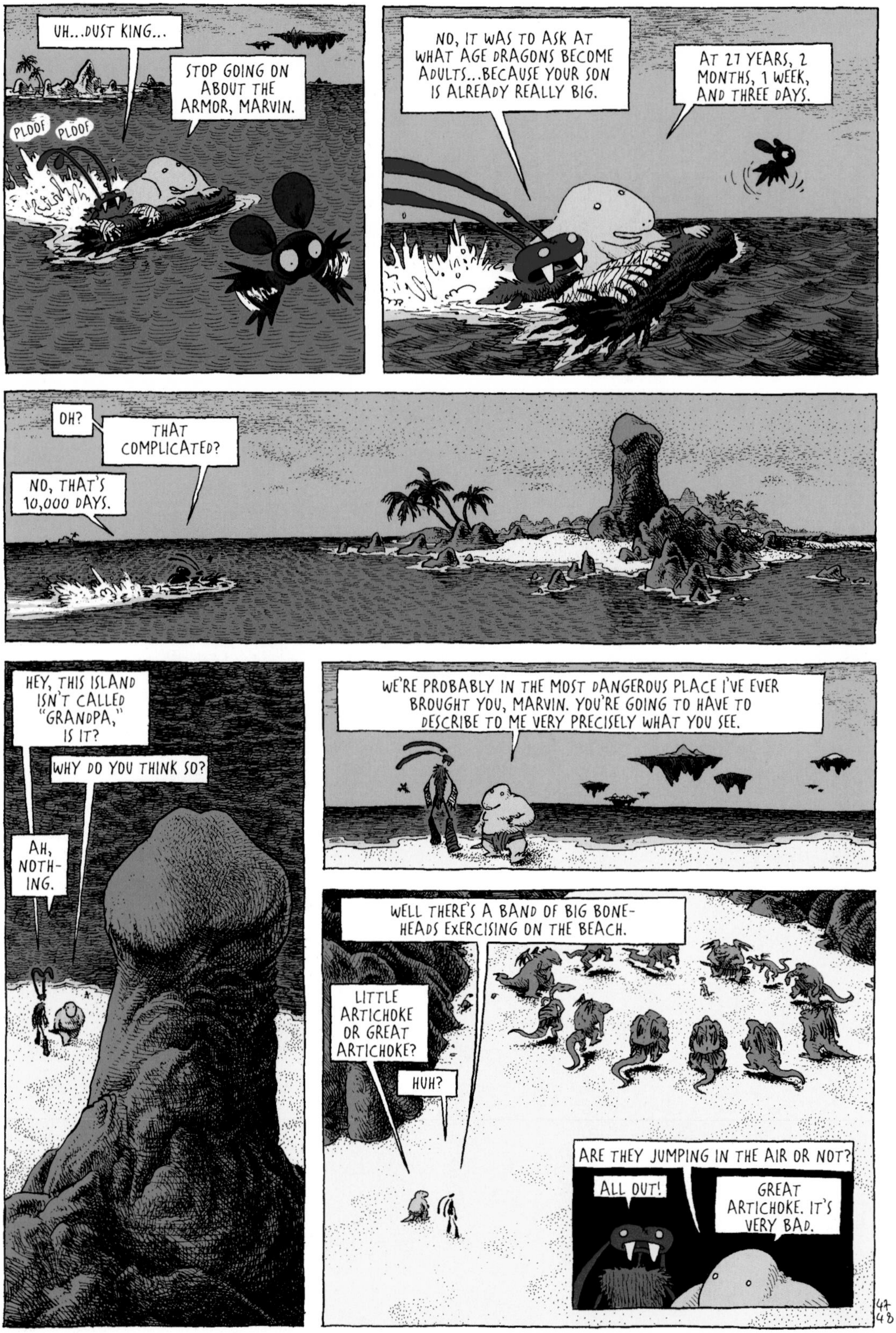
UH...DUST KING...
STOP GOING ON ABOUT THE ARMOR, MARVIN.
PLOOF
PLOOF
NO, IT WAS TO ASK AT WHAT AGE DRAGONS BECOME ADULTS...BECAUSE YOUR SON IS ALREADY REALLY BIG.
AT 27 YEARS, 2 MONTHS, 1 WEEK, AND THREE DAYS.
OH?
THAT COMPLICATED?
NO, THAT'S 10,000 DAYS.
HEY, THIS ISLAND ISN'T CALLED "GRANDPA," IS IT?
WHY DO YOU THINK SO?
AH, NOTHING.
WE'RE PROBABLY IN THE MOST DANGEROUS PLACE I'VE EVER BROUGHT YOU, MARVIN. YOU'RE GOING TO HAVE TO DESCRIBE TO ME VERY PRECISELY WHAT YOU SEE.
WELL THERE'S A BAND OF BIG BONEHEADS EXERCISING ON THE BEACH.
LITTLE ARTICHOKE OR GREAT ARTICHOKE?
HUH?
ARE THEY JUMPING IN THE AIR OR NOT?
ALL OUT!
GREAT ARTICHOKE. IT'S VERY BAD.
47
48

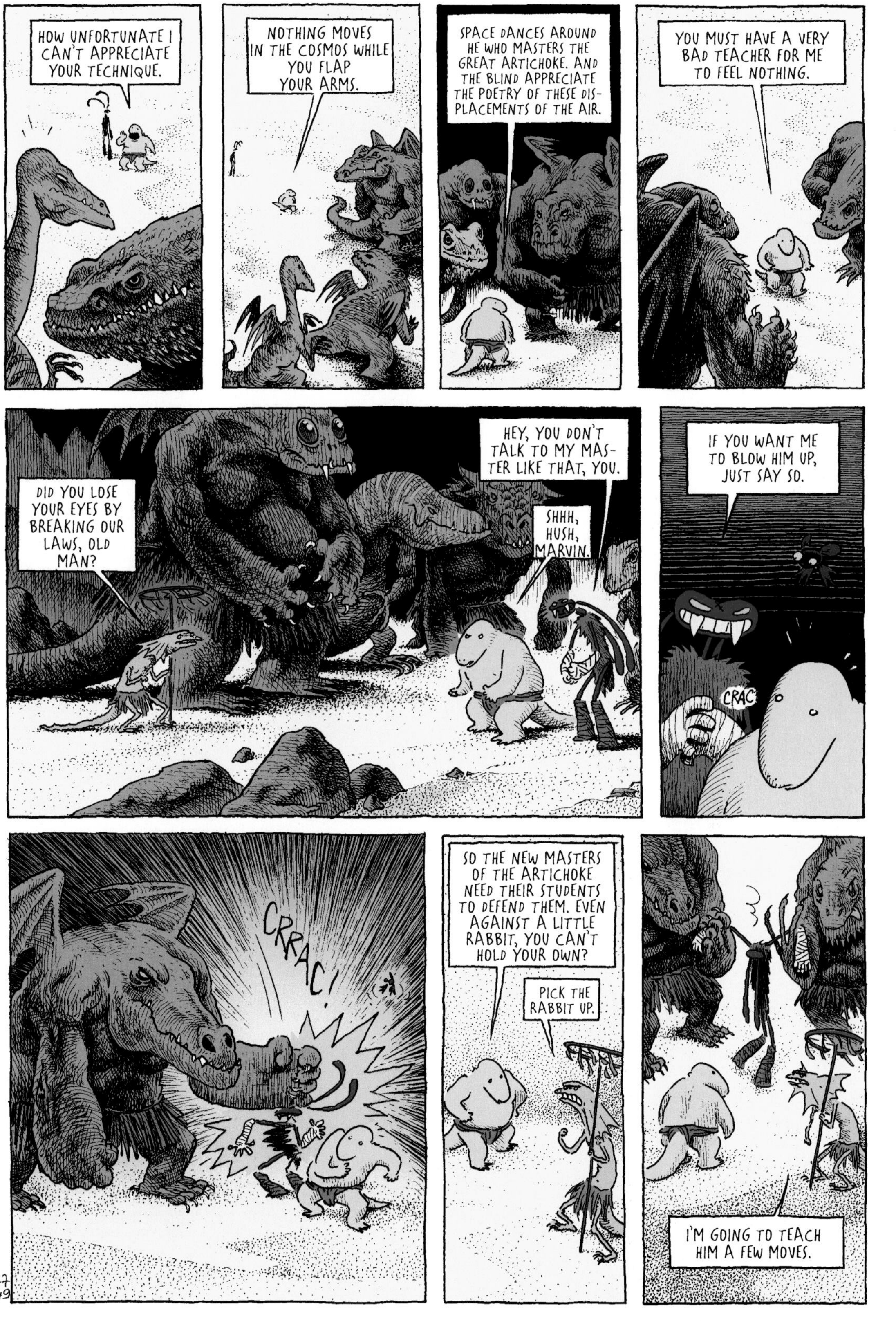
HOW UNFORTUNATE I CAN'T APPRECIATE YOUR TECHNIQUE.
NOTHING MOVES IN THE COSMOS WHILE YOU FLAP YOUR ARMS.
SPACE DANCES AROUND HE WHO MASTERS THE GREAT ARTICHOKE. AND THE BLIND APPRECIATE THE POETRY OF THESE DISPLACEMENTS OF THE AIR.
YOU MUST HAVE A VERY BAD TEACHER FOR ME TO FEEL NOTHING.
DID YOU LOSE YOUR EYES BY BREAKING OUR LAWS, OLD MAN?
HEY, YOU DON'T TALK TO MY MASTER LIKE THAT, YOU.
SHHH, HUSH, MARVIN.
IF YOU WANT ME TO BLOW HIM UP, JUST SAY SO.
CRAC
CRRAC!
SO THE NEW MASTERS OF THE ARTICHOKE NEED THEIR STUDENTS TO DEFEND THEM. EVEN AGAINST A LITTLE RABBIT, YOU CAN'T HOLD YOUR OWN?
PICK THE RABBIT UP.
I'M GOING TO TEACH HIM A FEW MOVES.

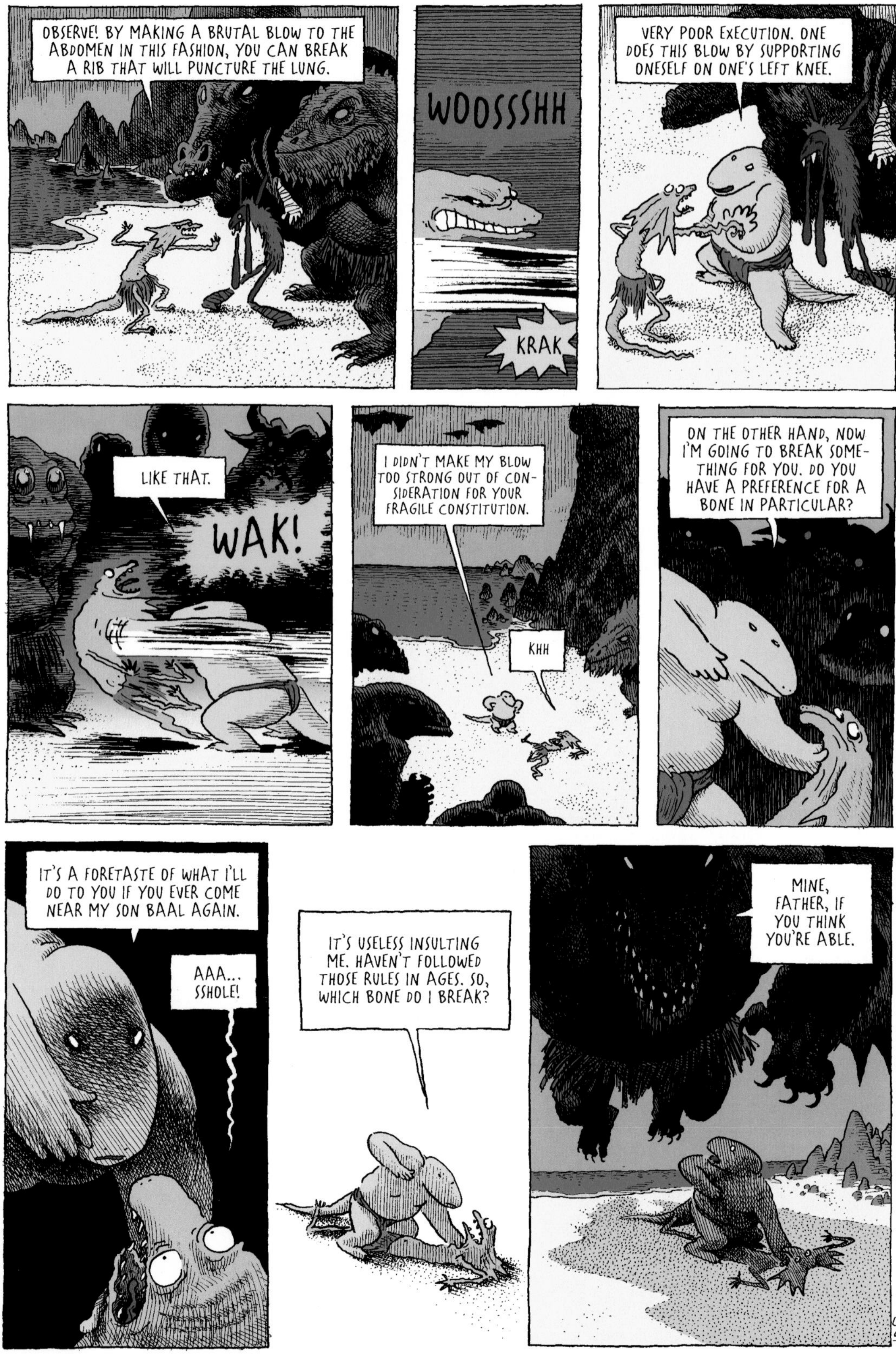
OBSERVE! BY MAKING A BRUTAL BLOW TO THE ABDOMEN IN THIS FASHION, YOU CAN BREAK A RIB THAT WILL PUNCTURE THE LUNG.
WOOSSSHH
KRAK
VERY POOR EXECUTION. ONE DOES THIS BLOW BY SUPPORTING ONESELF ON ONE'S LEFT KNEE.
LIKE THAT.
WAK!
I DIDN'T MAKE MY BLOW TOO STRONG OUT OF CONSIDERATION FOR YOUR FRAGILE CONSTITUTION.
KHH
ON THE OTHER HAND, NOW I'M GOING TO BREAK SOMETHING FOR YOU. DO YOU HAVE A PREFERENCE FOR A BONE IN PARTICULAR?
IT'S A FORETASTE OF WHAT I'LL DO TO YOU IF YOU EVER COME NEAR MY SON BAAL AGAIN.
AAA... SSHOLE!
IT'S USELESS INSULTING ME. HAVEN'T FOLLOWED THOSE RULES IN AGES. SO, WHICH BONE DO I BREAK?
MINE, FATHER, IF YOU THINK YOU'RE ABLE.

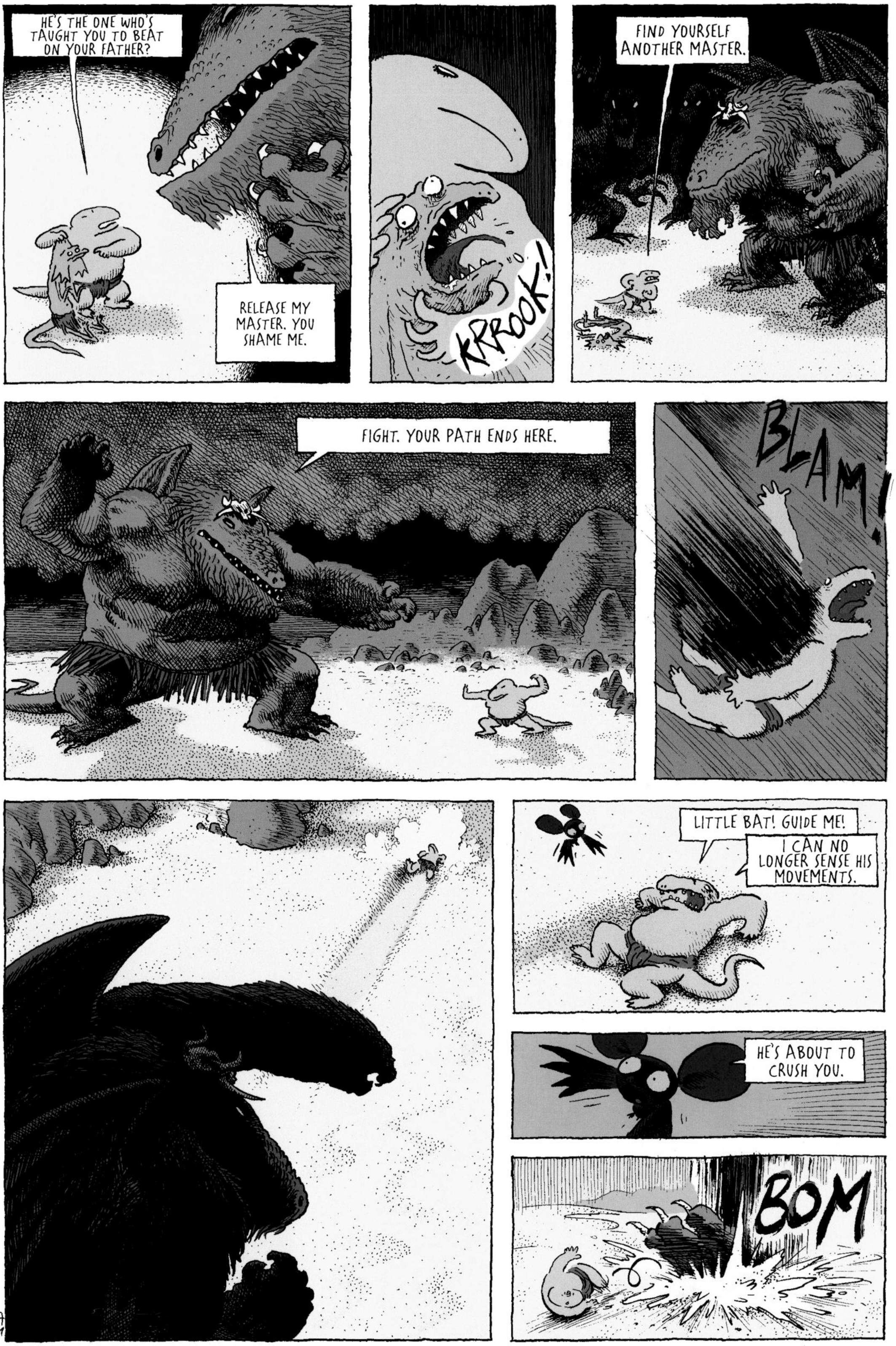
HE'S THE ONE WHO'S TAUGHT YOU TO BEAT ON YOUR FATHER?
RELEASE MY MASTER. YOU SHAME ME.
KRROOK!
FIND YOURSELF ANOTHER MASTER.
FIGHT. YOUR PATH ENDS HERE.
BLAM!
LITTLE BAT! GUIDE ME!
I CAN NO LONGER SENSE HIS MOVEMENTS.
HE'S ABOUT TO CRUSH YOU.
BOM

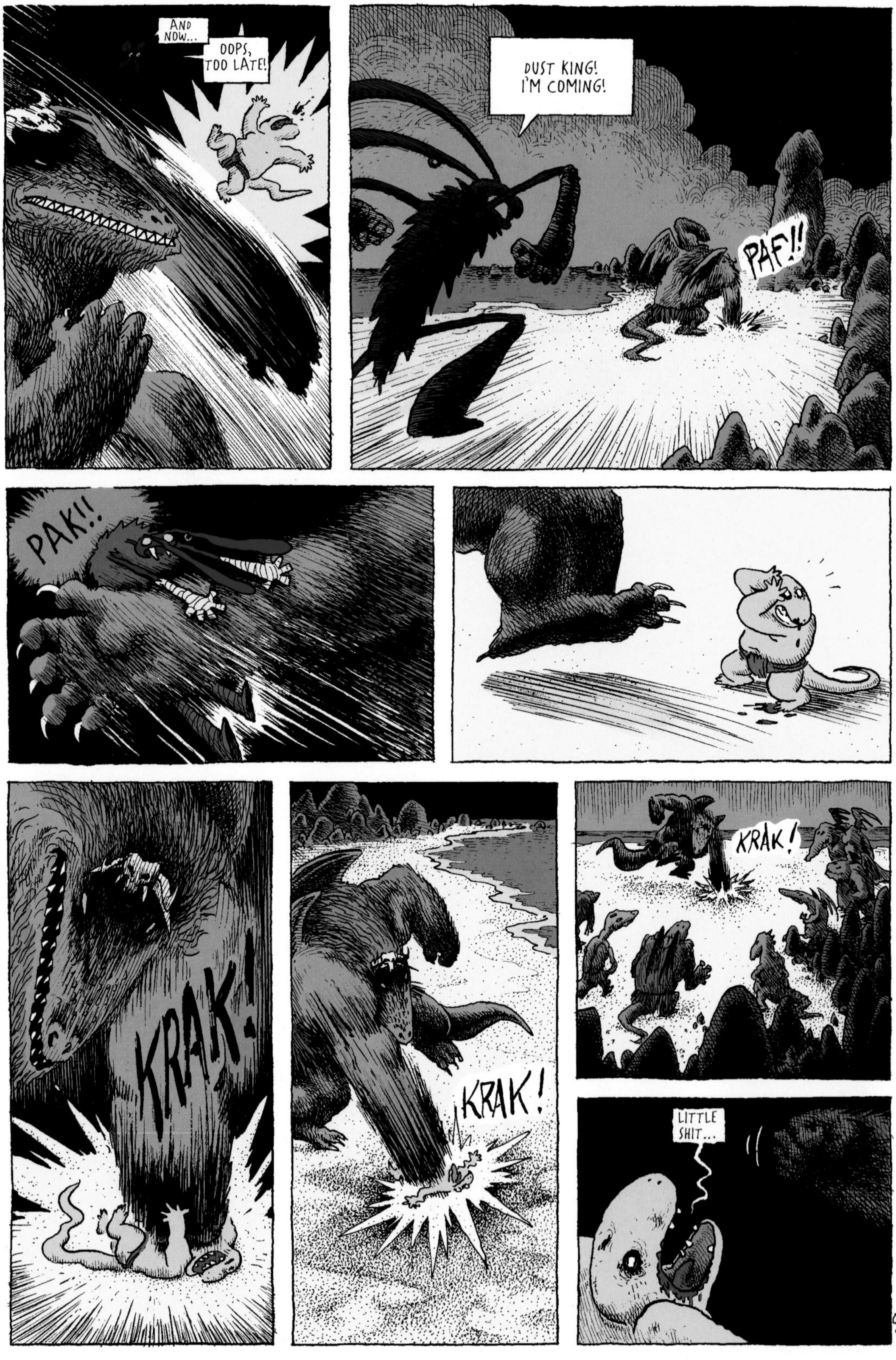
AND NOW...
OOPS, TOO LATE!
DUST KING! I'M COMING!
PAF!!
PAK!!
KRAK!
KRAK!
KRAK!
LITTLE SHIT...

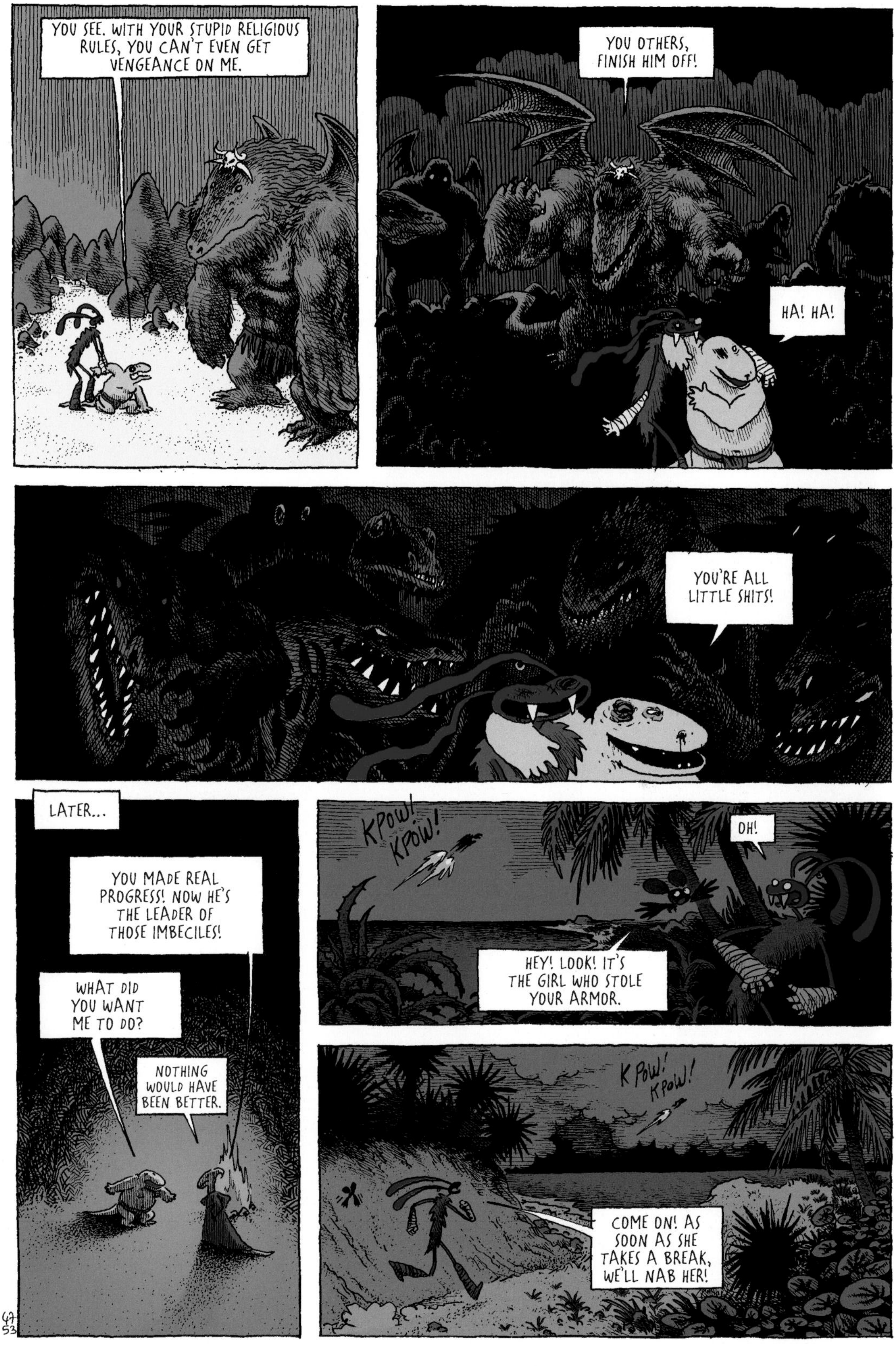
YOU SEE. WITH YOUR STUPID RELIGIOUS RULES, YOU CAN'T EVEN GET VENGEANCE ON ME.
YOU OTHERS, FINISH HIM OFF!
HA! HA!
YOU'RE ALL LITTLE SHITS!
LATER...
YOU MADE REAL PROGRESS! NOW HE'S THE LEADER OF THOSE IMBECILES!
WHAT DID YOU WANT ME TO DO?
NOTHING WOULD HAVE BEEN BETTER.
KPOW! KPOW!
OH!
HEY! LOOK! IT'S THE GIRL WHO STOLE YOUR ARMOR.
KPOW! KPOW!
COME ON! AS SOON AS SHE TAKES A BREAK, WE'LL NAB HER!

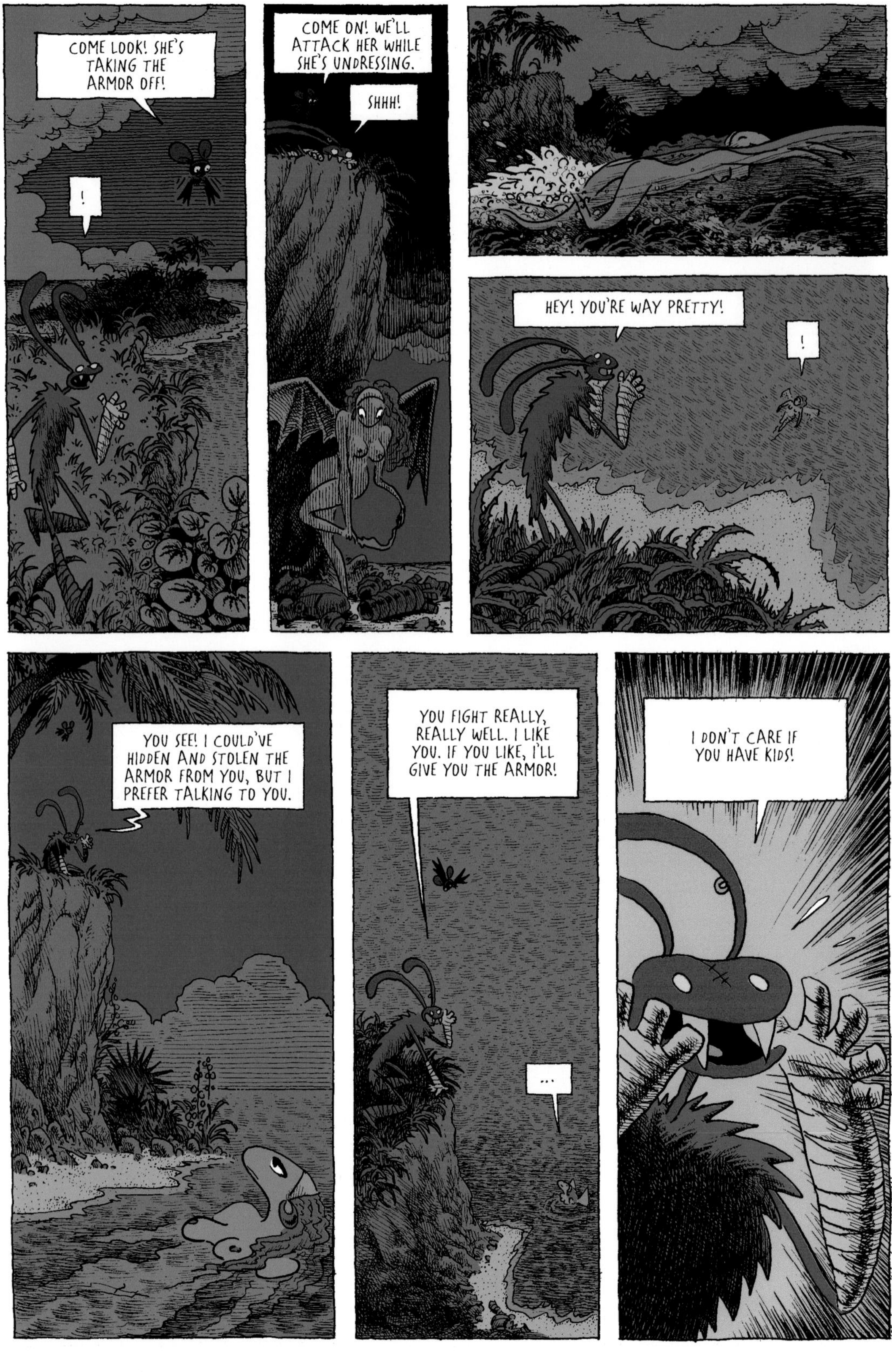
COME LOOK! SHE'S TAKING THE ARMOR OFF!
!
COME ON! WE'LL ATTACK HER WHILE SHE'S UNDRESSING.
SHHH!
HEY! YOU'RE WAY PRETTY!
!
YOU SEE! I COULD'VE HIDDEN AND STOLEN THE ARMOR FROM YOU, BUT I PREFER TALKING TO YOU.
YOU FIGHT REALLY, REALLY WELL. I LIKE YOU. IF YOU LIKE, I'LL GIVE YOU THE ARMOR!
...
I DON'T CARE IF YOU HAVE KIDS!

MASTER BAAL...

WOOSS

SORRY FOR BOTHERING YOU DURING YOUR MEDITATION, BUT YOUR WIFE HAS COME TO OUR ISLE.

WOOSS, DOESN'T SHE KNOW OUR RELIGION FORBIDS ME TO APPROACH HER?

OH NO, SHE DIDN'T WANT TO SEE YOU. SHE JUST WANTED TO SEND YOU A MESSAGE.

WOOSS...

SHE WANTED YOU TO KNOW THAT SHE'S GOTTEN ENGAGED WITH A RED RABBIT. WELL, NOT ENGAGED IN A RELIGIOUS SENSE, JUST THAT THEY'RE SLEEPING TOGETHER.

WOOSSSSSSSSSS

LIFE'S BEAUTIFUL, ISN'T IT?

PAPA!

PAPA!

CALL ME MARVIN.

PAPA!

PAPA!

HEY...ARE YOU NIMWITS OR WHAT?

NO, IT'S THEIR FATHER WHO'S COMING.

HUH?

BOM!

UH...I...

YOU WANT ME TO BEAT HIM UP?

NO, I'LL TAKE CARE OF IT.

TAKE A GOOD LOOK, I'M GONNA KILL YOUR LOVER.

GO AHEAD. IT DOESN'T MATTER.

PAPA!

PAPA!

KILL HIM. I'LL FIND ANOTHER ONE.

ARE THOSE ALL THE FEELINGS YOU HAD FOR ME?

I HAVE FIFTEEN KIDS TO RAISE. IF YOU'RE NOT AT HOME TO DO THE WORK, I'LL FIND SOMEONE ELSE.

ORMELLE, YOU KNOW I MARRIED GOD.

THEN SLEEP WITH GOD AND LEAVE ME IN PEACE.

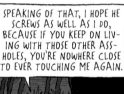

SPEAKING OF THAT, I HOPE HE SCREWS AS WELL AS I DO, BECAUSE IF YOU KEEP ON LIVING WITH THOSE OTHER ASSHOLES, YOU'RE NOWHERE CLOSE TO EVER TOUCHING ME AGAIN.

EXCUSE ME, BUT THERE'S A KID NEEDING A BOTTLE AND TWO OTHERS HAVE GONE CACA.

SO IF MISTER BONEHEAD WANTS TO GO DO HIS PRAYERS, LET HIM, BUT WE HAVE WORK TO DO.

OPEN YOUR MOUTH, DEAR. I'M GOING TO GIVE YOU SOME MORE CAKE.

STOP, MAMA, NOT IN FRONT OF THE KIDS.

PAPA!

YOU HAVE TO KEEP YOUR STRENGTH UP, YOU KNOW...YOU'LL HAVE TO BE GETTING UP EARLY TO DO BOTTLES.

GRANDPA!

GRANDPA!

OKAY, GIVE ME SOME.

GRANDPA DUST!

HOW COME CAKES FROM GRANNIES ARE ALWAYS SO GOOD.

MMM...

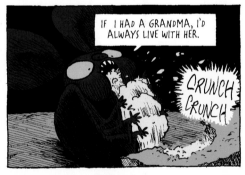

IF I HAD A GRANDMA, I'D ALWAYS LIVE WITH HER.

CRUNCH CRUNCH

COME...ORLONDOH WANTS TO TALK TO YOU.

HE'S HERE?

COME, I TELL YOU.

GRANDPA!

HERE'S MARVIN.

APPROACH, MARVIN.

MARVIN, I FOUND OUT WHAT YOU DID, AND I'M NOT PROUD.

DROP IT, ORLONDOH. INSTEAD, SHOW HIM THE NEW PATH.

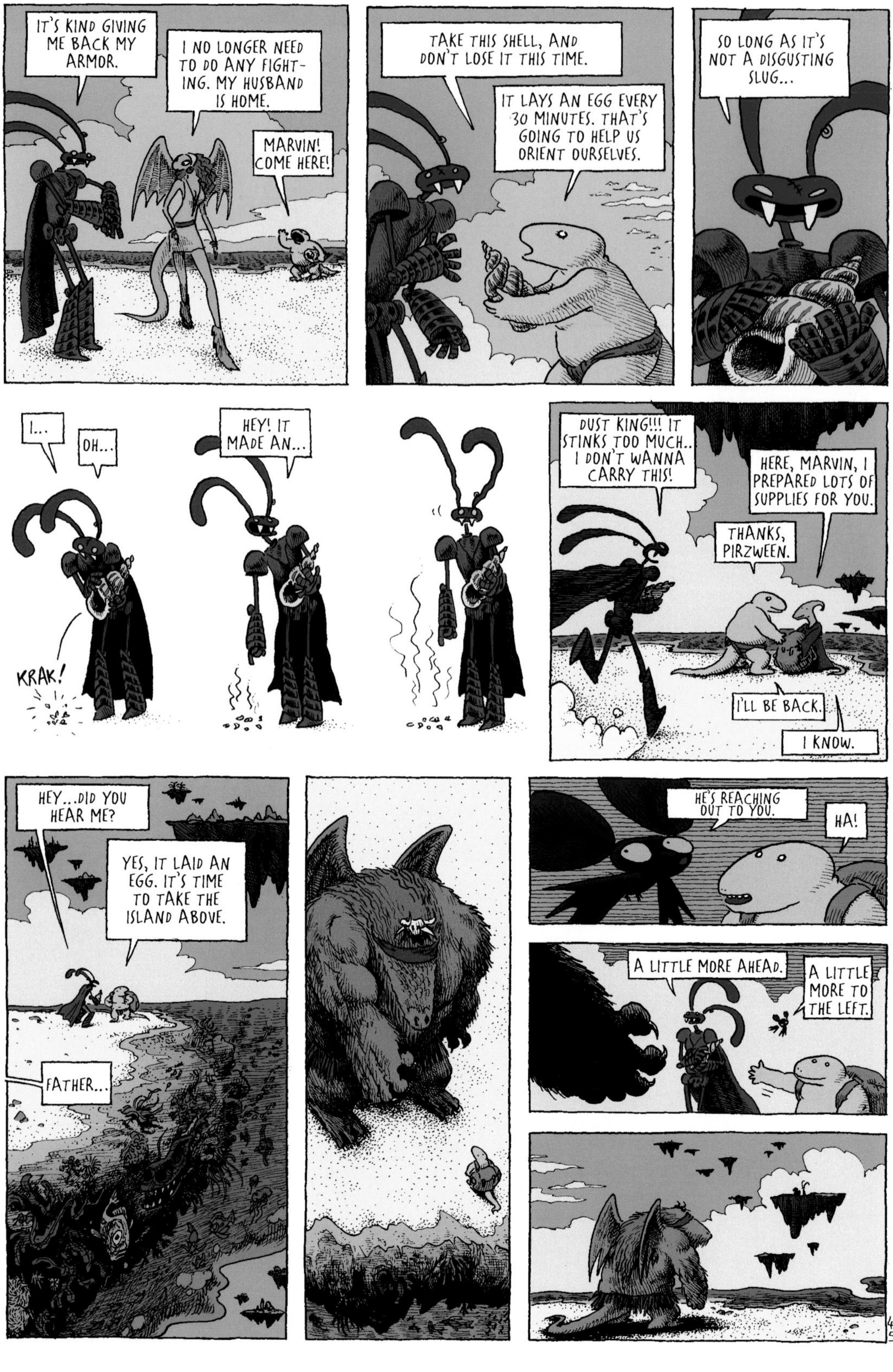
IT'S KIND GIVING ME BACK MY ARMOR.
I NO LONGER NEED TO DO ANY FIGHTING. MY HUSBAND IS HOME.
MARVIN! COME HERE!
TAKE THIS SHELL, AND DON'T LOSE IT THIS TIME.
IT LAYS AN EGG EVERY 30 MINUTES. THAT'S GOING TO HELP US ORIENT OURSELVES.
SO LONG AS IT'S NOT A DISGUSTING SLUG...
I...
OH...
KRAK!
HEY! IT MADE AN...
DUST KING!!! IT STINKS TOO MUCH.. I DON'T WANNA CARRY THIS!
HERE, MARVIN, I PREPARED LOTS OF SUPPLIES FOR YOU.
THANKS, PIRZWEEN.
I'LL BE BACK.
I KNOW.
HEY...DID YOU HEAR ME?
YES, IT LAID AN EGG. IT'S TIME TO TAKE THE ISLAND ABOVE.
FATHER...
HE'S REACHING OUT TO YOU.
HA!
A LITTLE MORE AHEAD.
A LITTLE MORE TO THE LEFT.

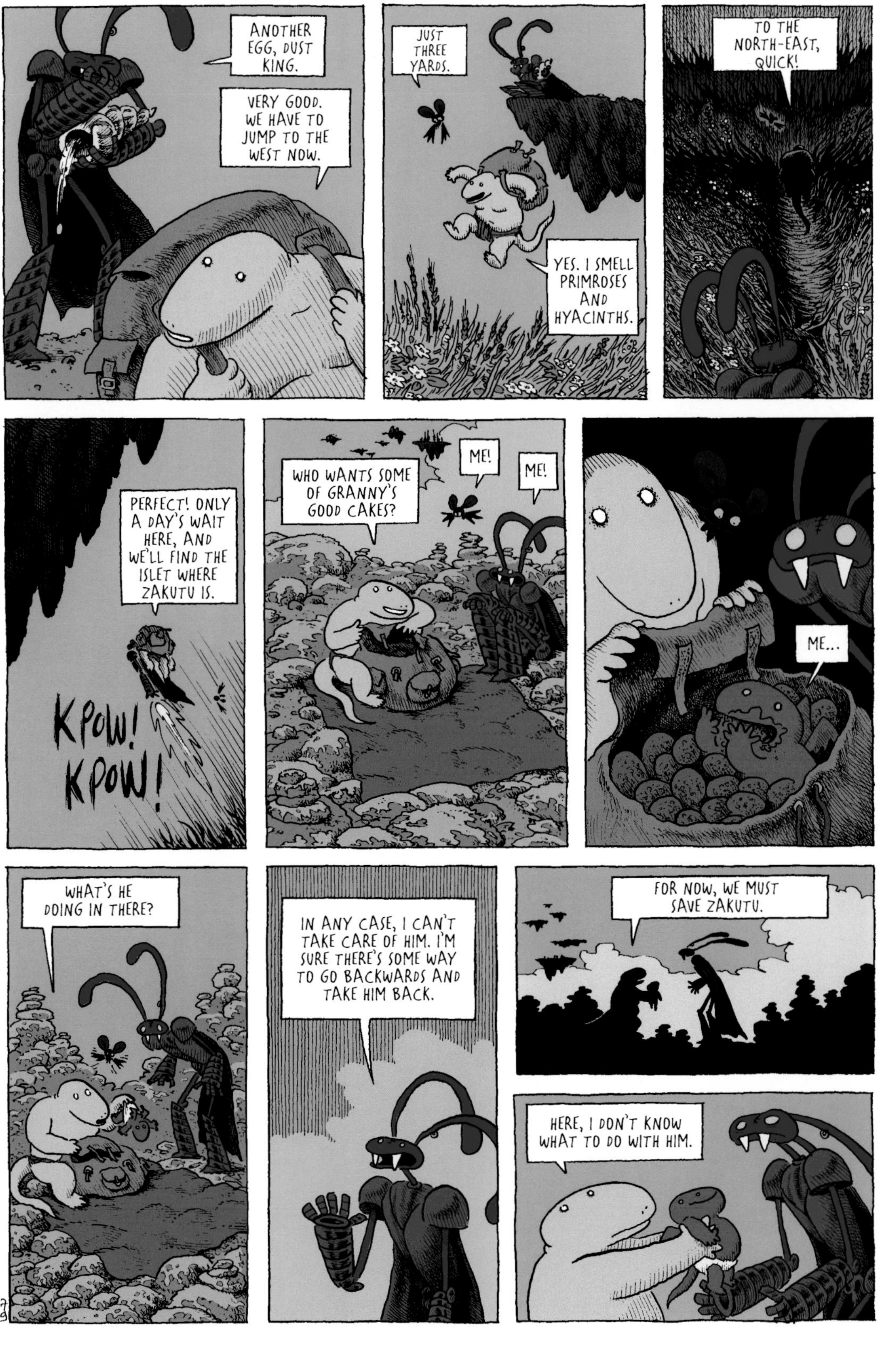
ANOTHER EGG, DUST KING.
VERY GOOD. WE HAVE TO JUMP TO THE WEST NOW.
JUST THREE YARDS.
YES. I SMELL PRIMROSES AND HYACINTHS.
TO THE NORTH-EAST, QUICK!
PERFECT! ONLY A DAY'S WAIT HERE, AND WE'LL FIND THE ISLET WHERE ZAKUTU IS.
KPOW! KPOW!
WHO WANTS SOME OF GRANNY'S GOOD CAKES?
ME!
ME!
ME...
WHAT'S HE DOING IN THERE?
IN ANY CASE, I CAN'T TAKE CARE OF HIM. I'M SURE THERE'S SOME WAY TO GO BACKWARDS AND TAKE HIM BACK.
FOR NOW, WE MUST SAVE ZAKUTU.
HERE, I DON'T KNOW WHAT TO DO WITH HIM.

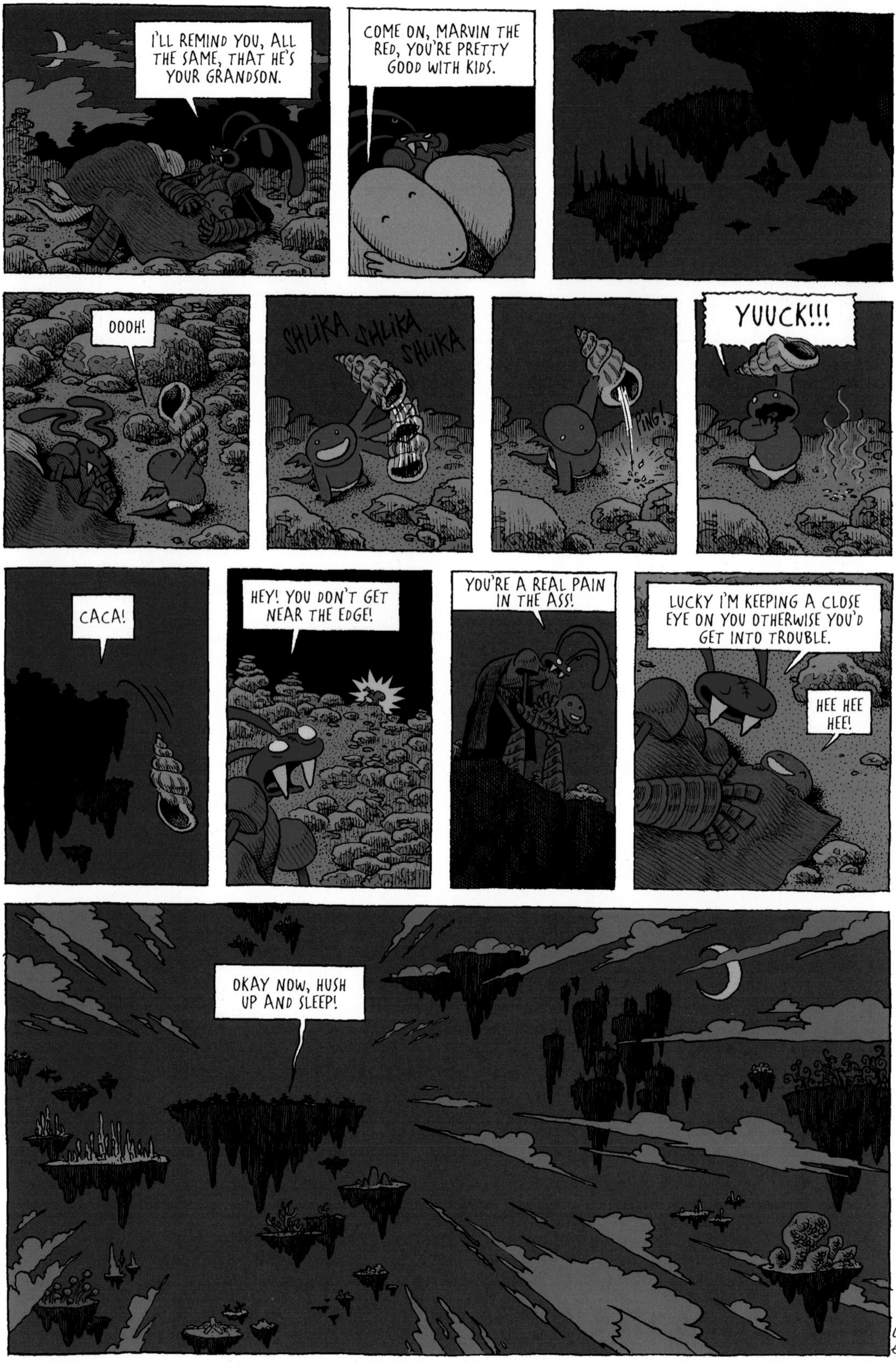
I'LL REMIND YOU, ALL THE SAME, THAT HE'S YOUR GRANDSON.
COME ON, MARVIN THE RED, YOU'RE PRETTY GOOD WITH KIDS.
OOOH!
SHLIKA SHLIKA SHLIKA
PING!
YUUCK!!!
CACA!
HEY! YOU DON'T GET NEAR THE EDGE!
YOU'RE A REAL PAIN IN THE ASS!
LUCKY I'M KEEPING A CLOSE EYE ON YOU OTHERWISE YOU'D GET INTO TROUBLE.
HEE HEE HEE!
OKAY NOW, HUSH UP AND SLEEP!

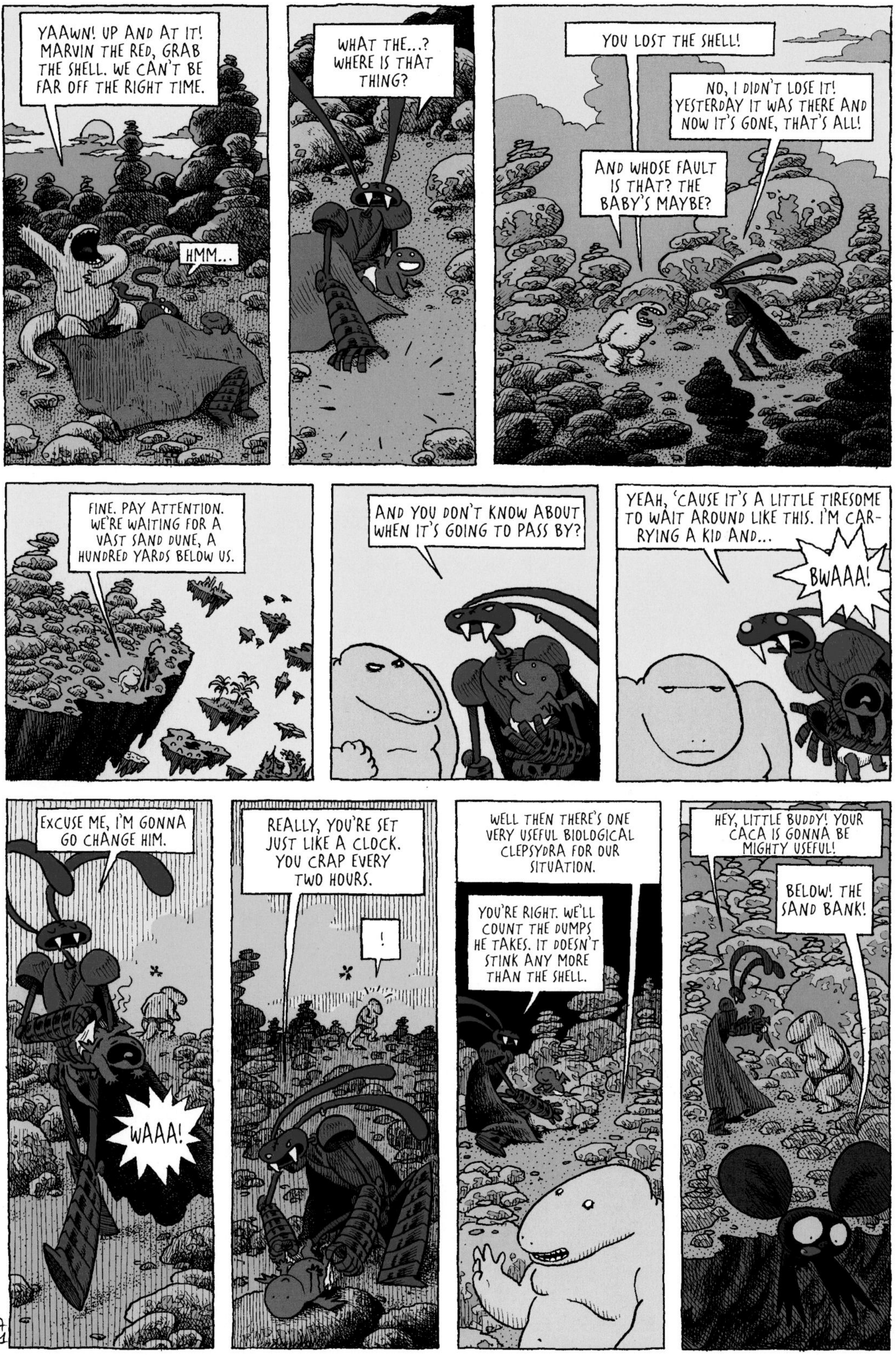
YAAWN! UP AND AT IT! MARVIN THE RED, GRAB THE SHELL. WE CAN'T BE FAR OFF THE RIGHT TIME.
HMM...
WHAT THE...? WHERE IS THAT THING?
YOU LOST THE SHELL!
NO, I DIDN'T LOSE IT! YESTERDAY IT WAS THERE AND NOW IT'S GONE, THAT'S ALL!
AND WHOSE FAULT IS THAT? THE BABY'S MAYBE?
FINE. PAY ATTENTION. WE'RE WAITING FOR A VAST SAND DUNE, A HUNDRED YARDS BELOW US.
AND YOU DON'T KNOW ABOUT WHEN IT'S GOING TO PASS BY?
YEAH, 'CAUSE IT'S A LITTLE TIRESOME TO WAIT AROUND LIKE THIS. I'M CARRYING A KID AND...
BWAAA!
EXCUSE ME, I'M GONNA GO CHANGE HIM.
WAAA!
REALLY, YOU'RE SET JUST LIKE A CLOCK. YOU CRAP EVERY TWO HOURS.
!
WELL THEN THERE'S ONE VERY USEFUL BIOLOGICAL CLEPSYDRA FOR OUR SITUATION.
YOU'RE RIGHT. WE'LL COUNT THE DUMPS HE TAKES. IT DOESN'T STINK ANY MORE THAN THE SHELL.
HEY, LITTLE BUDDY! YOUR CACA IS GONNA BE MIGHTY USEFUL!
BELOW! THE SAND BANK!

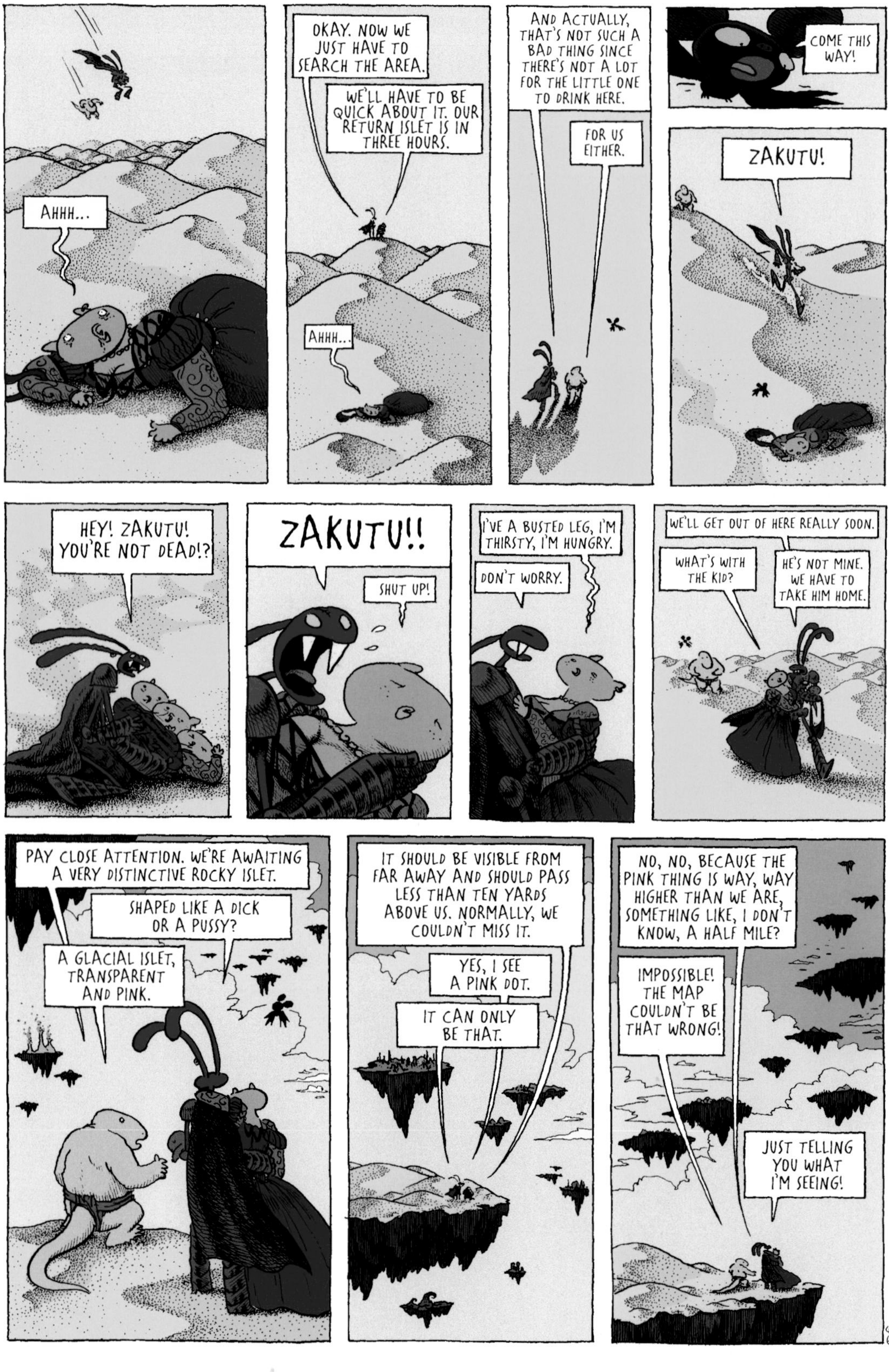
AHHH...
OKAY. NOW WE JUST HAVE TO SEARCH THE AREA.
WE'LL HAVE TO BE QUICK ABOUT IT. OUR RETURN ISLET IS IN THREE HOURS.
AHHH...
AND ACTUALLY, THAT'S NOT SUCH A BAD THING SINCE THERE'S NOT A LOT FOR THE LITTLE ONE TO DRINK HERE.
FOR US EITHER.
COME THIS WAY!
ZAKUTU!
HEY! ZAKUTU! YOU'RE NOT DEAD!?
ZAKUTU!!
SHUT UP!
I'VE A BUSTED LEG, I'M THIRSTY, I'M HUNGRY.
DON'T WORRY.
WE'LL GET OUT OF HERE REALLY SOON.
WHAT'S WITH THE KID?
HE'S NOT MINE. WE HAVE TO TAKE HIM HOME.
PAY CLOSE ATTENTION. WE'RE AWAITING A VERY DISTINCTIVE ROCKY ISLET.
SHAPED LIKE A DICK OR A PUSSY?
A GLACIAL ISLET, TRANSPARENT AND PINK.
IT SHOULD BE VISIBLE FROM FAR AWAY AND SHOULD PASS LESS THAN TEN YARDS ABOVE US. NORMALLY, WE COULDN'T MISS IT.
YES, I SEE A PINK DOT.
IT CAN ONLY BE THAT.
NO, NO, BECAUSE THE PINK THING IS WAY, WAY HIGHER THAN WE ARE, SOMETHING LIKE, I DON'T KNOW, A HALF MILE?
IMPOSSIBLE! THE MAP COULDN'T BE THAT WRONG!
JUST TELLING YOU WHAT I'M SEEING!

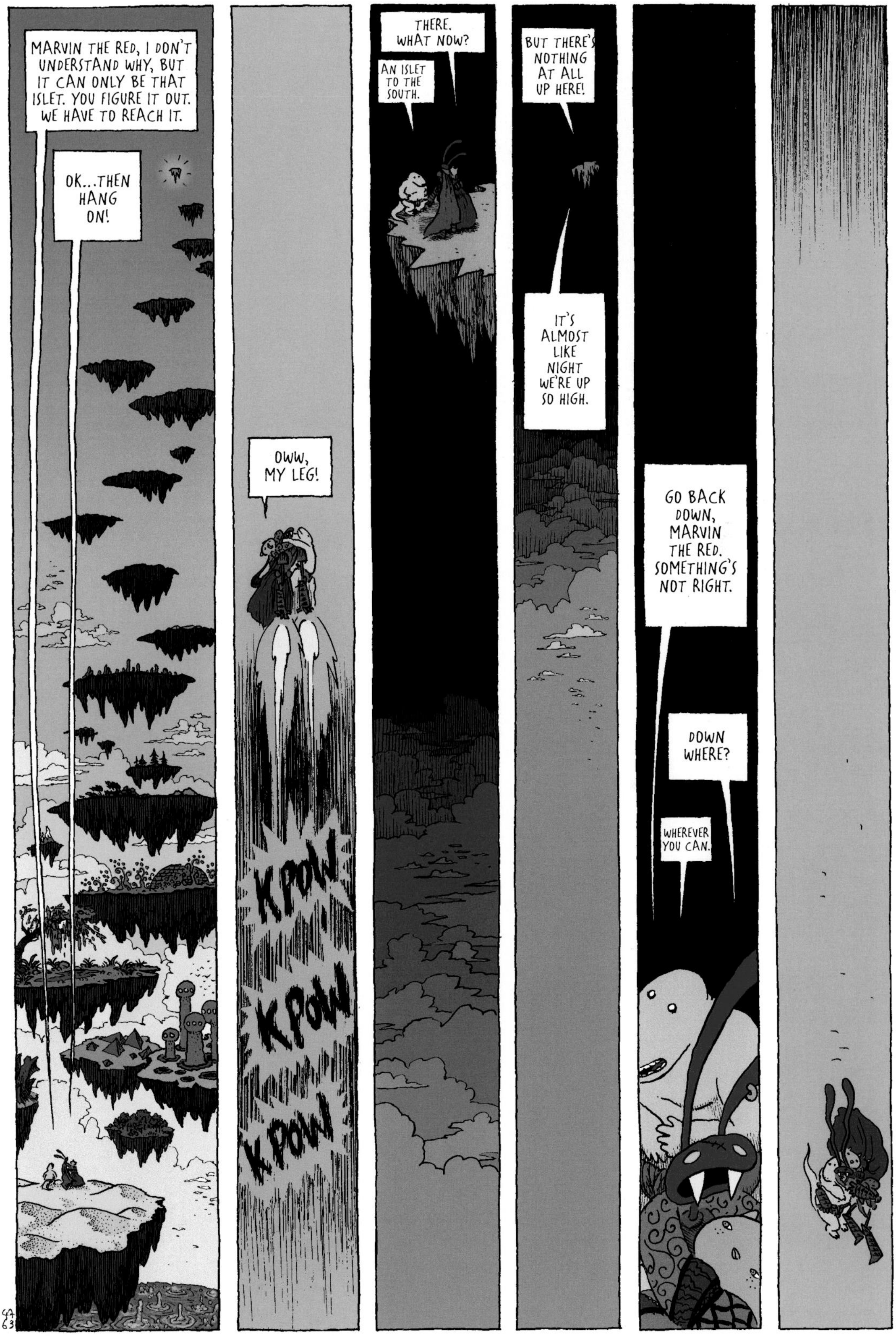
MARVIN THE RED, I DON'T UNDERSTAND WHY, BUT IT CAN ONLY BE THAT ISLET. YOU FIGURE IT OUT. WE HAVE TO REACH IT.
OK...THEN HANG ON!
OWW, MY LEG!
K POW
K POW
K POW
THERE. WHAT NOW?
AN ISLET TO THE SOUTH.
BUT THERE'S NOTHING AT ALL UP HERE!
IT'S ALMOST LIKE NIGHT WE'RE UP SO HIGH.
GO BACK DOWN, MARVIN THE RED. SOMETHING'S NOT RIGHT.
DOWN WHERE?
WHEREVER YOU CAN.

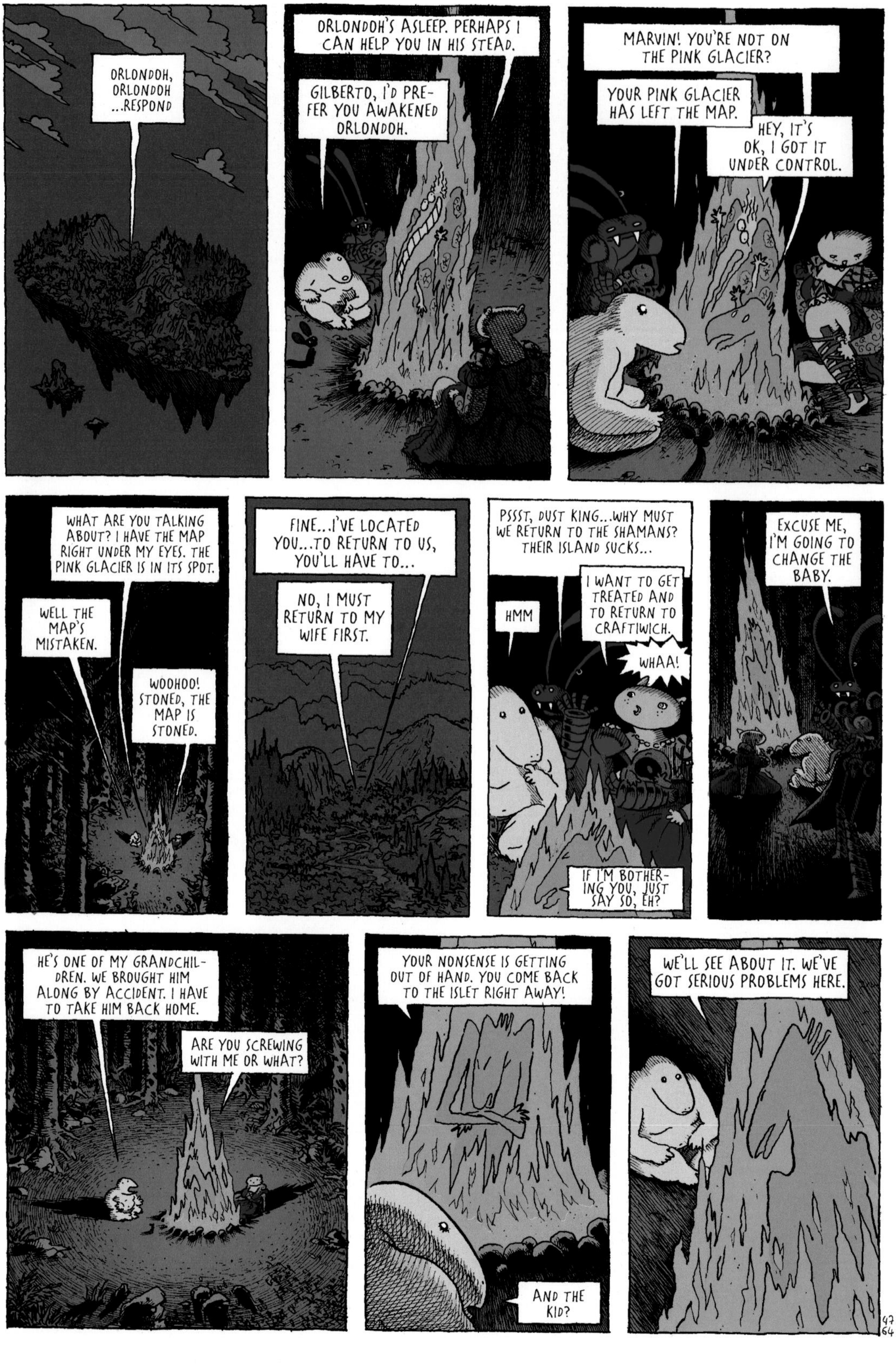
ORLONDOH, ORLONDOH ...RESPOND
ORLONDOH'S ASLEEP. PERHAPS I CAN HELP YOU IN HIS STEAD.
GILBERTO, I'D PREFER YOU AWAKENED ORLONDOH.
MARVIN! YOU'RE NOT ON THE PINK GLACIER?
YOUR PINK GLACIER HAS LEFT THE MAP.
HEY, IT'S OK, I GOT IT UNDER CONTROL.
WHAT ARE YOU TALKING ABOUT? I HAVE THE MAP RIGHT UNDER MY EYES. THE PINK GLACIER IS IN ITS SPOT.
WELL THE MAP'S MISTAKEN.
WOOHOO! STONED, THE MAP IS STONED.
FINE...I'VE LOCATED YOU...TO RETURN TO US, YOU'LL HAVE TO...
NO, I MUST RETURN TO MY WIFE FIRST.
PSSST, DUST KING...WHY MUST WE RETURN TO THE SHAMANS? THEIR ISLAND SUCKS...
HMM
I WANT TO GET TREATED AND TO RETURN TO CRAFTIWICH.
WHAA!
IF I'M BOTHERING YOU, JUST SAY SO, EH?
EXCUSE ME, I'M GOING TO CHANGE THE BABY.
HE'S ONE OF MY GRANDCHILDREN. WE BROUGHT HIM ALONG BY ACCIDENT. I HAVE TO TAKE HIM BACK HOME.
ARE YOU SCREWING WITH ME OR WHAT?
YOUR NONSENSE IS GETTING OUT OF HAND. YOU COME BACK TO THE ISLET RIGHT AWAY!
AND THE KID?
WE'LL SEE ABOUT IT. WE'VE GOT SERIOUS PROBLEMS HERE.

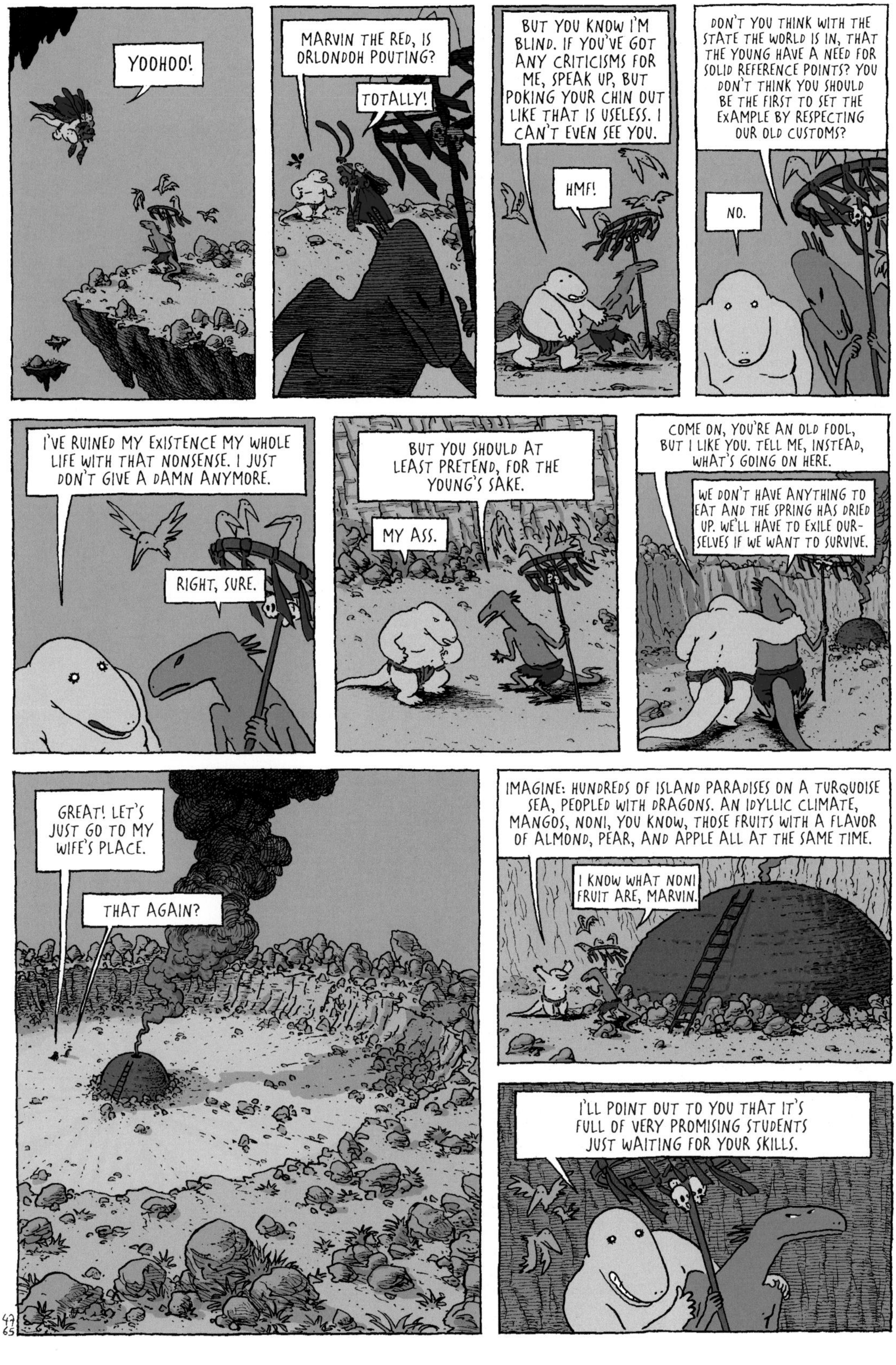

YOOHOO!
MARVIN THE RED, IS ORLONDOH POUTING?
TOTALLY!
BUT YOU KNOW I'M BLIND. IF YOU'VE GOT ANY CRITICISMS FOR ME, SPEAK UP, BUT POKING YOUR CHIN OUT LIKE THAT IS USELESS. I CAN'T EVEN SEE YOU.
HMF!
DON'T YOU THINK WITH THE STATE THE WORLD IS IN, THAT THE YOUNG HAVE A NEED FOR SOLID REFERENCE POINTS? YOU DON'T THINK YOU SHOULD BE THE FIRST TO SET THE EXAMPLE BY RESPECTING OUR OLD CUSTOMS?
NO.
I'VE RUINED MY EXISTENCE MY WHOLE LIFE WITH THAT NONSENSE. I JUST DON'T GIVE A DAMN ANYMORE.
RIGHT, SURE.
BUT YOU SHOULD AT LEAST PRETEND, FOR THE YOUNG'S SAKE.
MY ASS.
COME ON, YOU'RE AN OLD FOOL, BUT I LIKE YOU. TELL ME, INSTEAD, WHAT'S GOING ON HERE.
WE DON'T HAVE ANYTHING TO EAT AND THE SPRING HAS DRIED UP. WE'LL HAVE TO EXILE OURSELVES IF WE WANT TO SURVIVE.
GREAT! LET'S JUST GO TO MY WIFE'S PLACE.
THAT AGAIN?
IMAGINE: HUNDREDS OF ISLAND PARADISES ON A TURQUOISE SEA, PEOPLED WITH DRAGONS. AN IDYLLIC CLIMATE, MANGOS, NONI, YOU KNOW, THOSE FRUITS WITH A FLAVOR OF ALMOND, PEAR, AND APPLE ALL AT THE SAME TIME.
I KNOW WHAT NONI FRUIT ARE, MARVIN.
I'LL POINT OUT TO YOU THAT IT'S FULL OF VERY PROMISING STUDENTS JUST WAITING FOR YOUR SKILLS.

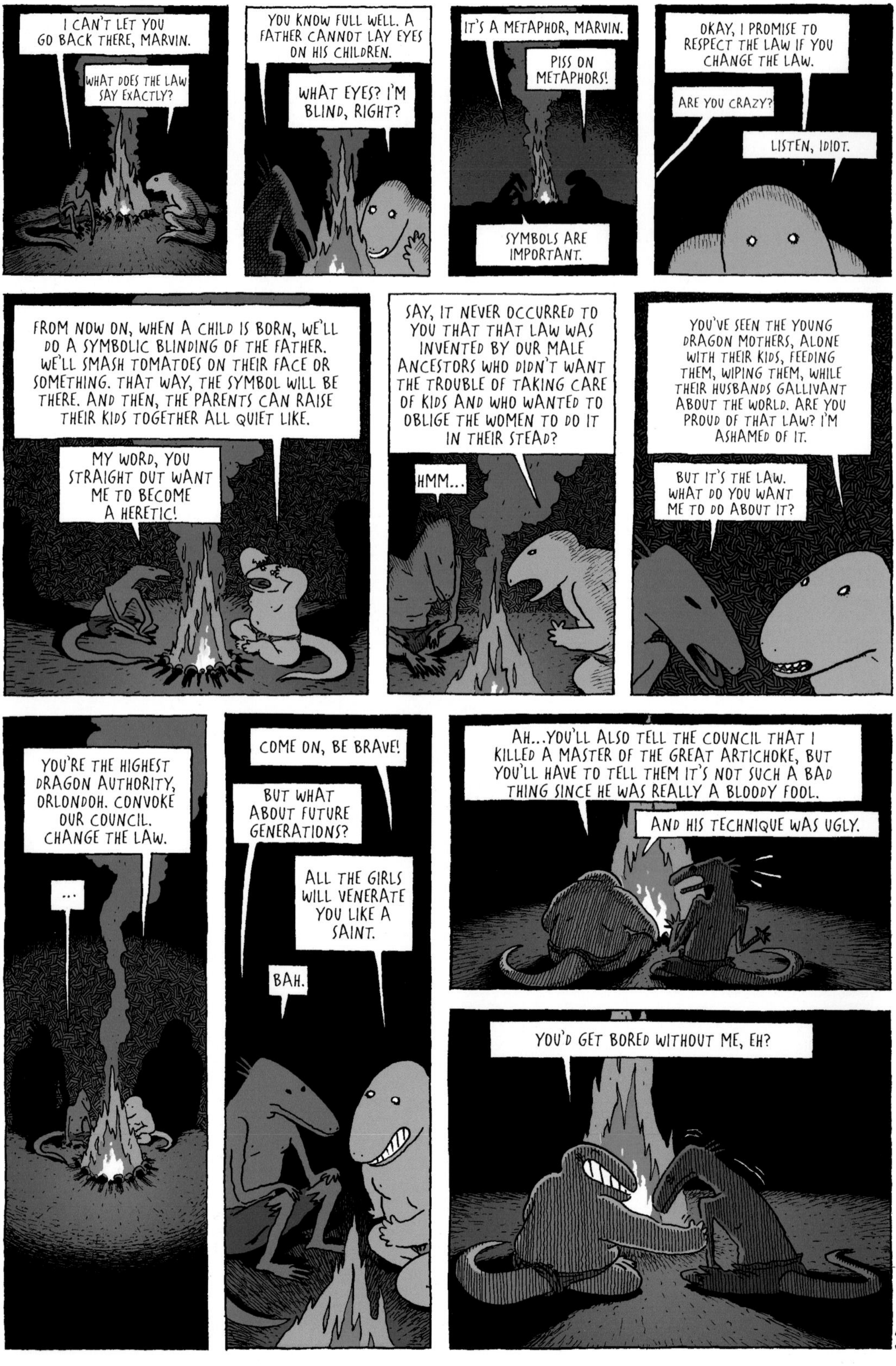

I CAN'T LET YOU GO BACK THERE, MARVIN.
WHAT DOES THE LAW SAY EXACTLY?
YOU KNOW FULL WELL. A FATHER CANNOT LAY EYES ON HIS CHILDREN.
WHAT EYES? I'M BLIND, RIGHT?
IT'S A METAPHOR, MARVIN.
PISS ON METAPHORS!
SYMBOLS ARE IMPORTANT.
OKAY, I PROMISE TO RESPECT THE LAW IF YOU CHANGE THE LAW.
ARE YOU CRAZY?
LISTEN, IDIOT.
FROM NOW ON, WHEN A CHILD IS BORN, WE'LL DO A SYMBOLIC BLINDING OF THE FATHER. WE'LL SMASH TOMATOES ON THEIR FACE OR SOMETHING. THAT WAY, THE SYMBOL WILL BE THERE. AND THEN, THE PARENTS CAN RAISE THEIR KIDS TOGETHER ALL QUIET LIKE.
MY WORD, YOU STRAIGHT OUT WANT ME TO BECOME A HERETIC!
SAY, IT NEVER OCCURRED TO YOU THAT THAT LAW WAS INVENTED BY OUR MALE ANCESTORS WHO DIDN'T WANT THE TROUBLE OF TAKING CARE OF KIDS AND WHO WANTED TO OBLIGE THE WOMEN TO DO IT IN THEIR STEAD?
HMM...
YOU'VE SEEN THE YOUNG DRAGON MOTHERS, ALONE WITH THEIR KIDS, FEEDING THEM, WIPING THEM, WHILE THEIR HUSBANDS GALLIVANT ABOUT THE WORLD. ARE YOU PROUD OF THAT LAW? I'M ASHAMED OF IT.
BUT IT'S THE LAW. WHAT DO YOU WANT ME TO DO ABOUT IT?
YOU'RE THE HIGHEST DRAGON AUTHORITY, ORLONDOH. CONVOKE OUR COUNCIL. CHANGE THE LAW.
...
COME ON, BE BRAVE!
BUT WHAT ABOUT FUTURE GENERATIONS?
ALL THE GIRLS WILL VENERATE YOU LIKE A SAINT.
BAH.
AH...YOU'LL ALSO TELL THE COUNCIL THAT I KILLED A MASTER OF THE GREAT ARTICHOKE, BUT YOU'LL HAVE TO TELL THEM IT'S NOT SUCH A BAD THING SINCE HE WAS REALLY A BLOODY FOOL.
AND HIS TECHNIQUE WAS UGLY.
YOU'D GET BORED WITHOUT ME, EH?

SEVERAL DAYS LATER, ABANDONING THE HOLE OF SPIRITS, THE SHAMANIC COUNCIL IN FULL REGALIA DISEMBARKS ON A BEACH PARADISE.

DO YOU SEE HOW CLASSY IT IS, SWEETIE?

I SAID I WANTED TO RETURN TO CRAFTIWICH.

DON'T WORRY. GILBERTO TOLD ME THAT CRAFTIWICH WILL PASS BY HERE IN SOMEWHERE AROUND TWO WEEKS. IN THE MEANTIME, WE'LL TAKE IT EASY. HEY, YOU KNOW, GILBERTO'S GOT SOME REALLY COOL STUFF...

I DON'T WANT TO SMOKE.

THANKS FOR BRINGING BACK MY BABY.

AH...YEAH

UH...

ZAKUTU, I'D LIKE TO INTRODUCE YOU TO THIS GIRL HERE, I DON'T KNOW HER NAME. SHE'S JUST A FRIEND.

YES, I IMAGINE THAT YOU WOULDN'T HAVE HAD SEX WITH THAT FISH FACE.

AH, NO NO NO, NO SEX AT ALL.

YOU LACK IMAGINATION, LARDASS.

OH, AND I DON'T GIVE A DAMN ANYHOW. YOU CAN DO WHAT-EVER YOU LIKE.

DID YOU HAVE TO SAY THAT!?

SHE'S THE ONE WHO INSULTED ME.

IF SHE WEREN'T YOUR FRIEND, SHE'D ALREADY BE DEAD.

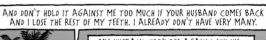

IS IT SO EASY TO FORGET WHAT THERE WAS BETWEEN US?

NO, BUT THERE, REALLY, IT WOULD HAVE BEEN MUCH BETTER FOR ME, IF YOU'D KEPT YOUR MOUTH SHUT.

AND DON'T HOLD IT AGAINST ME TOO MUCH IF YOUR HUSBAND COMES BACK AND I LOSE THE REST OF MY TEETH. I ALREADY DON'T HAVE VERY MANY.

MY HUSBAND TOOK OFF AGAIN WITH HIS STUPID BUDDIES.

HE'S INCAPABLE OF TAKING CARE OF A FAMILY.

YOU CAN COME TO MY PLACE IF YOU WANT.

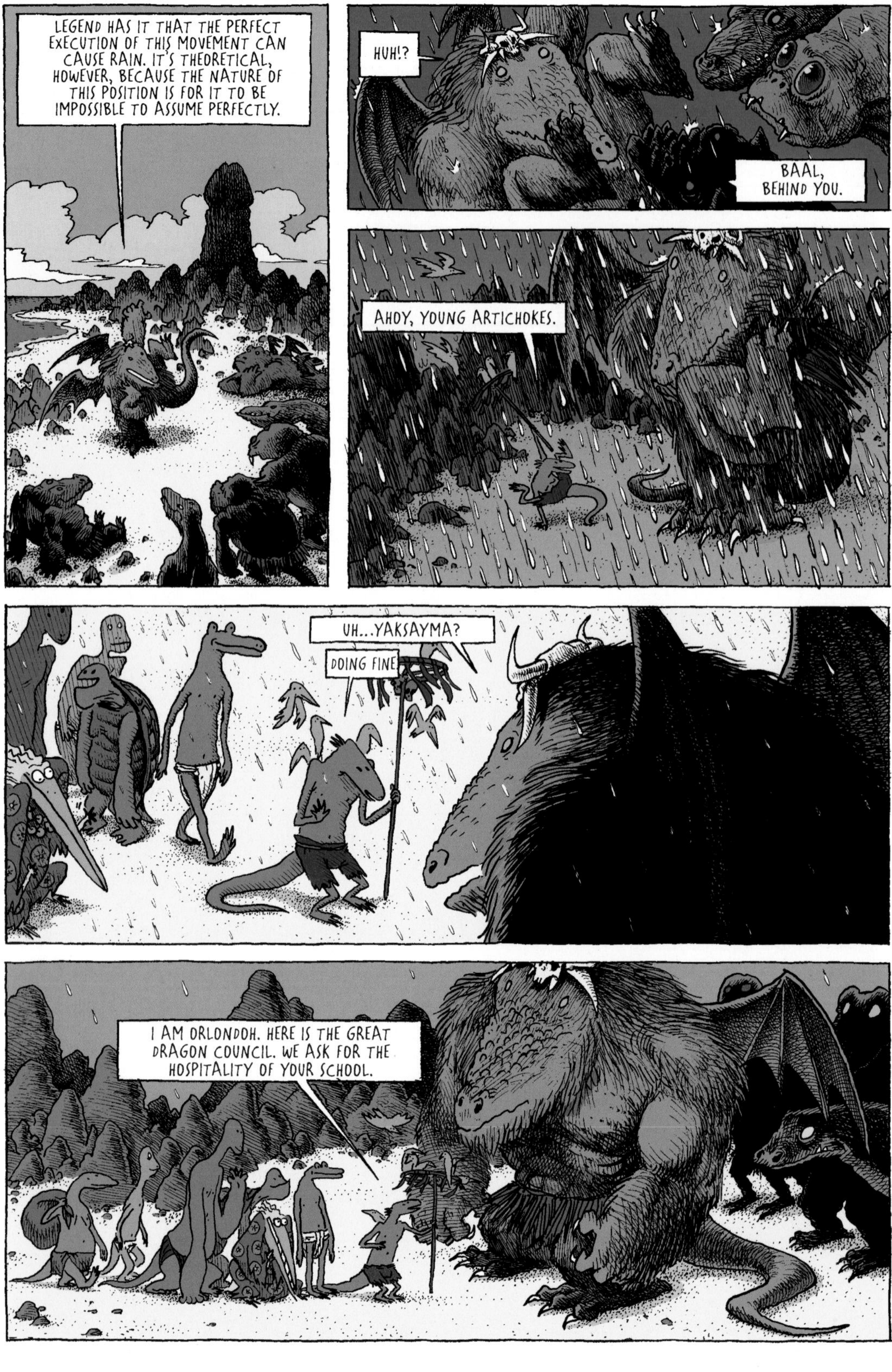
LEGEND HAS IT THAT THE PERFECT EXECUTION OF THIS MOVEMENT CAN CAUSE RAIN. IT'S THEORETICAL, HOWEVER, BECAUSE THE NATURE OF THIS POSITION IS FOR IT TO BE IMPOSSIBLE TO ASSUME PERFECTLY.
HUH!?
BAAL, BEHIND YOU.
AHOY, YOUNG ARTICHOKES.
UH...YAKSAYMA?
DOING FINE
I AM ORLONDOH. HERE IS THE GREAT DRAGON COUNCIL. WE ASK FOR THE HOSPITALITY OF YOUR SCHOOL.

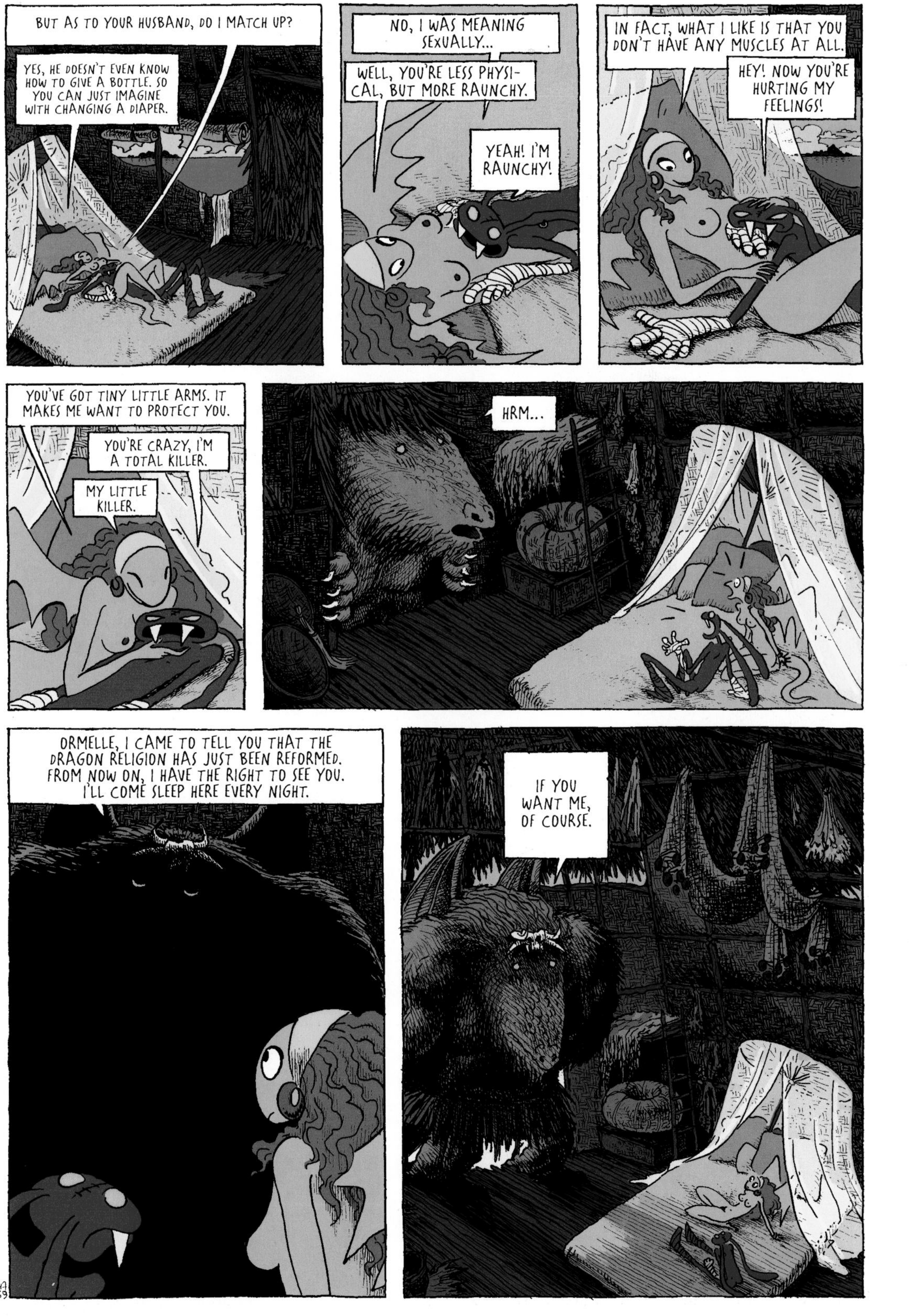
BUT AS TO YOUR HUSBAND, DO I MATCH UP?
YES, HE DOESN'T EVEN KNOW HOW TO GIVE A BOTTLE. SO YOU CAN JUST IMAGINE WITH CHANGING A DIAPER.
NO, I WAS MEANING SEXUALLY...
WELL, YOU'RE LESS PHYSI-CAL, BUT MORE RAUNCHY.
YEAH! I'M RAUNCHY!
IN FACT, WHAT I LIKE IS THAT YOU DON'T HAVE ANY MUSCLES AT ALL.
HEY! NOW YOU'RE HURTING MY FEELINGS!
YOU'VE GOT TINY LITTLE ARMS. IT MAKES ME WANT TO PROTECT YOU.
YOU'RE CRAZY, I'M A TOTAL KILLER.
MY LITTLE KILLER.
HRM...
ORMELLE, I CAME TO TELL YOU THAT THE DRAGON RELIGION HAS JUST BEEN REFORMED. FROM NOW ON, I HAVE THE RIGHT TO SEE YOU. I'LL COME SLEEP HERE EVERY NIGHT.
IF YOU WANT ME, OF COURSE.

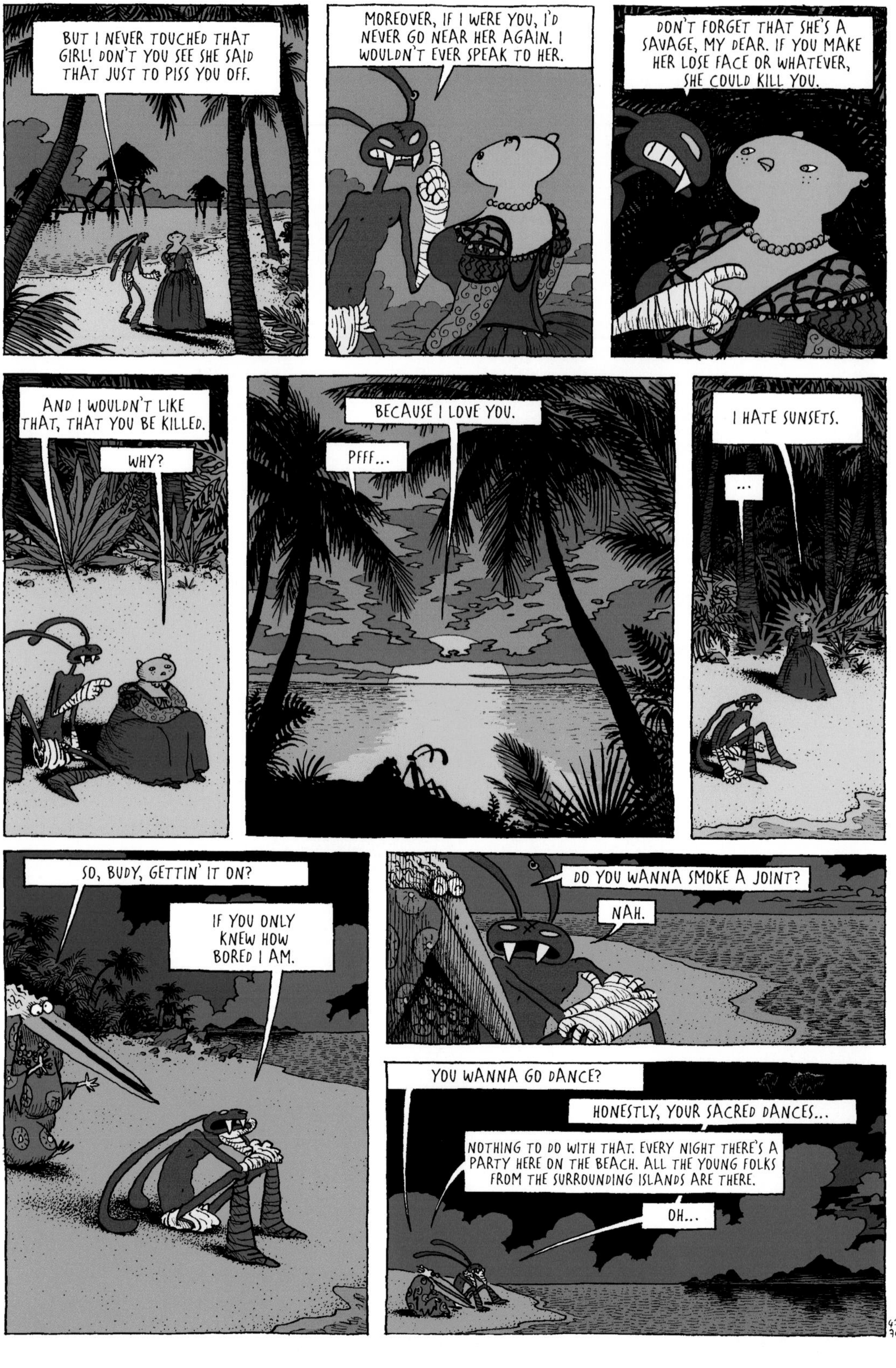

BUT I NEVER TOUCHED THAT GIRL! DON'T YOU SEE SHE SAID THAT JUST TO PISS YOU OFF.
MOREOVER, IF I WERE YOU, I'D NEVER GO NEAR HER AGAIN. I WOULDN'T EVER SPEAK TO HER.
DON'T FORGET THAT SHE'S A SAVAGE, MY DEAR. IF YOU MAKE HER LOSE FACE OR WHATEVER, SHE COULD KILL YOU.
AND I WOULDN'T LIKE THAT, THAT YOU BE KILLED.
WHY?
BECAUSE I LOVE YOU.
PFFF...
I HATE SUNSETS.
...
SO, BUDY, GETTIN' IT ON?
IF YOU ONLY KNEW HOW BORED I AM.
DO YOU WANNA SMOKE A JOINT?
NAH.
YOU WANNA GO DANCE?
HONESTLY, YOUR SACRED DANCES...
NOTHING TO DO WITH THAT. EVERY NIGHT THERE'S A PARTY HERE ON THE BEACH. ALL THE YOUNG FOLKS FROM THE SURROUNDING ISLANDS ARE THERE.
OH...

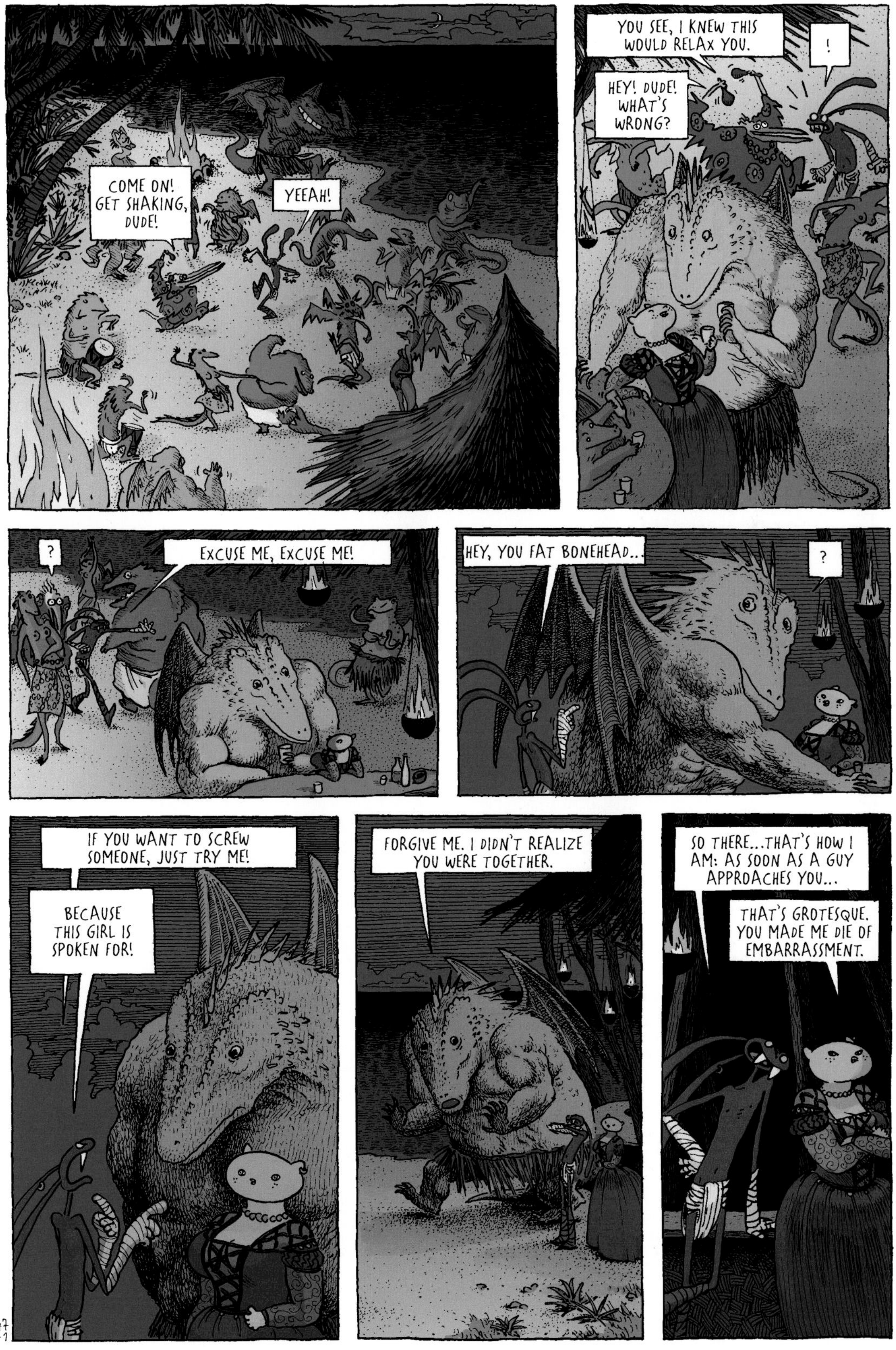
COME ON! GET SHAKING, DUDE!
YEEAH!
YOU SEE, I KNEW THIS WOULD RELAX YOU.
!
HEY! DUDE! WHAT'S WRONG?
?
EXCUSE ME, EXCUSE ME!
HEY, YOU FAT BONEHEAD...
?
IF YOU WANT TO SCREW SOMEONE, JUST TRY ME!
BECAUSE THIS GIRL IS SPOKEN FOR!
FORGIVE ME. I DIDN'T REALIZE YOU WERE TOGETHER.
SO THERE...THAT'S HOW I AM: AS SOON AS A GUY APPROACHES YOU...
THAT'S GROTESQUE. YOU MADE ME DIE OF EMBARRASSMENT.

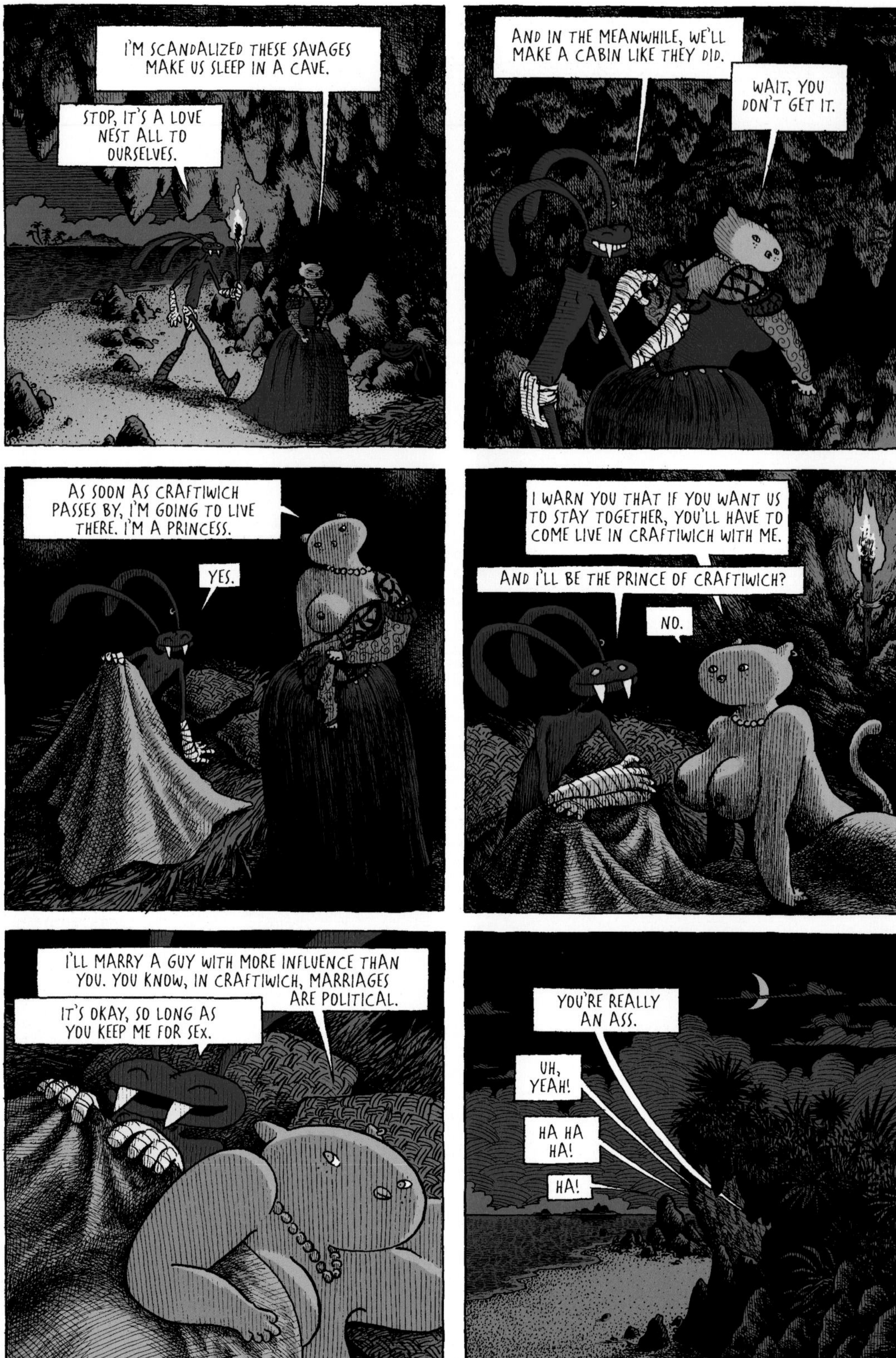
I'M SCANDALIZED THESE SAVAGES MAKE US SLEEP IN A CAVE.
STOP, IT'S A LOVE NEST ALL TO OURSELVES.
AND IN THE MEANWHILE, WE'LL MAKE A CABIN LIKE THEY DID.
WAIT, YOU DON'T GET IT.
AS SOON AS CRAFTIWICH PASSES BY, I'M GOING TO LIVE THERE. I'M A PRINCESS.
YES.
I WARN YOU THAT IF YOU WANT US TO STAY TOGETHER, YOU'LL HAVE TO COME LIVE IN CRAFTIWICH WITH ME.
AND I'LL BE THE PRINCE OF CRAFTIWICH?
NO.
I'LL MARRY A GUY WITH MORE INFLUENCE THAN YOU. YOU KNOW, IN CRAFTIWICH, MARRIAGES ARE POLITICAL.
IT'S OKAY, SO LONG AS YOU KEEP ME FOR SEX.
YOU'RE REALLY AN ASS.
UH, YEAH!
HA HA HA!
HA!

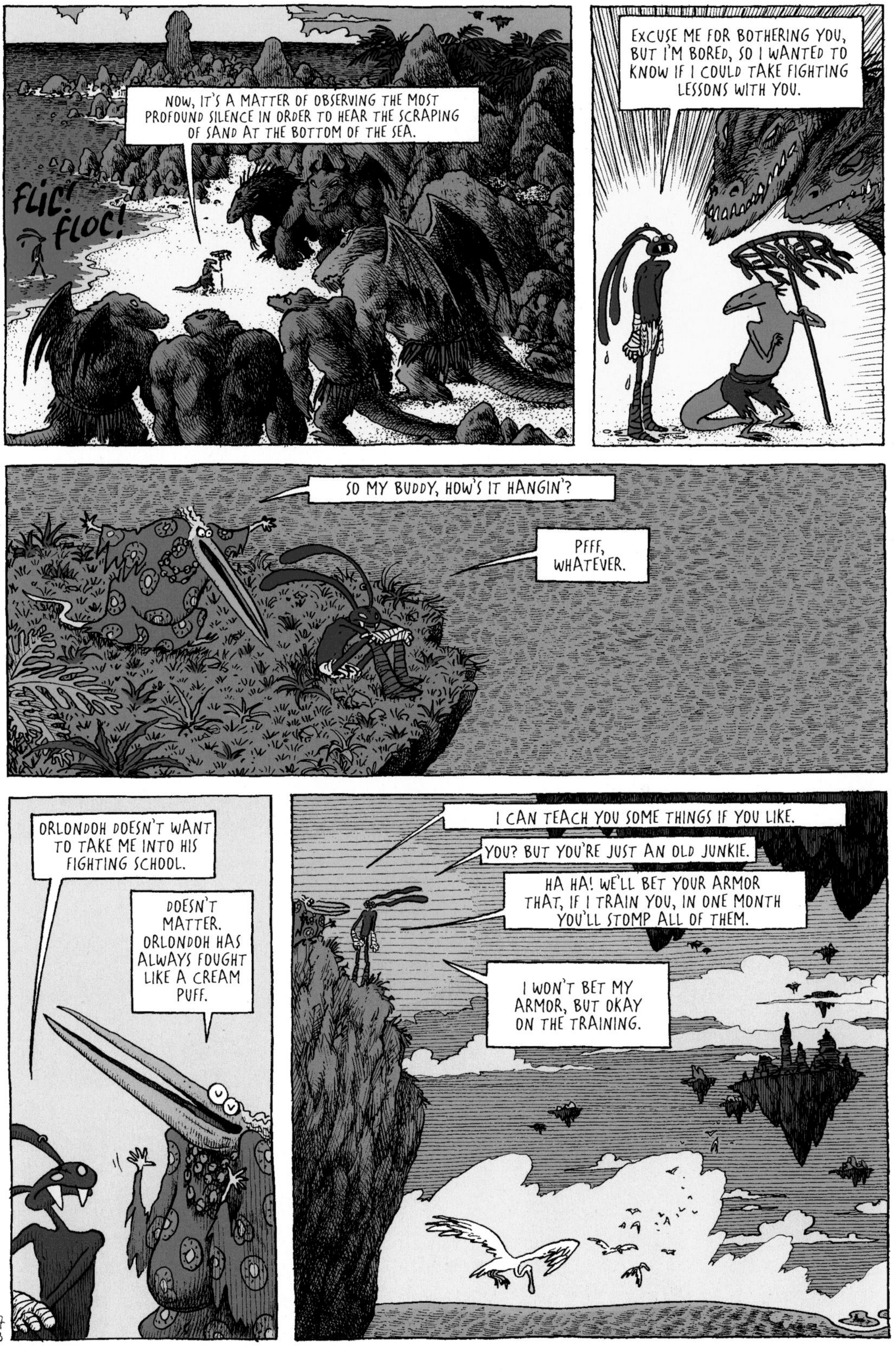
NOW, IT'S A MATTER OF OBSERVING THE MOST PROFOUND SILENCE IN ORDER TO HEAR THE SCRAPING OF SAND AT THE BOTTOM OF THE SEA.
FLIC! FLOC!
EXCUSE ME FOR BOTHERING YOU, BUT I'M BORED, SO I WANTED TO KNOW IF I COULD TAKE FIGHTING LESSONS WITH YOU.
SO MY BUDDY, HOW'S IT HANGIN'?
PFFF, WHATEVER.
ORLONDOH DOESN'T WANT TO TAKE ME INTO HIS FIGHTING SCHOOL.
DOESN'T MATTER. ORLONDOH HAS ALWAYS FOUGHT LIKE A CREAM PUFF.
I CAN TEACH YOU SOME THINGS IF YOU LIKE.
YOU? BUT YOU'RE JUST AN OLD JUNKIE.
HA HA! WE'LL BET YOUR ARMOR THAT, IF I TRAIN YOU, IN ONE MONTH YOU'LL STOMP ALL OF THEM.
I WON'T BET MY ARMOR, BUT OKAY ON THE TRAINING.

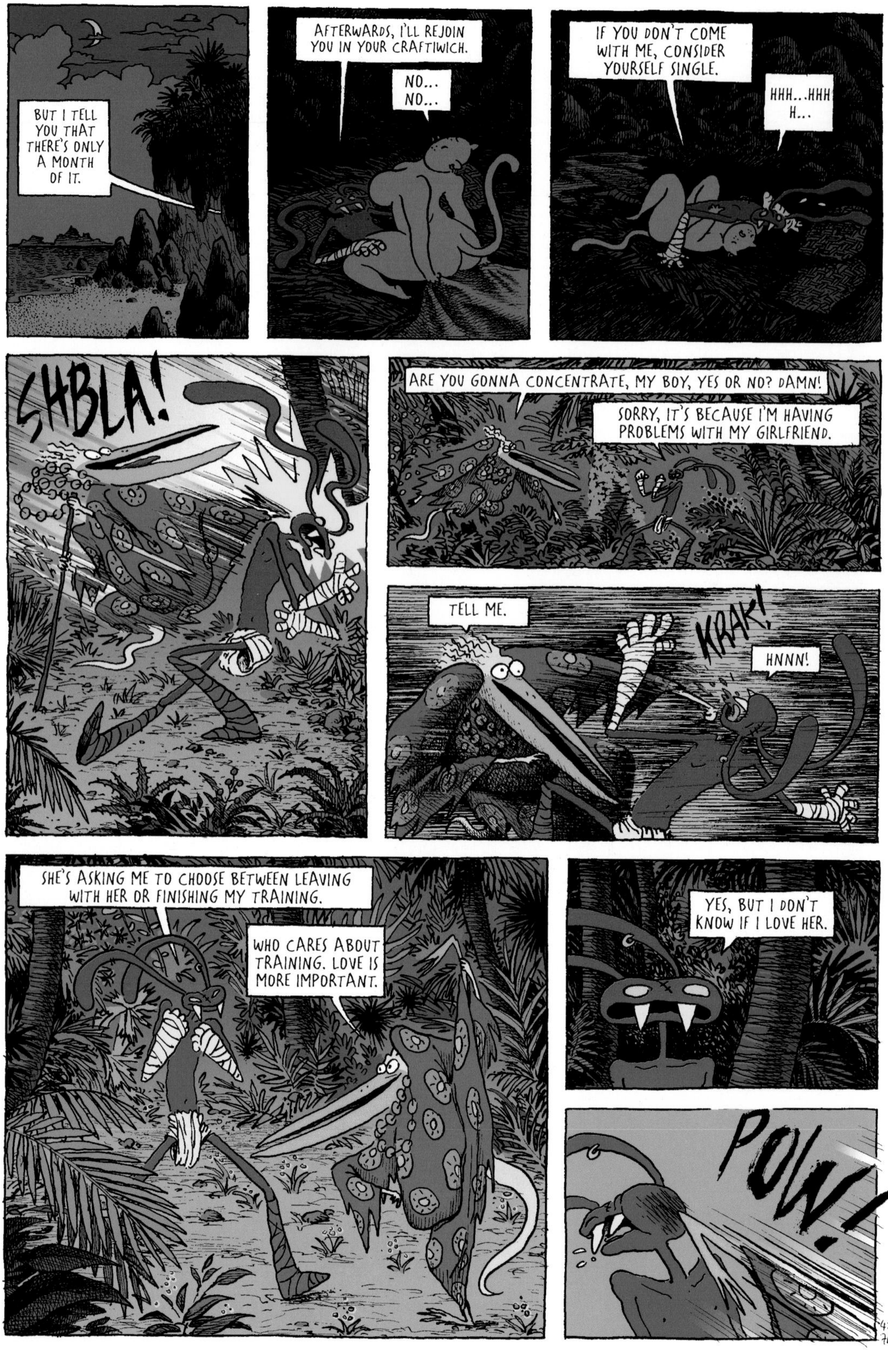
BUT I TELL YOU THAT THERE'S ONLY A MONTH OF IT.
AFTERWARDS, I'LL REJOIN YOU IN YOUR CRAFTIWICH.
NO... NO...
IF YOU DON'T COME WITH ME, CONSIDER YOURSELF SINGLE.
HHH...HHH H...
SHBLA!
ARE YOU GONNA CONCENTRATE, MY BOY, YES OR NO? DAMN!
SORRY, IT'S BECAUSE I'M HAVING PROBLEMS WITH MY GIRLFRIEND.
TELL ME.
KRAK!
HNNN!
SHE'S ASKING ME TO CHOOSE BETWEEN LEAVING WITH HER OR FINISHING MY TRAINING.
WHO CARES ABOUT TRAINING. LOVE IS MORE IMPORTANT.
YES, BUT I DON'T KNOW IF I LOVE HER.
POW!

NOW STOP WITH THE POUTING.

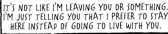

IT'S NOT LIKE I'M LEAVING YOU OR SOMETHING. I'M JUST TELLING YOU THAT I PREFER TO STAY HERE INSTEAD OF GOING TO LIVE WITH YOU.

GUYS ARE COWARDS.

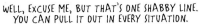

WELL, EXCUSE ME, BUT THAT'S ONE SHABBY LINE. YOU CAN PULL IT OUT IN EVERY SITUATION.

I'M SLEEPING.

DO YOU WANT ME TO COME WITH YOU TO PASS OVER TO THE OTHER ISLET?

NO.

AND HOW WILL YOU MANAGE IT? YOU DON'T HAVE ANY FLYING ARMOR, AND YOUR LEG ISN'T EVEN HEALED WELL!

I'VE MADE ARRANGEMENTS.

FLAP FLAP

!

IT'S NICE OF YOU TO TAKE ME.

IT'S THE VERY LEAST I CAN DO, MISS.

AND IT'S ALSO AN OCCASION TO SPEND SOME TIME WITH YOU.

DO YOU KNOW CRAFTIWICH?

I'VE NEVER LEFT MY ATOLL, MISS.

I INVITE YOU. YOU'LL BE MY BODYGUARD.

I WOULD HAVE TO ASK MY SHAMAN'S PERMISSION, MISS.

EXCUSE ME, MISS, BUT THIS CRAFTIWICH, ISN'T IT THE CITY WHERE THEY MAKE ARMOR LIKE THE RED RABBIT'S?

CERTAINLY.

DO YOU THINK I CAN HAVE A SET?

IF YOU'RE NICE.

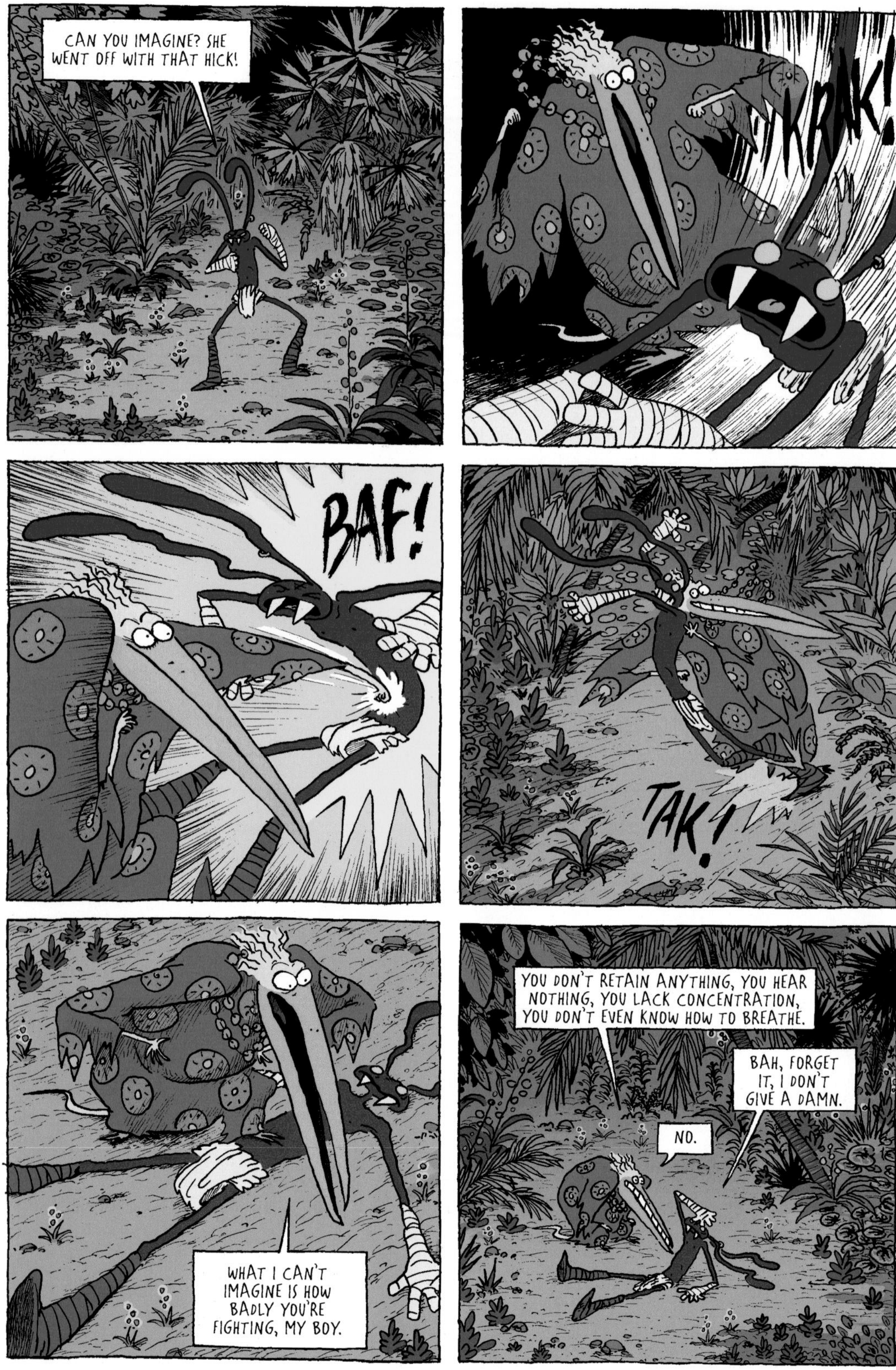

CAN YOU IMAGINE? SHE WENT OFF WITH THAT HICK!
KRAK!
BAF!
TAK!
WHAT I CAN'T IMAGINE IS HOW BADLY YOU'RE FIGHTING, MY BOY.
YOU DON'T RETAIN ANYTHING, YOU HEAR NOTHING, YOU LACK CONCENTRATION, YOU DON'T EVEN KNOW HOW TO BREATHE.
BAH, FORGET IT, I DON'T GIVE A DAMN.
NO.

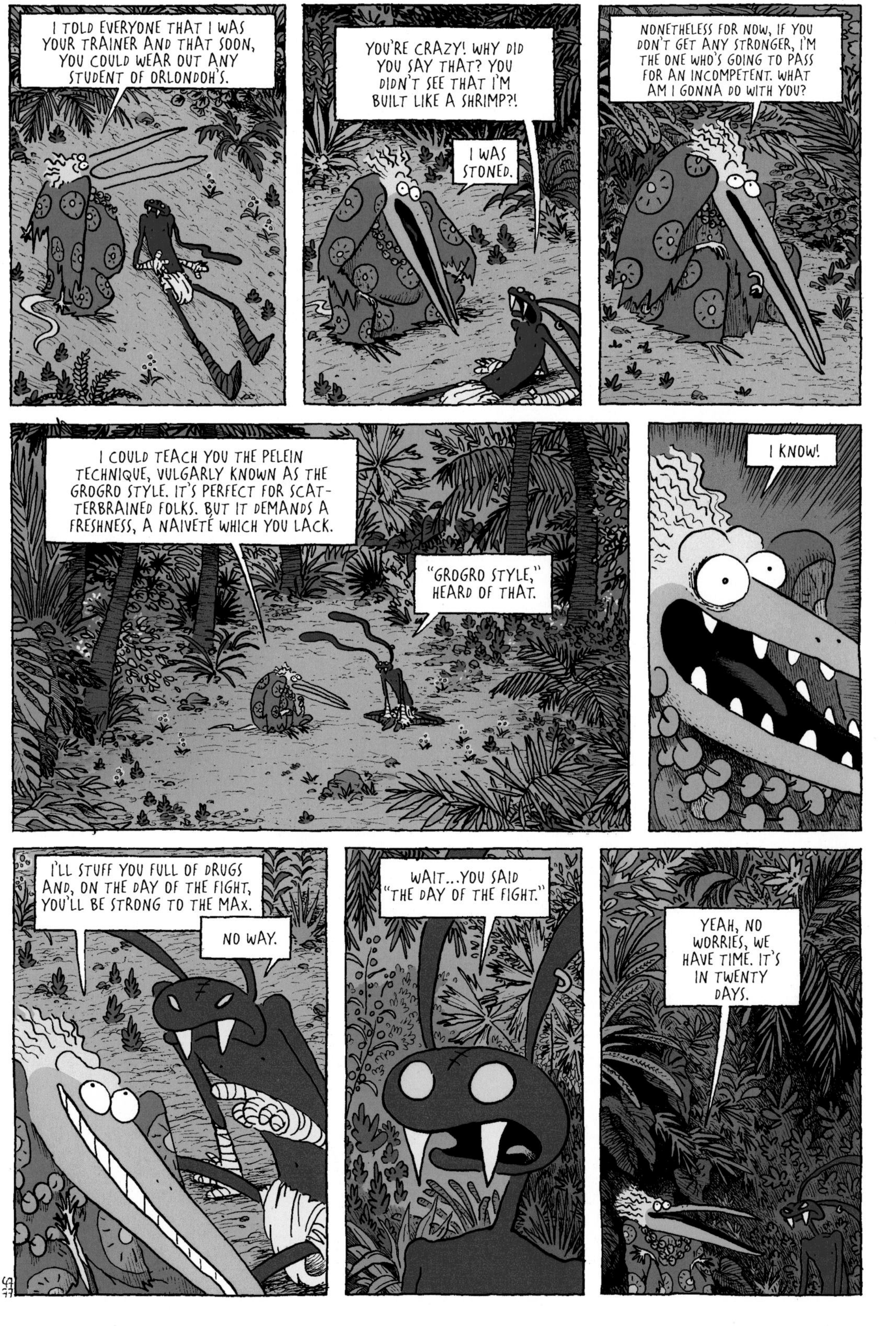
I TOLD EVERYONE THAT I WAS YOUR TRAINER AND THAT SOON, YOU COULD WEAR OUT ANY STUDENT OF ORLONDOH'S.
YOU'RE CRAZY! WHY DID YOU SAY THAT? YOU DIDN'T SEE THAT I'M BUILT LIKE A SHRIMP?!
I WAS STONED.
NONETHELESS FOR NOW, IF YOU DON'T GET ANY STRONGER, I'M THE ONE WHO'S GOING TO PASS FOR AN INCOMPETENT. WHAT AM I GONNA DO WITH YOU?
I COULD TEACH YOU THE PELEIN TECHNIQUE, VULGARLY KNOWN AS THE GROGRO STYLE. IT'S PERFECT FOR SCATTERBRAINED FOLKS. BUT IT DEMANDS A FRESHNESS, A NAIVETÉ WHICH YOU LACK.
"GROGRO STYLE," HEARD OF THAT.
I KNOW!
I'LL STUFF YOU FULL OF DRUGS AND, ON THE DAY OF THE FIGHT, YOU'LL BE STRONG TO THE MAX.
NO WAY.
WAIT...YOU SAID "THE DAY OF THE FIGHT."
YEAH, NO WORRIES, WE HAVE TIME. IT'S IN TWENTY DAYS.

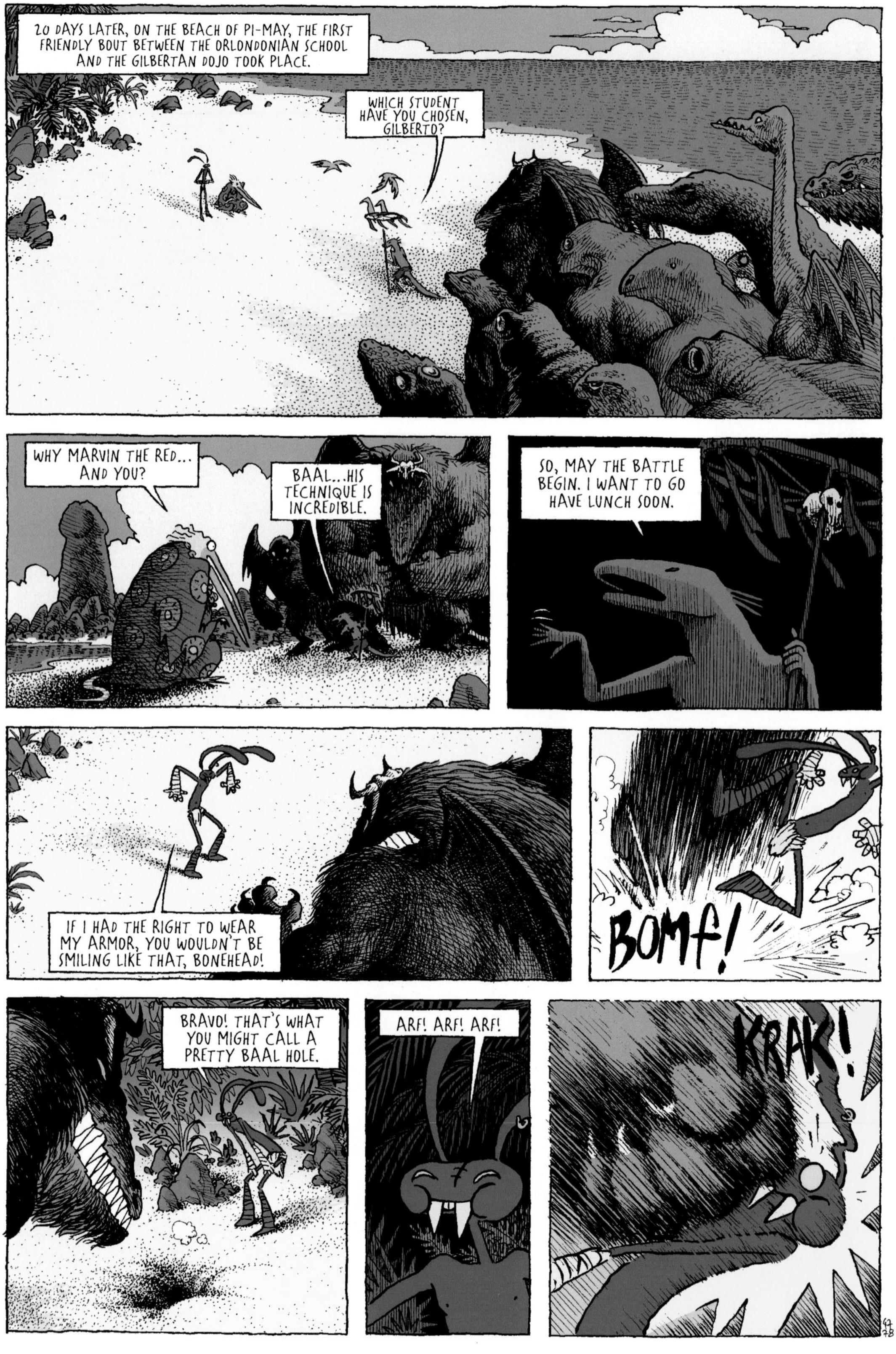

20 DAYS LATER, ON THE BEACH OF PI-MAY, THE FIRST FRIENDLY BOUT BETWEEN THE ORLONDONIAN SCHOOL AND THE GILBERTAN DOJO TOOK PLACE.
WHICH STUDENT HAVE YOU CHOSEN, GILBERTO?
WHY MARVIN THE RED... AND YOU?
BAAL...HIS TECHNIQUE IS INCREDIBLE.
SO, MAY THE BATTLE BEGIN. I WANT TO GO HAVE LUNCH SOON.
IF I HAD THE RIGHT TO WEAR MY ARMOR, YOU WOULDN'T BE SMILING LIKE THAT, BONEHEAD!
BOMF!
BRAVO! THAT'S WHAT YOU MIGHT CALL A PRETTY BAAL HOLE.
ARF! ARF! ARF!
KRAK!

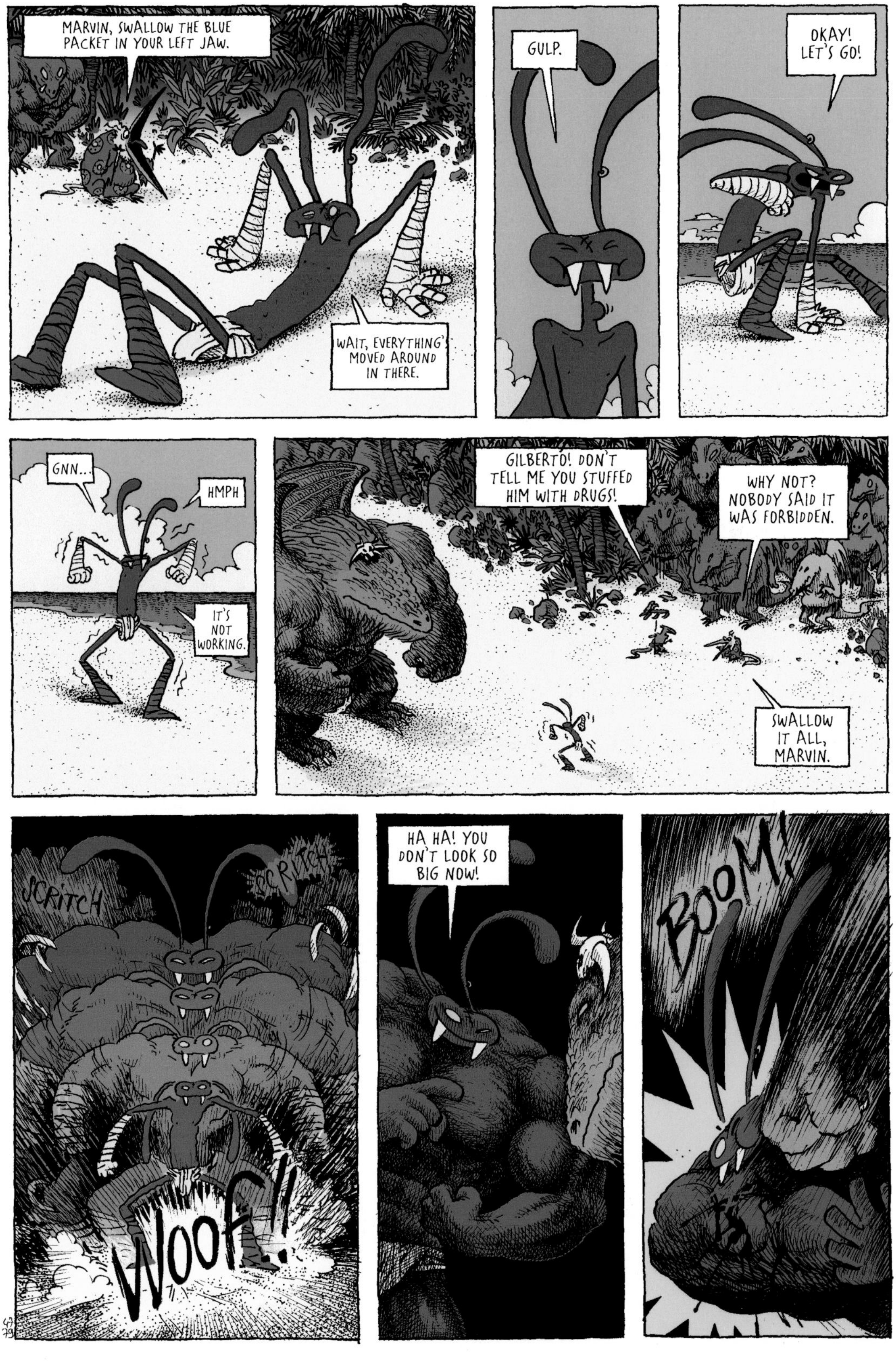
MARVIN, SWALLOW THE BLUE PACKET IN YOUR LEFT JAW.
WAIT, EVERYTHING'S MOVED AROUND IN THERE.
GULP.
OKAY! LET'S GO!
GNN...
HMPH
IT'S NOT WORKING.
GILBERTO! DON'T TELL ME YOU STUFFED HIM WITH DRUGS!
WHY NOT? NOBODY SAID IT WAS FORBIDDEN.
SWALLOW IT ALL, MARVIN.
SCRITCH
SCRITCH
WOOF!!
HA HA! YOU DON'T LOOK SO BIG NOW!
BOOM!

47
79

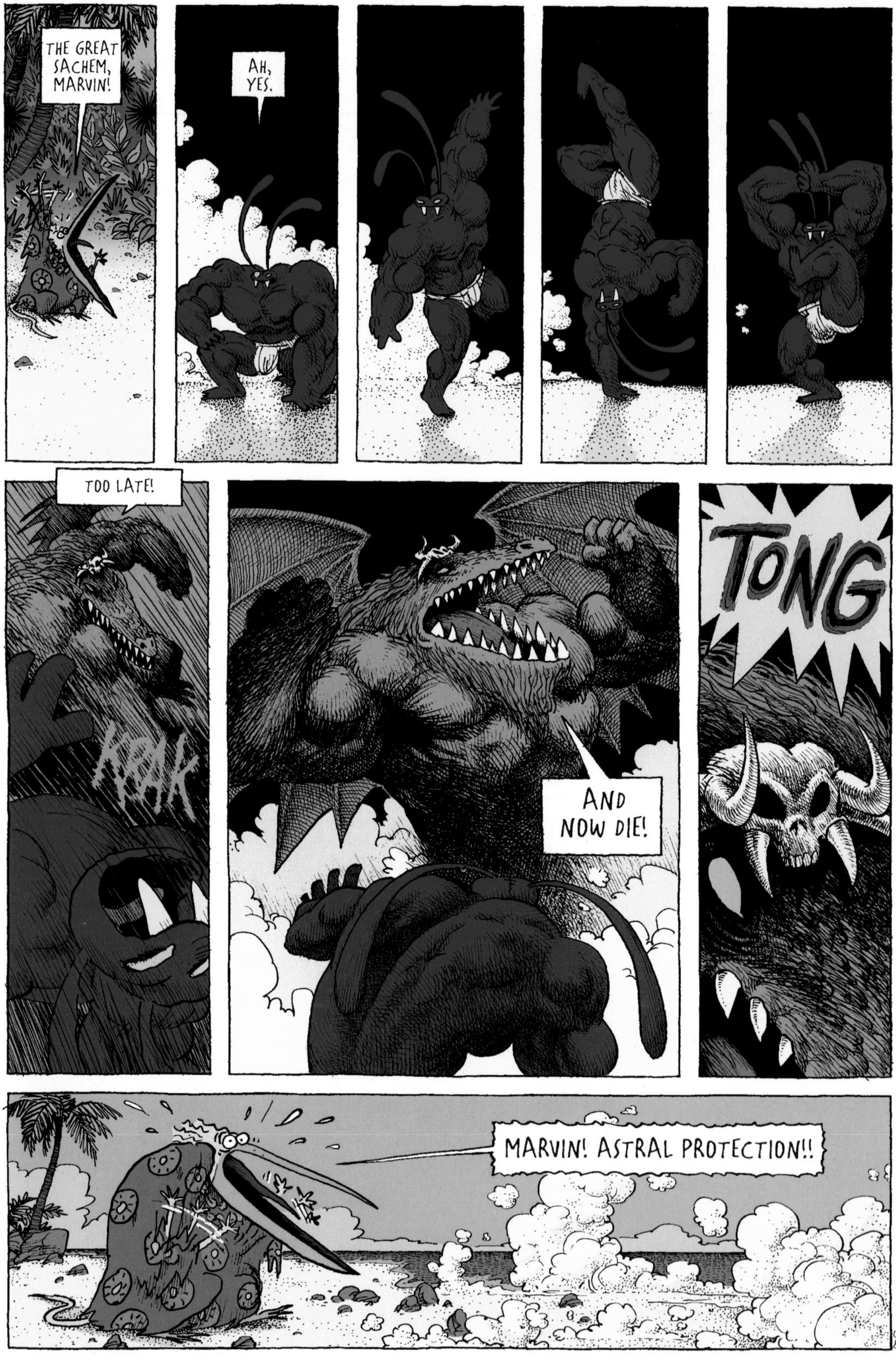
THE GREAT SACHEM, MARVIN!
AH, YES.
TOO LATE!
KRAK
AND NOW DIE!
TONG
MARVIN! ASTRAL PROTECTION!!

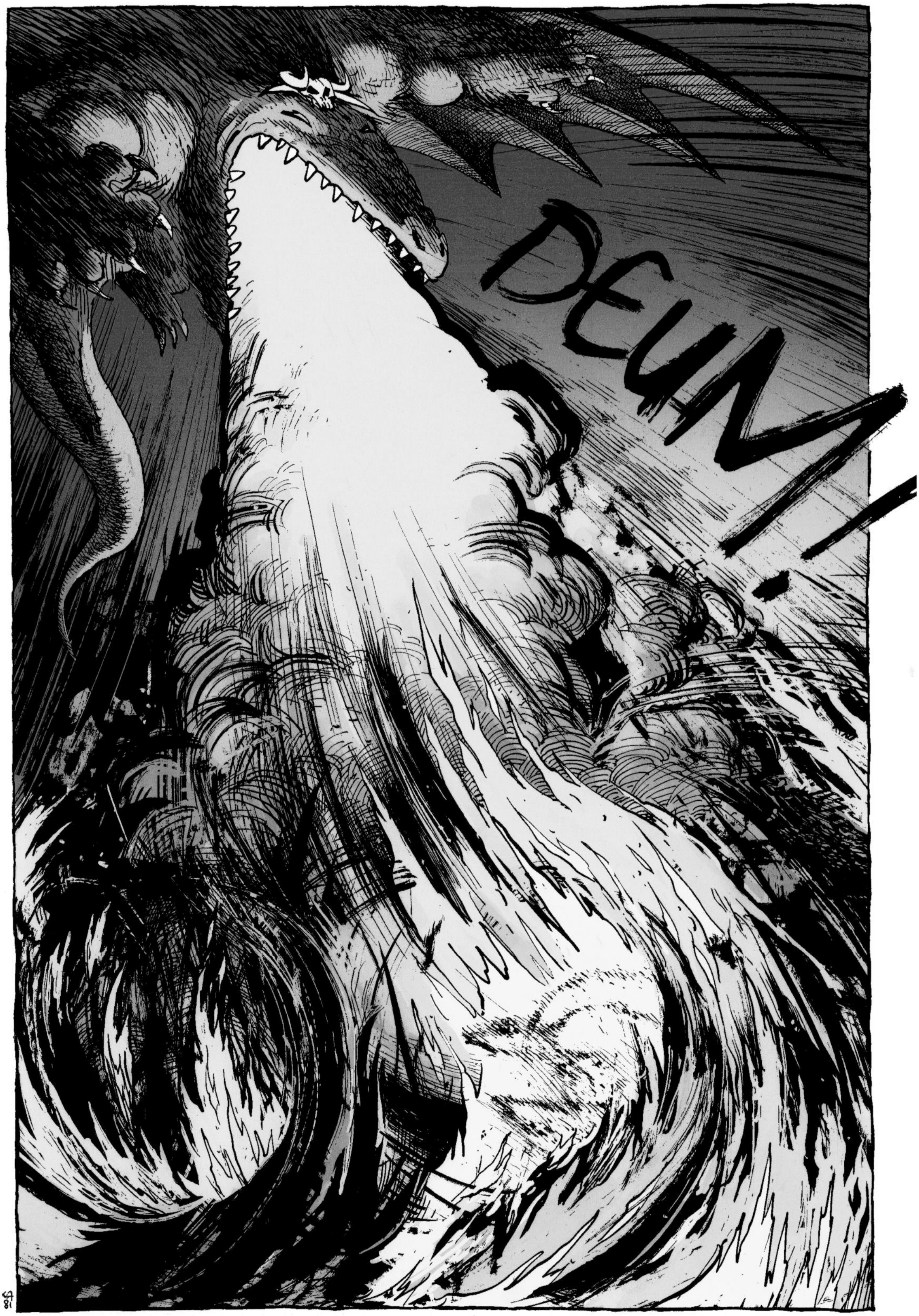
DEUM!!

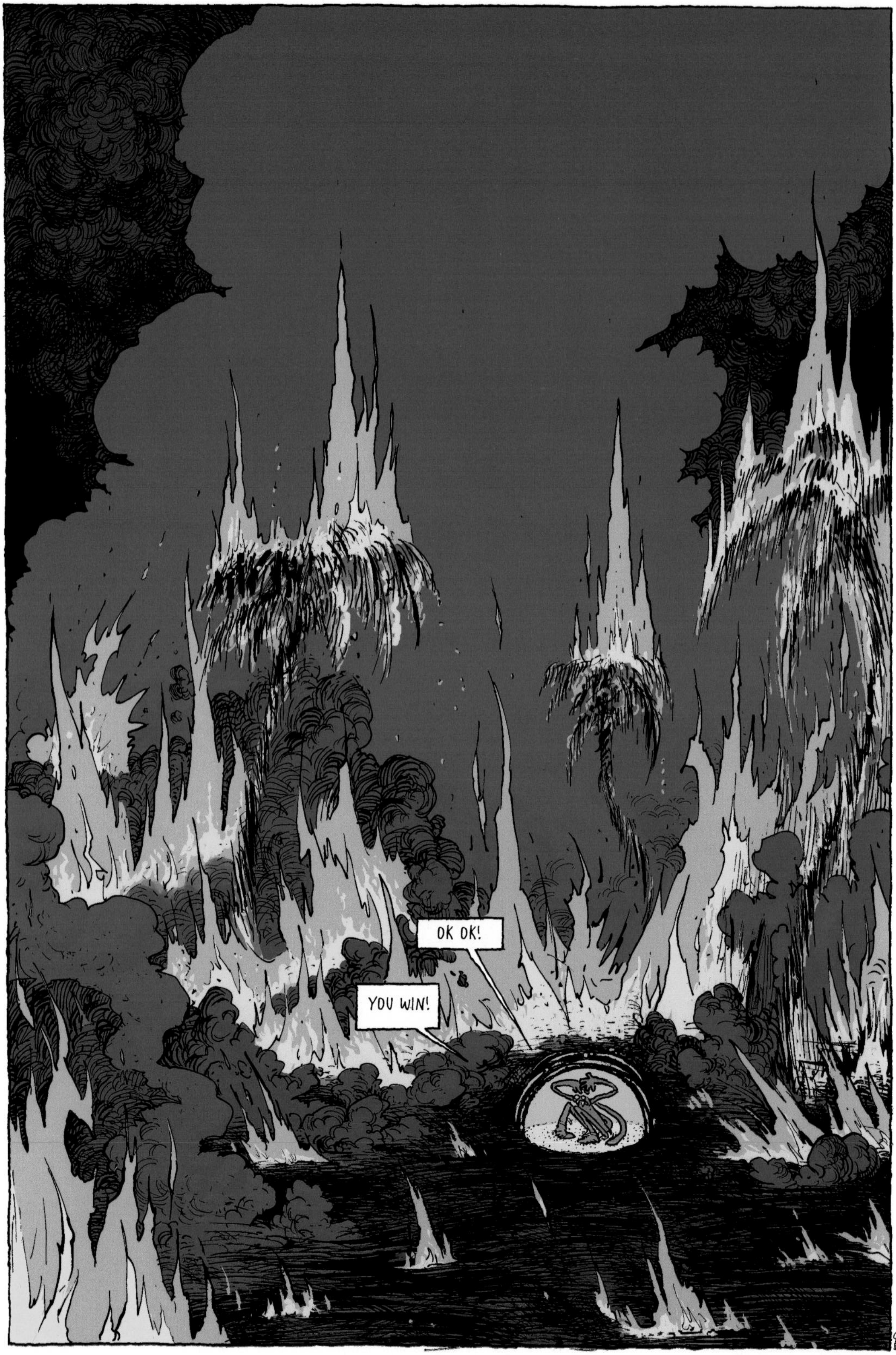
OK OK!
YOU WIN!

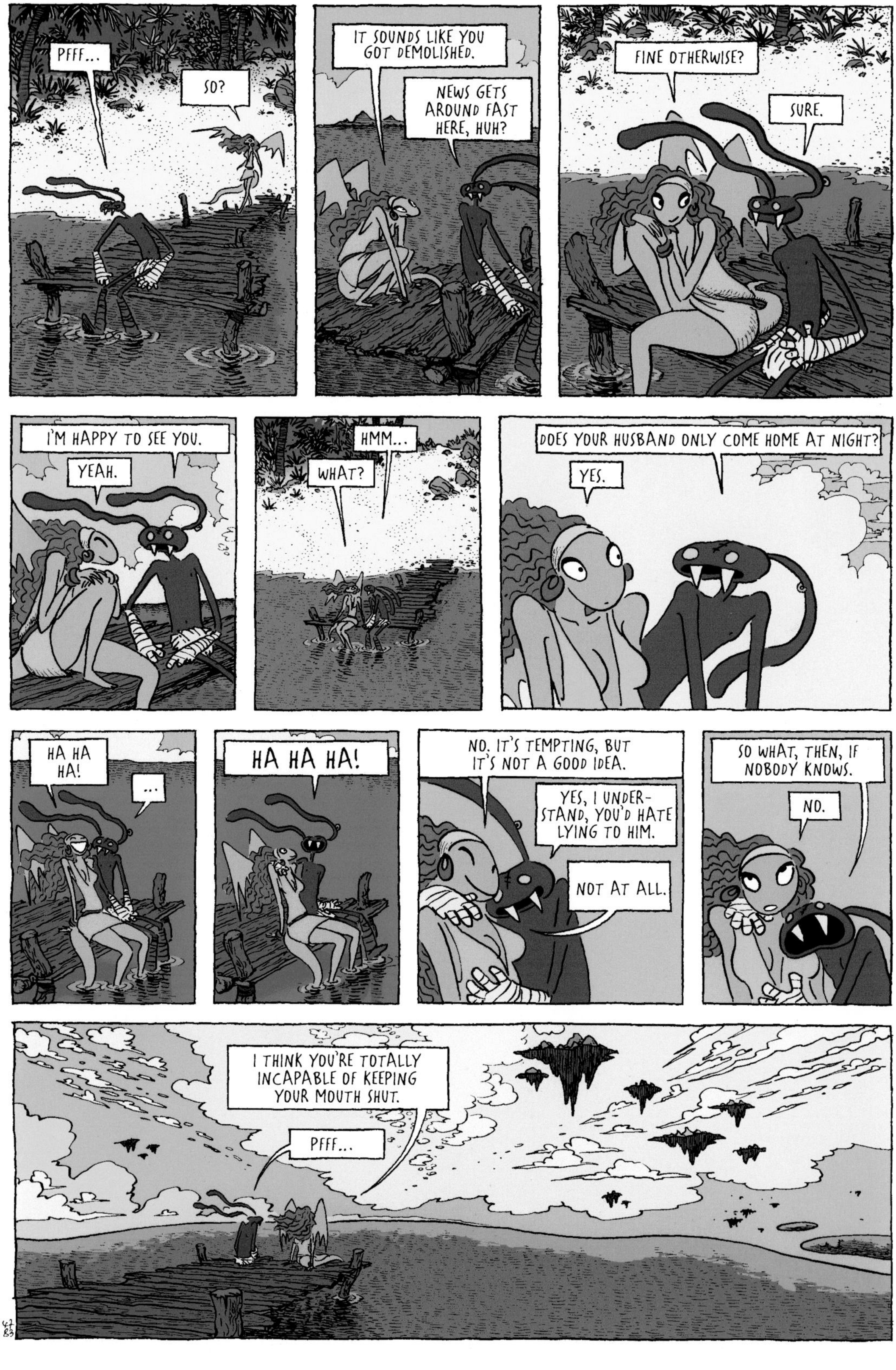
PFFF...
SO?
IT SOUNDS LIKE YOU GOT DEMOLISHED.
NEWS GETS AROUND FAST HERE, HUH?
FINE OTHERWISE?
SURE.
I'M HAPPY TO SEE YOU.
YEAH.
HMM...
WHAT?
DOES YOUR HUSBAND ONLY COME HOME AT NIGHT?
YES.
HA HA HA!
...
HA HA HA!
NO. IT'S TEMPTING, BUT IT'S NOT A GOOD IDEA.
YES, I UNDERSTAND, YOU'D HATE LYING TO HIM.
NOT AT ALL.
SO WHAT, THEN, IF NOBODY KNOWS.
NO.
I THINK YOU'RE TOTALLY INCAPABLE OF KEEPING YOUR MOUTH SHUT.
PFFF...

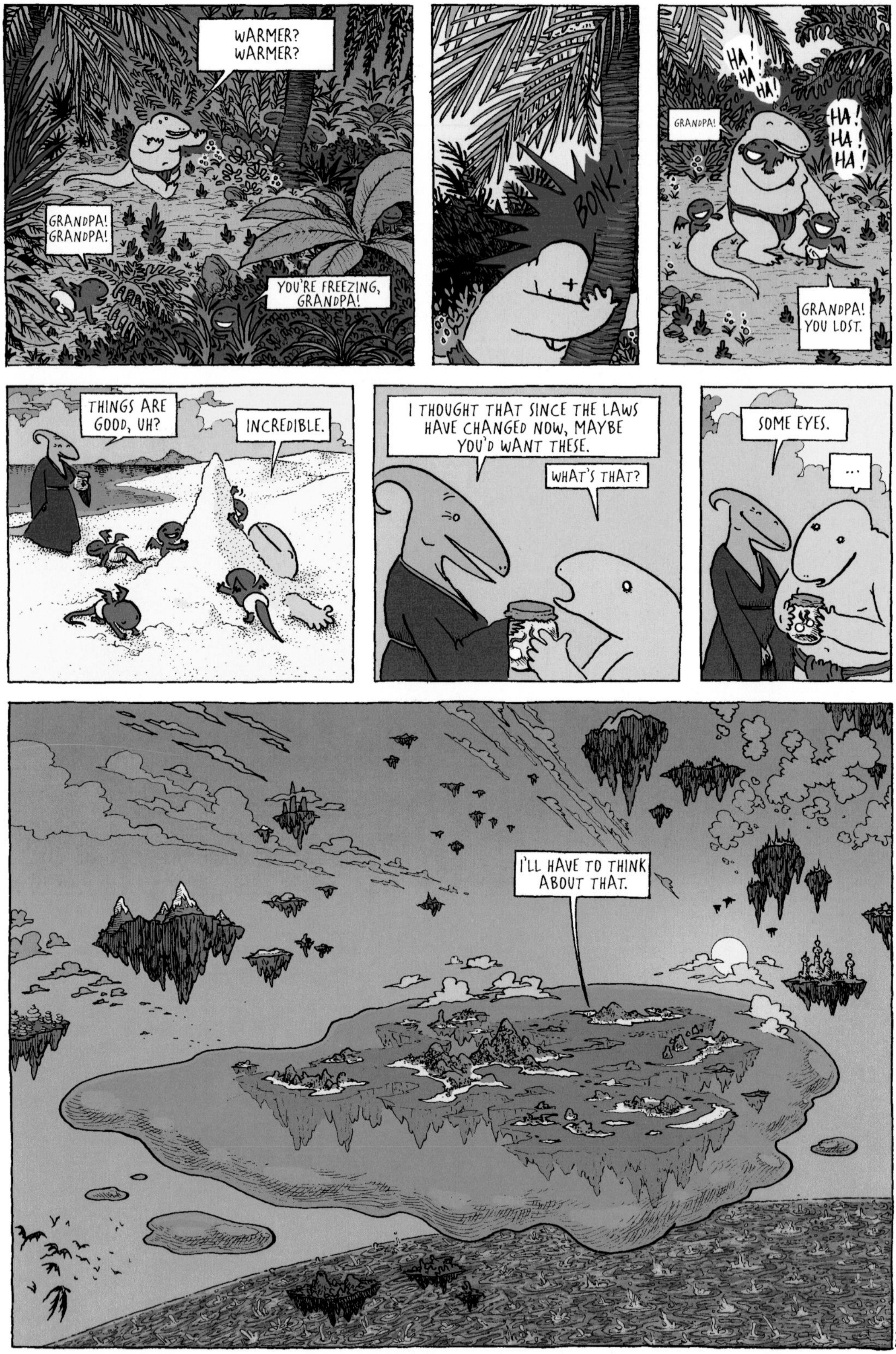
WARMER? WARMER?
GRANDPA! GRANDPA!
YOU'RE FREEZING, GRANDPA!
BONK!
HA! HA! HA!
GRANDPA!
HA! HA! HA!
GRANDPA! YOU LOST.
THINGS ARE GOOD, UH?
INCREDIBLE.
I THOUGHT THAT SINCE THE LAWS HAVE CHANGED NOW, MAYBE YOU'D WANT THESE.
WHAT'S THAT?
SOME EYES.
...
I'LL HAVE TO THINK ABOUT THAT.